Dear Dad

Happy
17th Birthday

I Love you
KID. Ken Harvey

Nov 2006

D0895317

SURVIVAL

BOOKS BY FRED BRUEMMER

The Long Hunt
Seasons of the Eskimo
Encounters with Arctic Animals
The Arctic
The Life of the Harp Seal
Children of the North
Summer at Bear River
The Arctic World
Arctic Animals
Seasons of the Seal
World of the Polar Bear
Seals (with Eric S. Grace)
Land of Dark, Land of Light (with Karen Pandell)
Les Animaux du Grand Nord (with Angèle Delaunois)
The Narwhal: Unicorn of the Sea
Arctic Memories: Living with the Inuit
Nanook and Nauja: The Polar Bear Cubs
(with Angèle Delaunois)
Kotik: The Baby Seal (with Angèle Delaunois)
Polar Dance: Born of the North Wind
(with Tom Mangelsen)
Seals in the Wild
Glimpses of Paradise

a refugee life

SURVIVAL

FRED BRUEMMER

KEY PORTER BOOKS

Copyright © 2005 by Fred Bruemmer

All rights reserved. No part of this work covered by the copyrights hereon may be reproduced or used in any form or by any means — graphic, electronic or mechanical, including photo-copying, recording, taping or information storage and retrieval systems — without the prior written permission of the publisher, or, in case of photocopying or other reprographic copying, a licence from Access Copyright, the Canadian Copyright Licensing Agency, One Yonge Street, Suite 1900, Toronto, Ontario, M6B 3A9.

Library and Archives Canada Cataloguing in Publication

Bruemmer, Fred
  Survival : a refugee life / Fred Bruemmer.

ISBN 1-55263-704-2

  1. Bruemmer, Fred. 2. World War, 1939–1945 — Conscript labour — Soviet Union. 3. World War, 1939–1945 — Prisoners and prisons, Soviet — Biography. 4. Germans — Soviet Union — Biography. 5. World War, 1939–1945 — Personal narratives, German. I. Title.

D805.R9B78 2005   940.53'18'092   C2005-903145-X

The publisher gratefully acknowledges the support of the Canada Council for the Arts and the Ontario Arts Council for its publishing program. We acknowledge the support of the Government of Ontario through the Ontario Media Development Corporation's Ontario Book Initiative.

We acknowledge the financial support of the Government of Canada through the Book Publishing Industry Development Program (BPIDP) for our publishing activities.

Key Porter Books Limited
Six Adelaide Street East, Tenth Floor
Toronto, Ontario
Canada M5C 1H6

www.keyporter.com

Text design: Ingrid Paulson
Electronic formatting: Beth Crane, Heidy Lawrance Associates

Printed and bound in Canada

05 06 07 08 09 5 4 3 2 1

For
Aurel and René
with love

CONTENTS

Preface

CHANGING WORLDS AND
CHANGING NAMES

IT MUST BE A VEXING, in fact sisyphean, task to produce an atlas. It is compiled with infinite care and labour, printed at great cost and, within a year, parts of it are already passé. Names change, borders change, some countries are born, others disintegrate. My *National Geographic Atlas of the World*, fifth edition, printed in 1981, is amazingly out of date — and so, according to our children, am I.

My father studied in Dorpat (now Tartu) in Estonia and then in St. Petersburg. When he returned as a young officer in Russia's imperial army at the beginning of the First World War, the city had been renamed Petrograd, because St. Petersburg sounded too German. It was Leningrad when I first visited it in 1974, and again St. Petersburg when I returned recently. The revolution had come full circle.

In my seventy-five years several empires have vanished and more than a hundred countries have been created. When I was born neither Israel nor Iraq existed. Stalin was already in control in the Soviet Union, and Hitler was four years away from absolute power in Germany.

When I went to school in the German town of Kalisch, I walked down the Hermann Göring Strasse and passed the Adolf Hitler Platz. Today, it is the Polish town of Kalisz and, I assume, nothing is named after Hitler. There is a Göring Street in Swakopmund, Namibia (where I once lived), but that was named after Heinrich Ernst Göring, the fat reichsmarshal's father, who, in 1885, was the Bismarck-appointed imperial commissioner of Deutsch-Südwest-Afrika, then the name of the future Namibia.

In the 1930s, at the time of the Great Terror, when Stalin ordered the murder of most of the friends and old comrades with whom he had built the Soviet Union, thousands of towns and villages had to be hurriedly renamed. After Stalin was safely dead, Khrushchev spoke publicly of his crimes, the cold-blooded murder of millions, and thousands of Stalin names were expunged. Stalingrad is still the name of a great Second World War battle, but the city today is called Volgograd.

In 1974, I returned to Riga, the city where I was born, in Latvia, then one of the socialist republics of the Soviet Union. I asked an old woman, a flower vendor, for the street where I grew up, using its Latvian name. She stared at me, as the people in the story stared at Rip van Winkle. "Dear God," she gasped in amazement, "where have you been?" For more than thirty years already that street had had a Russian name.

My wife, Maud, was born in 1937 in the Dutch East Indies. The major city was Batavia, a name derived from the Batavi, an ancient Germanic tribe that settled in the first century BC in the Rhine delta. Now the country is called Indonesia, and the former Batavia is its capital, Jakarta.

I grew up in a binomial society. In summer, we lived in the country. When I was off to a nearby village and Alma, our maid, asked in Latvian: "Where are you going?" I answered in Latvian "To Lielstraupe." When my mother asked the same question in German, I replied in German: "To Gross-Roop."

In this book I have used the names that at the time were most familiar to me. Where necessary, when other names are now familiar, I have added later or present names of cities, towns, or villages in brackets.

I HAVE KNOWN ANNA PORTER of Key Porter Books since 1971, when she was closely associated with the publication of my second book, *Seasons of the Eskimo*. Since then, she has encouraged me and has published most of my subsequent books. The present book was her idea. She urged me to write it, then guided it through to publication. I thank her for years of help and friendship.

Four of Canada's most respected authors, Modris Eksteins, Margaret MacMillan, Peter C. Newman, and Robert McGhee read the text. I am deeply grateful for their suggestions and remarks.

Patricia Kennedy, my manuscript editor, corrected and improved the text with the care and diligence of someone who truly loves language. Sheep don't like to be shorn, and authors, as a rule, don't like to be edited. Pat Kennedy did it with a gentle charm that I appreciate and an expertise that I admire.

My wife, Maud, shared with me, as always, the pleasures and frustrations that are part of writing a book.

Our sons, Aurel and René, who are of this time, helped their struggling parents, who are of times past, to cope with their computer. They are our future, and to them this book about my past is dedicated.

Fred Bruemmer
Montreal

INTRODUCTION

IN 1923, THE BRILLIANT DANISH ethnologist Knud Rasmussen stopped for a while at Bathurst Inlet, nearly in the exact centre of Canada's Arctic mainland coast, while making his epic three-year dog team trip from Greenland to Alaska. He found the isolated Inuit of Bathurst Inlet "inflammable" and "very temperamental," but also noted that "as poets [they were] perhaps the most gifted and inspired Eskimos I have ever fallen in with."

In the winter of 1969, I went to live with the Inuit of Bathurst Inlet for six months.

The dry arctic snow creaked and groaned underneath the ice-coated runners of our heavy sled. "*Kayornaktuk!* It is cold!" said Joseph Tikhek. "It will be good to get home." We had travelled for eight days by dog team, from Cambridge Bay on Victoria Island across windswept Dease Strait and over the rolling, rock-strewn icy plains of Kent Peninsula. Now we were nearing our destination, the winter camp of Joseph's family at Arctic Sound on the west coast of Bathurst Inlet.

I snuggled deeper into my heavy parka to escape the cutting wind, and worried. There had been no chance to warn the people at this remote camp of my arrival. Inuit were immensely hospitable. I had already spent part of the previous four years living with Inuit at other camps, sometimes for weeks, sometimes for a few months. But this time I meant to move in for six months with one of Canada's most isolated Inuit groups — one that was still leading a traditional way of life that in much of the Arctic had already vanished.

It was dark now. In the distance a husky howled dolefully. A faint orange light glimmered through the gloom. Our dogs, happy to be home, broke into a wild gallop. Fur-clad shapes rushed out to greet us.

"My mother will take care of the dogs," Joseph said. "Come into my father's house."

I followed him through a narrow passage of snow blocks into a large, double-layered tent. Children were sleeping on the raised, fur-covered snow platform at the rear. Moses Panegyuk, Joseph's father, smiled his welcome. "Tea is nearly ready," he said. We talked of the trip. Others crowded into the tent. Not by a word, not by a gesture, did anyone betray the slightest surprise or puzzlement at my unexpected presence. It would have been impolite. The stranger must be made welcome, not plied with questions. A sleepy, round face peeked out from underneath the furs on the sleeping platform and stared at me in wide-eyed wonder.

Aieee, kabloona! A white man! little Oched squealed and hid in fright, and we laughed and chatted, drank the sweet, scalding-hot tea and ate chunks of meat, squatting on the low snow benches at the side of the tent. "You will live with my grandfather," said Joseph, who had earlier slipped out of the tent, and now returned. So we walked through the crystal-clear, star-glittering night to the farthest tent of this four-tent community. Ekalun, Joseph's grandfather, was already in bed. With his narrow, powerful face, aquiline nose, and shaven head (except for a tuft of hair above his brow), he looked like a haughty Indian chieftain. The face was a mirror of the man, strong and self-reliant, fearless and free. There was kindness in that face, but also a hint of ruthlessness, and traces of that sardonic, mordant wit of which I would so often be the butt during the coming months.

Rosie Kongyona, Ekalun's wife, small and active, bustled busily over the pressure stove, the tattoo lines on her dark brow bunched into a concentrated frown as she tried to hurry the tea along.

"Ekalun," I said, "I have come for a long time. Is it all right?"

He waved his hand over the snow platform. "This is your home," he said simply. And my home it was for the next six months.

I liked camp life and its timeless rhythm. We lived according to mood, need, and weather. Ours was the primal time of hunters, not the clock-regulated existence of city-dwellers.

The camp community absorbed me, and I fitted easily into their lives. As a non-hunting male, I was an anomaly to them, but since I was harmless, happily ate their food, and made no special demands, the Inuit accepted me with easy nonchalance. I usually left camp each morning with the men to travel by dog team to the faraway seal-hunting grounds. While the fur-clad hunters, harpoon at the ready, stood statue-still above *agloos*, the seal breathing holes in the ice, I went for long, solitary walks. Sometimes I stayed in camp, watched the women work, or photographed the children.

The camp children were marvellously free and gloriously independent. They were a hardy, happy, self-reliant lot. They played together, built igloos, dragged a small sled up a nearby hill, piled on, and swooshed down. They harnessed a husky and went for sled rides. They rushed home, ate piles of seal meat, drank tea, and rushed out again.

At first they found me fascinating. They had seen whites, but no white person had ever lived at their camp before. They were curious though polite, but soon the novelty wore off, and they ignored me and went on with their busy little lives. They played and they helped their parents. They looked after the husky pups and played with them. Carrying alarmingly large, razor-sharp knives they cut bucketsful of freshwater ice to be melted into water. The boys learned to repair dog harnesses and helped to tie sled loads. The girls learned to sew fur clothing, using dried sinew as thread. In the past, their lives had moved nearly seamlessly from childhood into the world of adults.

While I watched the children and photographed their world, I was often reminded of my own childhood in rural Latvia in the 1930s. In summer we lived close to nature on a farm we called Quellenhof, and we were wonderfully free.

(Those northern experiences would grow into a children's book, *Children of the North*, that I wrote in 1979, ten years after living at Ekalun's camp. It was my book of joy and love, with a touch of nostalgia for simpler times, for their youth and for mine. It won a prize at the Bologna Book Fair in Italy.)

Inuit moulded their children's behaviour by praise and teasing. Ekalun, I realized with amusement, used the same technique with me. Slowly, with prods and praise, and with various subtle sanctions and rewards, he modified my behaviour to conform more closely to the culturally accepted norms of his society. At first he called me "*Kabloo*," short for *kabloona*, "white man," and later usually "*Amarok*," the wolf, the lone wolf, because of my long, solitary walks.

When Ekalun was a child, his culture had still been untouched, and whites were just a myth. He had been ten years old when his group of Inuit had been "discovered" by members of the 1913–1918 Stefansson-Anderson Canadian Arctic Expedition. It had been an amazing day, marking the arrival of an utterly alien people from another world. Ekalun remembered it with total clarity, and his first impression of whites had been that they were rich and rude.

To the Inuit, their wealth was beyond imagination. They had an abundance of wood and metal, both exceedingly rare and precious to Ekalun's people. It was as if extraterrestrials visited our world in chariots of diamonds and gold.

"What were they like, these first white men you met?" I asked Ekalun once.

He looked at me with an ironic smile. "They were just like you, *Kabloo*," he said. "Forever asking questions!"

I'm afraid I did ask a lot of questions and it sometimes annoyed him. But occasionally he liked to reminisce and would then talk for hours about a world that had already vanished. He was a married man before he acquired his first rifle. Before that, he had hunted sea mammals with a harpoon, and caribou with spear or bow and arrow.

Out of my time in Ekalun's camp grew my book *Seasons of the Eskimo: A Vanishing Way of Life*. It did well, went through many editions, was a Book-of-the-Month Club selection, and brought me a modicum of fame. *Maclean's* magazine called me the "Explorer-poet of the last frontier." My arctic work, wrote *Maclean's* editor Ernest Hillen, had made me "slowly and without fanfare, one of the least-known world-famous men in Canada."

It was, in some ways, the realization of my childhood hopes. Nearly seventy years ago, as a small boy in my hometown of Riga, Latvia, I had had two dreams: to grow up to be a *Naturforscher*, a "naturalist-biologist," and to travel.

I may have been influenced by the fact that, in the nineteenth century, so many of my countrymen, the Baltic Germans, living in the provinces of Estland, Livland, and Kurland of imperial Russia (now the republics of Estonia and Latvia), had been well-known biologists and explorers: Karl Ernst von Baer, who explored arctic Russia, especially the far-northern island of Novaya Zemlya, but as a scientist is best known as the founder of embryology; Jakob Baron von Uexküll, an early ecologist; Alexander Theodor von Middendorff, explorer of Siberia and recently honoured by the National Geographic Society as one of the hundred greatest explorers of all time; Ferdinand Baron von Wrangel, explorer and later governor of Russian-owned Alaska.

These were names I grew up with. We had their books at home. And, since the Baltic German nobility was such a small clan, I was probably remotely related to all of them.

My future at that time seemed simple and straightforward: high school, university, and someday, hopefully, a career in biology. Hitler and Stalin destroyed those hopes as they destroyed the hopes and lives of millions of others.

For me came the loss of my home, the murder of my parents, a work camp in the Soviet Union run by a corrupt and crazed sadist, and a miserable existence with a simple focus: to survive. That part of my life forms the core of this book.

For me, there were the post-war refugee years, emigration to Canada, work in a gold mine in northern Ontario, and long stints as writer and photographer first in Canada, then in Europe and the Middle East.

I married and returned to Canada. In the early 1960s, a magazine sent me north to Frobisher Bay (now Iqaluit) on Baffin Island to write an article about Inuit and their lives in the new towns that were being built. I met a people traumatized by transition, suspended between two worlds: one beloved but dying, the other new, alluring, but essentially alien.

Far from these nascent arctic towns, I was told, Inuit in remote camps "on the land" still lived modified forms of their ancient hunting culture. This, I felt, should be somehow preserved and recorded. Suddenly my scattered interests found a focus, and that is when I began to live with the Inuit. First came short trips of a few weeks, then longer ones to remote camps, like the one of Ekalun, and soon I spent six months of every year in the Arctic, commuting for thirty years between two worlds: the vanishing world of the traditional arctic hunter — from Greenland, across Canada's North to Alaska and Siberia — and my own home and family in Montreal.

I loved the Arctic, its rugged beauty, its haunting loneliness, its infinite space. It has the vastness of the sea, the grandeur of a Bach fugue. The Inuit call it *Nunassiaq*, the "beautiful land," and it became my second home. I would write more than a thousand articles about the Arctic and its people for magazines in Canada, the United States, and Europe.

In 1969, I wrote my first book, *The Long Hunt*, about a two-thousand kilometre dog-team trip I made with Inuit hunters from Grise Fiord on Ellesmere Island, Canada's northernmost village. It was their last, vast traditional polar bear hunt. Then it was a marvellous adventure, shared with men I greatly admired. Now it is part of the Inuit history that I recorded.

Fifteen years later, in 1974, my largest book, *The Arctic*, was published, my paean to the Inuit, those masters of the art of arctic survival, and their land. The response was gratifying. Wrote Dr. William E. Taylor, Canada's foremost arctic archeologist and then director of Canada's National Museum of Man in Ottawa: "This book is one man's thoughts and photographs of those immense stretches of land and sea, their nature, history, and inhabitants. It is the most comprehensive single book on its subject matter ever presented." *Life* magazine wrote, with considerable hyperbole: "Bruemmer [is] perhaps the greatest arctic expert in the world." Even though that was hardly true, it pleased me, especially considering the fact that, due to war and prison, I had not even finished high-school.

It has often occurred to me that the reason I felt such a strong and instant empathy with the Inuit — an empathy that led to some of my major work — was that my nature-linked ancestral life was destroyed as surely as theirs, and that their sense of family and community awoke in me memories of a beloved past.

In former books I have written extensively about the Inuit and their past. This book is about myself and my people, the Baltic Germans, an odd tribe that began seven hundred years ago with the crusades and lost its home in 1939, when the two great dictators of my time, Hitler and Stalin, signed an agreement of non-aggression and nine days later began the Second World War by invading Poland.

Chapter 1

THE BALTIC BARONS

I WAS TEN YEARS OLD when Hitler and Stalin divided my world and made me homeless. In one sweep, I lost what Germans call *Heimat* and Russians call *rodina*, the land to which one's soul belongs, and joined the uprooted of the world, whose home is everywhere and nowhere.

In the evening of August 23, 1939, watched by a benignly smiling Stalin, the foreign ministers of Germany and the Soviet Union, Joachim von Ribbentrop and Vyacheslav Molotov, signed in Moscow the Soviet–German Non-Aggression Pact.

They also signed a secret protocol. With the generosity of dictators giving away countries that do not belong to them, Hitler told Stalin: "You can have the Baltic states (the republics of Estonia, Latvia, and Lithuania), plus chunks of Finland and Romania. I want most of Poland. You can have the rest — and I want peace in the East while I conquer the West." Of course, the wording was a bit more subtle and diplomatic: they talked of "spheres of interest," but the meaning was clear and brutal. Nine days later, German troops invaded Poland and the Second World War began.

For my people, the Baltic Germans living in Latvia and Estonia and known collectively but inaccurately as the "Baltic

Barons" (some were barons, most were not) a seven-hundred-year era ended.

Once, wrote Professor Nicholas Riasanovsky of the University of California in his book on Czar Nicholas I (*Nicholas I and Official Nationality in Russia*), "the Baltic Barons, these descendants of the Teutonic Knights, formed an elite in the empire of the Romanovs." In the First World War many, including my father, despite their German roots, served in the Russian imperial army fighting against Germany and Austria. After the Russian Revolution, they defeated the Bolsheviks and freed Riga, the capital of the soon-to-be created Republic of Latvia.

In late 1939, with Soviet troops poised to occupy Latvia and Estonia, the Baltic Germans would naturally have been at the very top of Stalin's list of people to be exterminated. But a minor clause in the Ribbentrop–Molotov treaty allowed them to leave the land they had called home for seven centuries, to be resettled in Germany and in soon-to-be conquered Poland. It was to be the final chapter of their long history.

The past is prelude to our lives. To understand Scots and "auld lang syne," you had better know something about their history. To understand Baltic Germans, and me, you should know a bit about their seven-hundred-year history on the border between East and West.

That history begins with the Order of Teutonic Knights, founded in the Middle East in 1190 in the fading days of the great crusades. Defeated by the Muslims in the Holy Land, the Order sought new fields of endeavour and found them in the pagan lands of northeastern Europe.

The northeastern lands along the Baltic Sea, now occupied by the Republics of Latvia and Estonia, were then inhabited by Kurs, Letts, and Lithuanians, speaking Indo-European languages remotely related to India's Sanskrit, and by Livs and Ests, speaking Finno-Ugric languages akin to Finnish. They gave their names to three provinces called for the next seven hundred years Estland (Estonia), Livland (Livonia), and Kurland (Courland).

Albert von Buxhoeveden, a canon of the Bremen Cathedral in northwestern Germany, preached, with the encouragement of Pope Innocent III, the "Northern Crusade," to convert the pagans and gain land and power, and the Northern Crusade began in 1199 with twenty-three ships, each carrying about a hundred fighting men, mostly nobles from northern Germany. They formed the Order of Swordbrothers, and were the first to take up the Crusade, but then merged with the older, more experienced and more powerful Order of Teutonic Knights.

The conquest was quick and ruthless. Just two years later, in 1201, Bishop Albert von Buxhoeveden founded Riga. In the feudal fashion of the time, vassal knights were rewarded with estates.

While the Teutonic Knights advanced from the south the Danes under King Waldemar II occupied northern Estonia in 1219. But the Danes were badly overextended, and in 1343 they sold their share of Estonia to the Order for ten thousand marks in silver.

For three hundred years the Order of Teutonic Knights ruled supreme in the Baltic provinces. Mind you, nearby countries were preoccupied. In northern Russia, fragmented into city states and feuding tribes, people and rulers lived in terror of the Mongols and paid them tribute to avoid invasion and enslavement. The Swedes were busy fighting their neighbours. Poland was building its empire, which at one time extended from the Baltic to the Black Sea.

Defended by an elite army of warrior-monks, ruled by the Grand Masters of the Order, the provinces of Kurland, Livland, and Estland knew three centuries of relative peace and, for the German estate owners, prosperity. The principal towns, Riga and Reval (now Tallinn), were members of that powerful and immensely wealthy medieval union of trading cities known as the Hanseatic League, and their German burghers evolved into a comfortably patrician middle class.

This pleasant continuum of security, power, and privilege was abruptly threatened by two events: the Reformation and the rise of Russia. Beginning early in the sixteenth century in Germany, the Reformation spread rapidly to Scandinavia and to the Baltic provinces, where both the natives and the German nobility — including the Barons — became Lutheran. The knightly Order, essentially religious and Catholic, began to disintegrate.

At the same time, Ivan IV, grand duke of Moscow, the first ruler of Russia to call himself "czar" — and later known, with good reason, as Ivan the Terrible — defeated the Mongols in the south. Then he turned west to subjugate the German-ruled provinces, acquire their great wealth, and obtain access to the Baltic Sea. In 1558 his armies invaded Livland.

The Order, in disarray, implored the Holy Roman Emperor for help. None came. Desperate, the Order appealed to Sweden and Poland. Both agreed — on condition that henceforth they would rule the Baltic provinces.

Poland and Sweden, then among the mightiest powers in Europe, defeated the armies of the czar and halted, temporarily, Russia's "Drang nach Westen."

The last Grand Master of the Order of Teutonic Knights became the first duke of Kurland under Polish suzerainty. Livland and Estland became part of Sweden, and the Baltic Barons transferred their feudal fealty to Poland and Sweden. In return they retained all their ancient powers and privileges and continued to rule their lands with considerable autonomy.

Sweden, then a major power in Europe and forever at war, rewarded its mercenary officers from many lands with titles and with estates in the Baltic provinces. Many families from Sweden, France (mostly Huguenots), Scotland, Holland, and Germany settled in the Baltic lands and gradually became Baltic German.

The Northern War (1700–1721), the great collision between East and West, Russia and Sweden, crushed the Baltic provinces. During the conflict, the Baltic German nobility fought valiantly for its Swedish king, the young Charles XII, for more than half of the officers in the Swedish army were Baltic Barons. They fought against his many foes, defeated Russia's armies, and marched farther and farther into the immensity of Russia, to be finally annihilated at the battle of Poltava (1709) by the troops of Czar Peter the Great.

While the Baltic German officers (including several Bruemmers) died in the far-away Ukraine, their homeland was ravaged by Russian armies. Pleased with a job well done, the Russian commander-in-chief Boris Sheremetyev reported to Peter the Great: "Everything is destroyed. From Reval to Riga everything has been eradicated root and branch."

Sweden, defeated, ceded the Baltic provinces to Russia. Peter had gained his "window to the West," and he needed the Baltic Barons in his relentless drive to modernize and westernize an essentially eastern and archaic Russia. He came to Riga and in a lengthy document bestowed upon the Baltic German nobility all the rights and privileges they had possessed first under the Teutonic Order and then under Poland and Sweden. In the centrally governed, autocratic czarist empire, the Baltic provinces were anomalous islands of national, religious, and linguistic independence.

The Baltic German nobility was a small clan of about 1,500 estate-owning families. In the fourth generation, it was said, all were related. At home they enjoyed self-rule by elected members who served without pay. The Russian realm offered them immense opportunities for they were usually well educated, and spoke several languages: German, Russian, Latvian or Estonian, French, and often Latin and English. "Their superior education and managerial talents took them to the highest offices of tsarist Russia, where their influence in the civil and military services far exceeded their numbers," noted the Latvian-born Modris Eksteins, professor of history at the University of Toronto.

In 1867, when Mark Twain and America's first batch of tourists visited Yalta in the Crimea, they were invited for tea and talk by Czar Alexander II at his summer palace. In the czar's entourage Mark Twain met Baron Wrangel, who "used to be

Russian ambassador at Washington;" Baron Ungern-Sternberg, "the chief director of the railway system of Russia;" and General Count Todtleben, "the famous defender of Sevastopol" during the Crimean War. All were Baltic Germans and, Mark Twain noted, "everybody talks English."

During the 1812 war against Napoleon, sixty-nine generals of the Russian army were Baltic nobles, starting with the minister of war and later commander-in-chief Michael Prince Barclay de Tolly, a Baltic German of Scottish origin.

The Baltic Barons did well in the Russian realm and that aroused the hatred of the virulently nationalistic slavophiles. They regarded these Lutheran–Germans in their near-autonomous enclaves as evil, alien entities within the sacred body of holy Mother Russia. It was the ardent dream of the panslavists to destroy the Baltic Barons and, once that shield was removed, to assimilate the Ests and Letts of the Baltic provinces. "It is necessary at any price to Russify the Letts and Ests, and that as quickly as possible," wrote the Moscow professor and historian Michael Pogodin.

The Baltic Barons survived the attacks of the panslavists, only to be destroyed by two mighty forces that surged ahead in the late nineteenth century: Nationalism and Communism.

Like others of their class across Europe the Baltic Barons were complacently content. With some justification they regarded themselves as efficient and honest administrators, both of their estates and of the provinces they ruled, and as benevolent masters of the Ests and Letts.

The Ests and Letts, with equal justification, regarded the state of affairs very differently. Educated initially by Baltic German pastors in their own languages and later in their own schools, this new class of Ests and Letts was fervently nationalistic and saw the Baltic Barons as oppressors who had too much power and owned too much land.

The Communist message was simple and thrilling: it promised power to the proletariat and death to the barons.

The first blow came in 1905 when, without declaring war,
Japan attacked the city of Port Arthur and destroyed Russia's
Pacific fleet. Catastrophic defeats led to the first Russian
Revolution, which swept across the realm and engulfed the
Baltic provinces.

Led and encouraged by highly trained and often fanatic
Communist agitators, mobs of marauding peasants and workers
pillaged and torched the ancient baronial manors and, when
possible, killed the owners. One of the 181 estates they destroyed
was Alt-Kalzenau, the ancestral home of my family.

Alt-Kalzenau was an ancient estate. I have seen its name on a
Dutch map of 1612. But it was owned by Bruemmers for less than
a century. The family can be traced to the region of Bremen in
northwest Germany where, in 1200, they were referred to as
"knights." They came to the Baltic provinces as vassals of the Order
of Teutonic Knights and acquired estates. Younger sons served with
merit but no great distinction in the armies of the Order, plus those
of Sweden and of imperial Russia. Older sons through the generations ran the estates. They were the quintessential country squires,
and in 1905 their world went up in flames.

The men who destroyed Alt-Kalzenau were probably
workers from a nearby city, for they not only looted and burned
the manor, they burned the stables, with the horses, the cattle,
the pigs, the chickens. My father rarely spoke of that time. That
the revolutionaries plundered the manor and set it aflame he
could understand. That they burned the animals he could not
forgive.

Life went on. My grandparents had fled to Riga. They
returned and rebuilt. But their world was coming to an end.
Soon the Baltic Barons, the lords and lairds of Livland, Estland,
and Kurland, would rule no more.

My father served as a cavalry officer in Russia's imperial army in the First World War. An Austrian bullet shattered his right arm, which healed but remained stiff and from time to time the old wounds opened and more bone splinters emerged.

In 1917, the empire of the Romanovs collapsed. Czar Nicholas II abdicated in March. On November 17, 1917, the Bolsheviks under Lenin seized power.

In the brutal civil war that followed, the Bolsheviks were at first victorious in the Baltic provinces. They arrested 570 Baltic noblemen to be sent to Siberia and death. One of them was my father, who had recently married.

When my mother tried to see him in prison, she met an unexpected friend. One of the Red Guards was a young worker from her parents' estate. They were of about the same age and had known each other from childhood. As an ardent revolutionary he was probably in favour of shooting Baltic Barons. But not the husband of his "young lady"! He arranged my father's escape and my parents hid with a loyal Estonian forester until the danger was over.

By a fluke of history, the other Baltic noblemen, already in Siberia, also survived. Lenin, fighting a civil war on many fronts, had to have peace with Germany and he instructed Leon Trotsky, his commissar for foreign affairs, to sign at Brest–Litovsk (now the city of Brest on the Polish–Belarus border) a treaty with Germany. One very minor clause demanded the release of the Baltic nobles. Lenin, anxious to oblige, sent an urgent telegram to Siberia: "Don't kill the Baltic Barons!" All returned home.

In the Baltic provinces the Bolsheviks were finally defeated, leaving a trail of death and devastation. My grandfather, the last Bruemmer of Alt-Kalzenau, died in 1919 in a Bolshevik prison, from maltreatment and starvation. My grandmother survived the prison, so weak she could no longer walk, and died a few months later.

Fighting the Bolsheviks were the armies of the just-proclaimed Republics of Latvia and Estonia and the "Landeswehr," a Baltic German army of volunteers. Its last commander, at England's insistence, was Colonel Harold Alexander, later the famous Second World War Field Marshal Earl Alexander of Tunis.

Of the Landeswehr, Alexander said in his farewell address: "I am proud to have commanded an Army composed entirely of gentlemen." He liked the life and the land so much, he even contemplated buying an estate in Latvia.

But the time of estates was over. Estland, Livland, and Kurland became the Republics of Estonia and Latvia, and the first thing they did was to confiscate without compensation the roughly two thousand estates of the Baltic nobility.

From being a wealthy, nearly autonomous upper class in the immense Russian empire, with all its opportunities, they became abruptly an impoverished, disliked, but — like the Jews — tolerated minority in two small, struggling, new-born countries. And that ended the ancient world of the Baltic Barons.

Chapter 2

THE PLACE OF THE SACRED SPRING

ACCEPTING THE END OF HIS WORLD and the finality of estate confiscation, my father in the 1920s had begun to build a new life. He leased the fifty hectares that remained from our family estate and ceded our house to the Latvian state. The family home, Alt-Kalzenau, rebuilt after being burned by revolutionaries in 1905, an old-fashioned manor of Edwardian elegance, was gutted and made into a dairy.

My father had studied medicine. The First World War and his service in Russia's imperial army had interrupted his studies. After the war he began an entirely new career. Together with a relative, Manfred von Vegesack, known for his business acumen, he started an insurance company and later a bank in Riga.

He was successful but paid a bitter price, for we rarely saw him — even in the winter months in the city. He worked long hours. He smoked incessantly, Russian *papirosy*, tube cigarettes with hollow cardboard stems. In 1934, when he was forty-two years old, he had a massive heart attack. He recovered but suffered from angina pectoris and, when the pain was bad, took tiny white nitroglycerin pills.

Adults and children then lived in separate worlds. My parents never discussed business, money, problems, plans, or children in our presence. If they did, they spoke French. The first French words I learned were le petit, "the little one." When I heard those words I knew my parents were talking about me. Despite this separation, there was a lot of love and also deep respect. As a small child I kissed my father's hand.

My mother was tall, loving, and easy-going. History fascinated her. She read a lot, was an expert on the history of Eastern Europe in general and Russia in particular, and corresponded with historians who shared her interests. Among my parent's friends were many emigré Russians who had fled from the Soviet Union, and one, a princess who had studied history in St. Petersburg, was a frequent visitor. When I first met her, I was impressed by her exuberance and elegance and, as I bowed to kiss her hand, by the beautiful rings she was wearing. Later I noticed she had on only her wedding ring, and asked my mother why she no longer wore those lovely rings. "She had to sell them," my mother said matter-of-factly. "They are very poor."

Life in Riga must have been difficult and not only for refugee princesses. Before the First World War, Riga was one of the wealthier cities of Europe and the wealthiest city in Russia after St. Petersburg. In 1914, it had a population of 530,000. In 1920, devastated by war and civil war, now capital of the new republic of Latvia, its population had shrunk to less than 200,000.

And just to the east was the menace of a Russia ruled by Bolsheviks. Even as a small child I was aware of it. Every night, before I went to sleep, my mother would come to my room. It was a nice warm moment. She would sit on my bed, I would snuggle up to her, we would talk a bit, and then I would say my prayers. I finished by asking God to protect my father and mother, my sisters, Heddy and Hella, my brother, Arist, and ended the prayer with a special appeal: "*Und, lieber Gott, bitte beschütze die armen Russen!* (And, dear God, please protect the poor Russians!)." They, I knew, were ruled by evil men.

My sister Heddy, nine years older than I, lived in a world remote from mine. She wore soft felt Marlene Dietrich hats, then in fashion, she danced, she went to parties and, at home, listened raptly to schmaltzy German *Schlager* "(hits)" or catchy jazz played on a wind-up gramophone, which whined on and on when the needle got stuck in a groove.

My brother, Arist, eight years my senior, was awesomely industrious. He was a good carpenter, liked to repair things, make things, invent things. On our birthday wish-lists Heddy asked for clothes, Hella asked for dolls, I asked for books, and Arist wanted tools.

Hella, four years older, blonde, happy and very kind, was my playmate and, because hot water was precious, also my bath-mate. Saturday was bath day. The large tub was filled with water and we romped and splashed until the bathroom was flooded, then hurriedly mopped up before angry adults came.

Children were left to amuse themselves. Hella and I built "houses" with chairs and blankets, raced our tricycle up and down the lengthy corridor of our Riga apartment, or went skating at the rink in a nearby park.

Hella wore Heddy's castoff clothes and I got hand-me-downs from Arist. In former days children's clothes were preserved in presses and worn through several generations. Now clothes were given to other families or, when totally worn, to the ragman who came once a month and chanted in the courtyard: "Rags, bottles, and shoes! Rags, bottles, and shoes!"

We rarely went out. Until I was ten, I saw only one film: Walt Disney's "Snow White and the Seven Dwarfs," and found the queen-witch so frightening that I had nightmares for weeks.

The great thrill of the winter in town was our annual visit to the circus. It was a magic evening, full of thrills and fantastic skills, of scantily clad girls and dashing men atop wildly gallop-ing horses, and always a Russian trainer who danced with his muzzled bears and rewarded them with sugar cubes. The stars of the show were the clowns, Ripsi and Pipsi, wonderfully funny for us children, but exciting for the adults, for they were the only men in Latvia who dared to poke fun at the government.

Independent Latvia started in 1918 as a multiple-party democracy, to be replaced, in the mid-1930s, by an authoritarian regime that tolerated neither opposition nor criticism. Only the clowns, enjoying the ancient "freedom of fools" that protected court jesters, could speak the truth. Most of it was way beyond my understanding but I do remember one skit. We went to the circus shortly after the government had passed a very unpopular law.

Ripsi came into the middle of the arena and erected a long, low barrier. His chum, Pipsi, dashed in from the other side and was about to leap over the barrier to greet him.

"Stop!" called Ripsi in a solemn voice and pointed at the barrier. "That's the law. You must not cross it!"

"But how can I reach you?" wailed Pipsi.

"Easy," said Ripsi, the scarlet lips moving in his chalk-white deadpan face. "You do what all the big shots do. You walk around it!"

As part of a policy of ethnic tolerance, Germans and Jews in Latvia were allowed to have their own schools. Since we were Baltic Germans, Heddy and Hella went to a girls' school where modern languages, Russian, English, and French, were stressed, while Arist and I went to the gymnasium where the emphasis was on the classic languages, Latin and Greek. Living in Latvia, we also learned Latvian in school, but really as a foreign language. In the city, Latvians, Germans, and Jews lived their separate lives in their separate worlds. We shopped in German at German stores, went to German doctors, had German friends, and spoke German with our dentist, who was Jewish. In my class of about twenty, only another boy and I spoke fluent Latvian because we spent part of the year in the country.

As a small boy I had one big problem: I was passionately interested in animals and natural history, and no one I knew understood or cared. I lived in this solitude until I was six, and met my Uncle Nicko, and then a wonderful life began. He was Nikolai von Transehe, a good biologist and an excellent but eccentric teacher.

Every Saturday after school I went to his apartment. The aunt served us cake and real coffee with lots of milk. This was a real treat. (At home only my mother drank real coffee, imported and very expensive. Everyone else got bitter ersatz coffee made of roasted chicory roots.) On one visit, Uncle Nicko looked at me sternly and asked: "How do birds fly?" That had been the subject of his lecture the previous Saturday and now he made me repeat it, corrected, explained, got more and more animated, and imitated the flight of swans with flailing arms.

On Saturday evenings he took me along to the regular meeting of the Naturforscherverein zu Riga, the Riga naturalists' society, founded in 1845 and still very Victorian. Most men were dressed in suits and ties, and some of the older gentlemen wore frock coats. There was usually one lecture, often illustrated with somewhat misty lantern slides of dancing cranes or grazing elks, followed by questions and lengthy discussions. All the members were seriously enthusiastic and none seemed to find it odd that I was there.

When I was seven, Uncle Nicko got me a "job" at Riga's Museum of Natural History. For a while, in a back room, I helped two paleontologists clean and assemble the skeletons of prehistoric fish that came from a quarry near Riga. They could never agree which bone should go where, argued, consulted books, and each tried to tell me in detail why he was right.

Once my writing was good enough, I helped to relabel the entire public portion of the collection. The old labels, in German and Latin, had to be replaced by new labels in Latvian, German, and Latin. (When I returned to the museum forty years later, the labels had been changed again. Now they were in Russian, Latvian, and Latin.)

In 1929, the year I was born, my father bought a farm in northwest Latvia, which we called Quellenhof, "the place of the sacred spring." From a triangular cleft at the base of the rust-red sandstone cliffs beneath our house burbled and rushed a spring of abundant, ice-cold, crystal-clear water. Latvian women from near and far came to this spring, filled bottles with its sacred water, washed their hands and faces, and chanted strange songs that were really prayers to the ancient pagan gods of forests and springs.

Latvia in the 1920s and 1930s was a land of small farmers, and since children were needed to help with the farm work, winter holidays at Christmas and Easter were short and summer holidays marvellously long, from the end of May well into September.

In May our orderly city life would come to an end, for about May 20 we would leave for Quellenhof and freedom. Just covering the eighty-five kilometres from Riga was an adventure, and the trip took most of the day.

We went by train to Sigulda (which we called Segewold), a very slow train that stopped at many stations. From Sigulda we continued by bus. The driver, as a rule, stopped at a local pub "just for a drink," and sometimes drank so much he could no longer walk. He would be carried out and shoved behind the steering wheel. There followed a brutal screeching of gears, the bus lurched forward, someone said in a solemn voice, "May God protect us!" and the farm women bent their kerchiefed heads in silent prayer.

Cars were still rare in rural Latvia. People were in awe of them and horses were terrified and bolted. When we travelled by horse-drawn cart and heard the distant drone of a car, we stopped, slipped a bag over the horse's head, and held it firmly until the danger had passed.

It was usually evening by the time we reached Quellenhof and had a joyful reunion with all the people who worked there. Then we rushed to the stables, said "Hello" to the horses, petted the cows, admired new calves and scratched the pigs. We kicked off our shoes and socks and for the next four months we were barefoot and free (*des petits sauvages*, "little savages," a disapproving city aunt told my mother).

Life on the land then was simple and largely self-sufficient. We had no electricity, no radio, no running water, and a sort of in-house outhouse, a smelly closet not far from the dining room. Almost all our food was grown in Quellenhof; berries and mushrooms came from the forests and moors; fish and crayfish from the lakes and the river. People made their own clothes; most families still owned spinning wheels and looms.

The first morning of every summer in Quellenhof, I woke up at dawn and listened to the concert of the birds: the chatter and whistling of starlings, the harsh shriek of jays, the mellow fluting of orioles, and the joyous two-syllable calls of the cuckoo that were counted by every country girl, for the number of times the first cuckoo of spring called was the number of years to her wedding.

All spring, summer, and fall we could do whatever we wanted, but because we did not have to work, we wanted to work. Heddy helped with the house and the garden. Arist was always busy, making wooden rakes and pitchforks for haying, repairing machines, building chairs and tables. His carpentry shop smelled of freshly cut wood and of the brownish glue, made of hides, hooves, and bones, that was heated in a *bain-marie*–type gluepot.

Hella and I did mainly the things that were fun. When in spring manure was spread, we drove the carts between stables and fields, moist manure squelching up between our toes.

We helped with haying. Hay was vital, it was the main winter fodder for horses and cattle. For its harvest and storage, timing and weather were all important, and Fricis, the senior worker, my mother, and all the other men would anxiously study the portends: the amount of dew in the evening, the colour of sunsets, the shifting of clouds and winds, the best phase of the moon. When all seemed right, the hay was cut on the wide riverine meadows, dried, raked into conical haycocks, and loaded with pitchforks onto broad wagons. I led the horses, the men pitched up the hay, and Hella and Ella, Fricis's daughter, trampled down and adjusted the load to make it as large as possible, and then, with the utmost caution, we drove the towering hay wagon home to be stored in lofts and barns. The nights were light in our northern land, and we all worked around the clock to bring in the hay and celebrated afterwards with a great feast on our lawn, with marvellous food and lots of home-brewed beer.

Hella and I always needed money and our allowances were slim. I got ten santims (ten cents) a week. One year Hella wanted a pretty dress. My dream was much more expensive: a large book, the *Birds of Europe* that I had admired at Uncle Nicko's. My mother promised me that if I earned the immense sum of five lats (about five dollars) during the summer, she would pay the rest, and I would get the book for Christmas.

As soon as the wild strawberries ripened, I would spend days collecting them. I knew all the best spots in forest clearings and at the edge of forest meadows. As I picked the ripe red berries, I watched birds, found the nests of bumblebees, watched busy, yellow-furred undertaker beetles bury a dead mouse, and once, at dusk, saw a mother shrew closely followed by all her furry, thimble-sized baby shrews.

In the fields I gathered ergot, a dark, potent, poisonous, usually inch-long fungus that grew in rye ears together with grains. I could sell ergot to a pharmacy in Riga, since it was used in many medications.

I spent long days on my knees to gather the spores of club mosses that grew in the forest and at the edge of the moors. I shook the stalks above a sheet of paper, then let the tiny, bright-yellow spores glide into a bottle. It took a week to fill a bottle. The spores were used to coat pharmaceutical pills to keep them from sticking to each other. The spores were also used in fire-works, for they burned with a brilliant green flame.

The most wonderful night of the year was June 23, Midsummer Night's Eve, St. John's Eve, and in rural Latvia the Festival of Fire and of the ancient gods. All year long, on the same traditional meadow spot near the river, wood was piled up into a huge pyre in preparation.

One year my father came from Riga, together with Dr. Stender, a close friend and well-known doctor, and Fricis and I went by cart to the bus station to pick them up. Dr. Stender looked at me, brown, scratched, and scrawny and asked: "Does the little guy have tuberculosis?" He used the complex name, but I knew what he meant. Consumption was still common in Latvia. People coughed terribly and there was blood on their lips. They became weak and died.

The adults talked. I sat behind them and sulked. Three kilometres from Quellenhof I jumped off the cart, easily outpaced the gently trotting horse, and was waiting for them when they arrived. Dr. Stender smiled. "The little guy does not have t.b.," he said in a loud voice.

In the evening we gathered on the meadow, not only our family and the people of Quellenhof, but families from several nearby farms, for on this spot, since time immemorial, people had gathered to celebrate the summer solstice with a mighty fire.

All wore beautifully made wreaths, crowns, and chaplets of leaves and flowers. Those of my mother and father, host and hostess of the night, were made of oak leaves. I, as the youngest, lit the fire. A hole had been left at the base of the pyre. I crawled in and set fire to the mass of birch bark in the centre.

For a while, little happened: some crackling and wisps of smoke. Then the flames spread and rose, soared up with a rush and a roar, golden sparks danced high in the sky and we stared at the flames and drank home-brewed beer. Some people sang the ancient songs of gods and goddesses of pagan times.

Much later, when the fire had burned down, they threw dry fir and juniper branches onto the glowing coals and, as the fire shot up again, the young men raced across the meadow and jumped through the sheet of flames.

I was too young to jump. But two men took me by the arms, raced with me towards the fire, yelled "Close your eyes!" and threw me through the flames. For one instant I was engulfed by heat and light, then others caught me on the far side and brushed sparks from body and head.

In 1938, Hella was allowed to bring her best friend, Karin von Haken, to Quellenhof. Both were at the *backfisch* age and talked, laughed, and giggled a lot. They had absolutely no use for a little brother, and I spent more and more time with an old woman the people called *ragana*, "the witch," but only behind her back.

She was our cattle herder. Early in the morning she opened the stable, and the cows, calves, and heifers wandered off to feed all day in the forest and on some of the meadows. Most of the herding was done by her dog, a clever, devoted brownish-brindled mutt.

The *ragana* could not read or write, but she had spent her entire life in the forests and had an immense knowledge of animals and plants. She knew where the owls nested and, when she called, an owl looked out of its hole in one of the ancient oaks. A weasel lived in a pile of stones; when we passed she squeaked like a mouse, and the weasel zipped out and tried to find it. For lunch, she made a sort of stew of mushrooms, milk from one of the cows, herbs, leaves, and roots in a sooty pot over a small fire. We ate it with chunks of dark rye bread and she told me stories about the elves and trolls that lived in the woods.

She was also a healer. In fall, the season for making jams and jellies, berries boiled in shiny, copper-bottomed pots on the large wood stove in the kitchen. Alma, our young maid, slipped, fell on the red-hot stove and burned her lower right arm. She screamed with pain, soothed the burn with pork fat, and wrapped the arm in a rag.

The wound festered but only when it was very bad did she tell my mother, who immediately took her to a doctor in the nearest town. He looked and said at once that gangrene had set in. Only prompt amputation could save her life. "Never!" cried Alma. Without an arm, no man would marry her. She would rather die. They returned to Quellenhof, and Alma went to the witch.

She had known Alma would come and was prepared. She had collected herbs, leaves, and roots and had peeled the bark off an arm-thick elder tree.

Alma's arm looked awful, black, spongy, and puffy, and it smelled like carrion. The *ragana* covered the lower arm with a thick poultice of crushed plants, encased it in alder bark, its sap blood-red, and sealed it with heated pine resin. Then she wrapped the arm in clean linen, made a sling, and told Alma not to use the hand and arm.

Ten days later, while all of us anxiously watched, the old woman cut the bark cast and cautiously removed it. The arm was healing. The poultice, they said, had sucked out the infection. Another poultice plus alder-bark sheaths was applied and the next time the witch took it off, pink skin covered the wound. The arm healed and the next spring Alma got married.

1939 WAS DIFFERENT. A new bus awaited us at Sigulda station. The driver wore a uniform. He did not stop at the pub. He was cold, efficient, and sober.

Electricity had reached Quellenhof. A simple machine near the spring pumped water to houses and stables. Water was no longer carried in pails with shoulder-yokes, but now came from taps. The electric pump throbbed near the sacred spring, and the women no longer gathered to wash their hands and faces and pray to the ancient gods.

Hella and Karin read *Vom Winde Verweht* (*Gone with the Wind*) and talked about Scarlett O'Hara and Rhett Butler.

Heddy, for some reason I did not grasp, remained in Riga.

There was now a radio in the living room. It ended our isolation and brought the world to Quellenhof.

I had a new friend, Stanka, a seasonal contract worker from Poland.

Stanka was only twenty or so and a happy, cheerful man. He came from eastern Poland, the part that had once belonged to Russia (and today is Russian again) and, in addition to Polish, spoke fluent Russian, so at least my parents could talk with him.

I still spent most of my days alone in the forest, watching birds, collecting insects, swimming in the Brassle River, but in the evening I often visited Stanka, in his room in the carpentry building. In a way we were both a bit lonely. I did not speak Russian, but had heard it so often at home that now, with Stanka's help, I learned it quickly. We roasted little sausages over the fire and he taught me the lovely, melancholy folk songs of Russia.

Life went on in its ancient rural rhythm that flowed with the season, but something was wrong. My father came several times from Riga, and my parents talked, but only in private. There was a tension I had never known before — not in Quellenhof, where we had lived alone and where nothing ever seemed to change.

In the fall, a car came to Quellenhof, the first car, I think, that ever came to visit us. That evening Stanka was teaching me the old Russian song of the "Twelve Robbers" when suddenly my father came to the room. "Heddy got engaged," he said. "You must come and congratulate them." I had met the groom and found him fascinating. He was the only man I knew who had hunted tigers. His name was Reinhold von Löwis of Menar. He belonged to a well-known Baltic German family of Scottish origin. The family name, centuries ago, had been Lowis, and they had owned the castle of Menar in Scotland.

After the First World War, Reinhold, like many Baltic Germans, had found the situation in Latvia hopeless. He emigrated to Holland, studied, and became a planter on Sumatra in the Dutch East Indies. In 1939 he came to Europe on one of the long holidays planters were granted every few years, visited us in Riga, for we were old family friends and remote relatives, courted Heddy, and now they were engaged. They would marry and move to Sumatra, a world away from us.

A few days later, on September 1, German troops attacked Poland and the Second World War began. Stanka packed his things. He had to return to Poland, he said, and fight the Germans.

We left Quellenhof in mid-September. I sat on the old wooden cart next to my mother, and only when we were far from Quellenhof did she quietly tell me that we would never return. The Bolsheviks would invade Latvia, she explained. All Baltic Germans had to leave.

It slowly sank in. We would never return to Quellenhof! I started to cry. My mother held me very close but did not talk, for there was nothing to say.

The last months in Riga were confused and hectic. Movers came and crated furniture and belongings. Traders came to buy the things we were leaving. Our schools were closed. The museum was closed. The adults were worried, upset, busy.

My godfather, my mother's brother, Karl von Wahl, usually called Uncle Karluscha, had moved to Riga as representative of a large German company. He was tall, charming, and generous and spoiled us with expensive liquor-filled chocolates that we had never tasted before.

He took us to the circus. It was still marvellous, but somehow no longer so funny. In one of their skits, Ripsi and Pipsi dressed as Baltic Germans and, speaking a Chaplinesque Germanic gibberish, came out with a large crate and packed into it the replica of one of our well-known churches. It was more sad than funny. Even the Letts, who resented the Baltic Germans, did not laugh. Our world was suddenly filled with fear.

In all, 84,000 Baltic Germans left Latvia and Estonia, and 2,180 remained. One of them was Uncle Karluscha. Unlike us, he had German citizenship and felt safe. He would die in a Siberian slave labour camp in 1942.

In mid-November it was our turn. We filed aboard a ship that in pre-war times had carried loads of bananas. As the ship left Riga harbour, everyone stood on deck and stared at the receding city, the vanishing land. Few cried. They just stood and stared, their faces sad and empty, and then they went down and lay on the straw the crew had spread for us in the former banana rooms.

I remained on deck. I had never been on a ship before and found it exciting. There was a nearly full moon and the moonlight glinted on the rolling waves. Lights and land disappeared. The ship began to rise and fall, twist and yaw, I felt suddenly cold, then hot, rushed to the railing, and was miserably seasick.

Chapter 3

THE POLISH ESTATE IN GERMANY

POOR POLAND. WHEN I REACHED it in the winter of 1940, it had just been divided for the fourth time by its rapacious neighbours.

Long ago, a powerful Poland extended from the Baltic Sea to the Black Sea. For about thirty years in the fifteenth century Poland was the largest state in Europe.

By 1773, however, weakened by external conflicts and internal dissensions, Poland was so reduced that Russia, Austria, and Prussia each took a fat slice of it. That was the First Partition of Poland. In the Second Partition, in 1793, they took some more, and two years later, in the Third Partition, they took the rest. Austria now owned Galicia in the southeast, Prussia the northwestern portion, and Russia owned the centre and the east.

Poland was reborn after the First World War. The Treaty of Versailles awarded Poland the eastern part of Prussia, Austria ceded Galicia, and the Soviet Union, defeated by the Polish army under Marshal Józef Pilsudski in 1920, yielded the east. This state of affairs would not last long.

On September 1, 1939, German troops invaded Poland from the west. On September 17, 1939 (as agreed between Hitler and Stalin), Soviet troops invaded Poland from the east. It was over in less than a month. On October 19, 1939, Germany incorporated western Poland, the region that had once belonged to Prussia. It became one of the twenty *Gaue*, "administrative regions," of the Reich, the Warthegau, named after the river Warthe (Warta). The Soviet Union took back the eastern portion of Poland. The centre became the "Generalgouvernement Polen," a sort of rump Poland, ruled by a German governor general.

The Warthegau, now German, was "cleaned." The entire Polish upper class — estate owners, factory owners, administrators — and most of the middle class — lawyers, teachers, professors — were arrested and deported to central Poland. Only workers remained, foremen, some experts essential to run the industry, plus some doctors, dentists, and a few priests.

All cities, towns, villages, estates, streets, squares, rivers, lakes, and forests got German names, usually those they had had during Prussia's reign, or their names were Germanized: the town of Kalisz became Kalisch, nearby Ostrów Wielkopolski became Ostrowo.

The vacuum created by the deportation of Poles from the Warthegau was filled by Germans from the Reich and by Germans from eastern Europe. Since so many Baltic Germans had once owned estates, the administration of many of the now-vacant Polish estates was assigned to them. My father would receive one of these assignments.

When our "banana boat" from Riga docked in Gotenhafen (Gdynia) near Danzig (Gdansk) we were quartered with a family in Pomerania for a while. Heddy, since her civil marriage a citizen of neutral Holland, met up with Reinhold. Their church wedding was in Pomerania, and I drank too much champagne (so cool and clear and bubbly). They spent their honeymoon in Italy and then went on by ship to Sumatra. Heddy sent us a postcard from Egypt.

Although Arist was at the wedding, soon afterwards he left us. To avoid the draft, he volunteered for the Wehrmacht (army) and went off to a panzer training school near Berlin.

In late January 1940, my parents, Hella, and I were sent to Posen (Poznan). Soon after, my father returned from a trip, and said the estate assigned to us was now called Kleingraben (its Polish name had been Hankova), and we would leave in two days.

We travelled by train to Ostrowo. There two coaches awaited us: a shiny, black brougham and an open landau, each pulled by two magnificent Arab horses. The coachman held the door open for us and Hella and I climbed into the velvet-lined brougham.

The wheels rattled on the cobbled roads. We stared out of the windows. The land was flat, snowy, empty. Mop-headed osier willows lined the road. Flocks of rooks flew above the white land.

Finally we passed through the small village for the workers on the estate, its thatched roofs covered with snow, and drove through the great gate and up the broad gravel drive, flanked by manicured beech hedges, that led to the manor.

Seven people stood on the manor steps, six women and one man. The man was Staszek, the foreman. He bowed and, in German, welcomed us to . . . He started with the Polish name and then said "Kleingraben." He introduced us to the others, the house servants. They bowed and curtsied awkwardly, then showed us to our rooms. Dinner, they said, would be served in half an hour.

The dining-room table was very long. We sat at one end: my mother at the head of the table, my father on her right, Hella on her left, and I next to Hella. Large-globed lamps spread a soft light over the fine linen tablecloth, the china plates, the silver.

The food came by dumbwaiter from the large kitchen in the basement. Maugosza, the senior housemaid, served. I watched my parents closely. I had never been served before.

It was wonderful — and it was awful. This was not home, not our home. It belonged to others who had been brutally evicted. A little girl had lived in "my" room. She was about my age. Her schoolbooks were there; some of her clothes; her shoes; a large sketchbook with childish drawings of her life, her parents, her house — the house in which we now lived.

Kleingraben was a large estate of about a hundred people. It had a very long byre, with rows and rows of cows and, at the end, in separate stalls, two massive bulls. The great farm wagons were pulled by four-horse teams, guided by teamsters with long whips that they could crack like rifle shots. There were stables full of heavy workhorses, a large piggery, and the stable for the coach and riding horses, several of them thoroughbred Arabs.

The people were deferential but remote, although language was not a problem. Until 1919 this region had been part of Prussia, and all the older people spoke German. Several workers had served in the German army in the First World War. Staszek had been a sergeant in the Kaiser's army at the same time that my father was an officer in the army of the Czar.

Maugosza, deeply devoted to her absent masters and hence deeply resentful of our presence, was coldly efficient. However, Rosa, the maid who looked after the bedrooms, just couldn't be cold. She was a tall, angular woman, with a narrow face, deep-set eyes, and long dark hair.

"What is your name?" she asked me.

"Friedel," I answered, for that's what the family called me.

"Fridek," Rosa said and Fridek I remained all the time we were in Kleingraben (in Quellenhof I had been "Fricit"). She was very kind and loved me with that special love of a childless woman.

In March, a desperate man came to see my father. His name was Pan Grabowski and until recently he had been the teacher in a nearby rural school. Now Polish schools were closed; the teachers were deported to work in German industry, and their families were sent to central Poland.

My father phoned friends, lawyers who worked in administration, then saw the top Nazi Party people in Ostrowo. He stressed the size and importance of Kleingraben as a food producer. He probably dropped names. The Party people first objected, then shrugged — one Pole more or less was not really that important — and graciously obliged.

Pan Grabowski got that vital *Ausweis* "identity card" saying his work was *kriegswichtig* "essential for the war effort." He came to Kleingraben as accountant-manager and moved with his family into an empty flat.

On Pan Grabowski's first day in Kleingraben my father invited him to dine with us. This turned out to be a mistake, for it offended the servants' rigid sense of class. We might be usurpers, but we were *szlachta*, "nobility," and we belonged. Pan Grabowski, the village teacher, did not belong and Maugosza served him with evident reluctance and icy arrogance. I often ate at his home, but Pan Grabowski never dined with us again.

In spring, the "phoney war" ended; the "sitzkrieg" abruptly became the "blitzkrieg." On May 10, 1940, German troops invaded Holland, then Belgium and France, and we no longer heard from Heddy in the Dutch East Indies. Until then, she had written several letters, letters from another world: wild boars had invaded her garden and the servants had cried: *Babi! Babi!* ("pig" in Malay). A python had nearly strangled her dog. It had been killed, and Reinhold had promised her python-skin shoes and an elegant purse. One evening a tiger had walked past their house. Now Heddy belonged to an "enemy nation." Our letters to her were returned with the stamped words CANNOT BE DELIVERED.

My Polish improved rapidly, and soon it was fluent but rural. But there were a few words I could not manage. In May, cockchafers emerged en masse, elegant, deep-brown beetles that were extremely voracious and stripped the new leaves from bushes, trees, and our elegant beech hedge. All the village children came to collect and kill the beetles, for they got a few pennies per jar, and they teased me when, as expected, I kept mispronouncing the cockchafer's Polish name *chrzaszcz*. (Later I learned that this word is part of one of Poland's favourite tongue twisters: *W Szczebrzeszynie chrzaszcz brzmi w trzcinie.* In Szczebrzeszyn the cockchafer buzzes in the weeds.)

That spring, Hella and I began to ride. Hella's horse was Kalina, an exquisitely elegant glossy-black, purebred four-year-

THE POLISH ESTATE IN GERMANY • 47

old Arab mare, who loved to race but at first refused to jump. In full gallop, even at a small ditch, she put on the brakes and Hella went flying.

My horse, misnamed Konczik, "little horse," also four years old, half-Arab, half-Trakehner, was long, tall, and powerful, a dark-dappled grey who just loved to jump.

Hella rode with a saddle. For me, my father and Staszek, the former cavalrymen, agreed it would be best at first to ride bare-back with only a cinched saddle blanket. Over the months, riding three to four hours every day, I developed a vise-like hold, clung to Konczik like a limpet, and slowly became as one with the horse. I always talked with Konczik, and his ears flicked back and forth. I grew to know his every mood and sensed every movement of his powerful body.

One day in fall, when the grain had been harvested and the stubble fields were yellow and bare, we walked slowly to a broad, water-filled ditch, Konczik had a good look. Then we backed up two hundred yards or so, I shouted "Go!" and he raced forward. I could feel his body tense, and with an immense fluid motion, he soared up and over the ditch and raced on. We jumped ditch after ditch, raced back and jumped them again.

With the beginning of the school year in September, Hella moved to a girls' boarding school in Wreschen (Wrzesnia), a small town near Posen. I remained in Kleingraben to be educated by a private tutor, Fräulein von Klot, who had been a teacher at a German school in Latvia. She was middle-aged, grey-haired, plumpish, and taught with great enthusiasm the subjects that interested her (and fortunately me): history, geography, and literature. Biology was my own passion. We skimmed lightly over mathematics, physics, and chemistry but added mythology and botany to the curriculum.

My great love was entomology. In Riga already I had admired the museum's large collection of insects. Now Pan Grabowski who, as a young man, had collected insects, presented me with two cases: one of beetles and one of moths and butterflies, beautifully mounted and labelled. They became the core of my growing collection.

Kleingraben had a very large park, an oasis of trees in the vast expanse of flat fields. Behind the manor house, a traditional Polish *dwor*, a lovely white neo-classical building with four white columns at the entrance, was an elegant English park and garden. Beyond that was the "wild park," and that was my enchanted realm, for it was full of old trees and tangled bushes, home to a great variety of birds, beetles, butterflies, and moths. In one corner of the park was a pond partially covered by weeds and full of frogs, water beetles, ferocious-fanged nymphs, and zippy whirligig beetles. A pair of moorhens built their floating nest among the reeds. I watched them for hours, sitting on the low branches of an ancient oak at the very edge of the pond.

On March 6, 1941, we celebrated my father's fifty-ninth birthday. Hella came. Arist was on furlough. The cook made a wonderful meal. We had just reached dessert when the first shot rang out. For an instant my parents froze, for they had lived through revolutions. Then they relaxed and we went out.

On the drive and lawns in front of the house stood, widely spaced, the twelve senior teamsters with their long whips. From the manor steps, Staszek directed them. They swung the whips outward in a great sweep and then, upon command, with perfect precision, cracked their twelve long whips in unison. Fifty-nine times. It was their traditional homage to the lord of the manor, and I could see that my father was deeply moved.

My mother said something to the maids and they now came with bottles of schnapps and a large tray with glasses, beautiful crystal glasses from my mother's family's estate in Estonia. Staszek, followed by the other men, walked up the stairs, each one took a full glass of liquor from the tray, raised it towards my father, drained it, and smashed the glass on the ground. Horrified, I watched my mother. Her gracious smile was a bit frozen, but it never wavered.

Amidst a world at war, Kleingraben was a remote island of peace, concerned with its own affairs. My father always rose early, made an extensive tour of the estate in his dogcart pulled by Maijka, a snow-white Arab mare, and discussed the daily chores with the workers and foremen. He had a short rest after lunch, and the rest of the day he talked crops, yields, accounts, plans, crop rotations, transport, and all the myriad other things involved in running a large estate with Pan Grabowski and Staszek.

Maugosza and the head gardener reported every morning to my mother, but it was simply a polite formality. They suggested this, they suggested that, my mother agreed, and all went about their work as they had always done.

FROM TIME TO TIME government inspectors came. Some were Nazi Party appointees and, my mother said cynically, came mainly for lunch, for our cook was well-known for her superb cuisine. They asked a few questions, thanked us for lunch, and left. Others were hard-working professionals. They asked for — and got — detailed accounts, and counted every pig and piglet.

After dinner we sat in the "small salon." Only for rare receptions and parties did we use the "large salon" and the ballroom, with its intricate parquet floor and glowing crystal chandeliers. We talked of the day's events. Once I found the nest of a hoopoe, a marvellous bird with a salmon-pink body, a large, black-tipped crest, and a delicate, slightly curved bill, but no one shared my enthusiasm. All listened politely to my tales of birds and beetles and marvellous moths, and then went on to talk about people and horses.

My mother read, mostly books dealing with Russian history. Fräulein von Klot knitted another pullover for one of her nephews. My father and I played bezique, a card game popular in nineteenth-century France and England. Winning depended on luck and on the ability to memorize all cards played. (Much later I read that bezique was also Churchill's favourite card game. He and Lady Churchill would play it during quiet evenings at home.)

One day I was surprised to see the "Parteiabzeichen," the Party pin, on my father's dresser. It seemed so totally out of character that I asked my mother in amazement: "Is father a member of the Party?" "Yes," she explained. "He had to join in order to protect our people."

Some months later that extra clout may have saved Rosa. Admirably loyal, she and other house servants had, without telling my parents, sent food parcels to the owners of Kleingraben now living in central Poland. Under the laws of the Reich, this was a serious crime. Rosa's name was the only one on the parcels as "sender," and now the police came to arrest her.

My father went with her to Ostrowo and managed to get her released on bail, pending trial and sentencing in two weeks. They were two anxious weeks. A Pole accused of a serious crime was nearly certain to be sentenced to a long term in prison. Or worse.

I do not know what my father did, whom he saw, what strings he pulled, what the lawyers that he hired managed to arrange, but two weeks later he returned from the trial together with Rosa. The judge had been brief. The accused was a very simple person and had acted in ignorance. Finally the saving words, "and in view of the fact that her work is *kriegswichtig*," Rosa was released with an admonition "never to do it again" and a fine, which my father paid.

We were still sitting in the salon after their return, talking, relieved, when Maugosza, the senior maid, normally coldly efficient and remote, came in, walked up to my father, made a deep curtsy, kissed his hand, and walked out again.

ON JUNE 22, 1941, four days before my twelfth birthday, Germany attacked the Soviet Union with three million men, 3,300 tanks, and 2,770 aircraft. One of those tanks was commanded by Arist, now a lieutenant. For a while we received letters that said little except "I am well." One evening in late fall the telephone rang.

Arist had been wounded. He was in a military hospital in Breslau (Wroclaw) in Silesia.

My parents left next day and returned a week later. Arist had been severely wounded, but his unusual first name (due to my grandfather's love for Greek history and heroes such as Aristides and Aristotle, both my father and brother were named Arist,) had probably saved his arm.

Somewhere in the eastern Ukraine, Arist had been standing in the turret of his tank looking for enemy vehicles when a Russian soldier rose and shot. Since Arist was holding binoculars, the bullet pierced both his lower and upper arm. The upper arm was a flesh wound. In the lower arm, blood vessels and nerves were torn.

The wounds were dressed at a field station, and with other wounded he was loaded onto a train heading west. The train stopped in Breslau, where orderlies walked through the train to take out emergency cases. Arist would not have been one of them, but one orderly stopped and said loudly: "This guy's got the same name as our *Chefarzt* (chief surgeon)!" The chief surgeon turned out to be Dr. Arist Stender, my father's godson and the son of the Dr. Stender who had visited us in Quellenhof.

They took Arist to the Breslau hospital, and Dr. Stender operated immediately. For a long time Arist's hand would look like a closed claw and, without nerves, was without motion or feeling. Slowly the nerves, their sheaths repaired, regrew, and after nearly two years of intense therapy in rehabilitation clinics Arist would regain the use of arm and hand. Later he said that the Russian soldier who shot him had probably saved his life. He missed the war years 1942 and part of 1943, years of immense German casualties. Of Arist's Riga class of nineteen boys, only four survived the war.

In the fall of 1941, Fräulein von Klot acquired a second student and I a perfect friend. Wolf Lackschewitz came from a Baltic German family of doctors and naturalists. His great-grandfather was Alexander Theodor von Middendorff, the famous explorer of northernmost Siberia. Bilau, the estate administered by his father, was fifteen kilometres from Kleingraben. When his tutor broke her hip during the summer, my parents invited Wolf to spend the next school term with us.

After my family's indifference to most things biological, it was marvellous to be with someone who shared my fascination with nature. We collected beetles and butterflies. We raised caterpillars in glass containers and spent hours each day collecting leaves for them. When winter and snow put a stop to our insect studies, we became obsessed with another project: to learn the behaviour of animals by following and "reading" their tracks in the snow. Very much in the mould of late-nineteenth-century "young naturalists," we took lengthy notes of all we observed and wrote detailed nature diaries.

But in 1942, Fräulein von Klot had reached the end of her qualifications. She could not teach us English, Latin, and other subjects required at our school level. Wolf went to a boarding school in northern Germany, and I was enrolled at the high school in the town of Kalisch, a one-and-a-half-hour bicycle ride away from Kleingraben. I could come home on weekends, but during the week I lived at a boarding home run by two middle-aged Baltic German teachers. I shared a room with three boys.

I had not been in a school since Riga, more than three years before, and this was a totally different school, a totally new world. It already began badly when on the first day in the corridor I greeted a teacher politely with "Good morning." He stopped me and said sternly, "The German greeting is 'Heil Hitler'! Remember that." I tried to remember.

Our classroom teacher, Fräulein Reiss, called my name to be registered. I stood up. The other boys regarded me with that mixture of curiosity and hostility that the established group has for the "new boy," the outsider.

She asked the standard questions: name, age, place of birth. "Confession?"

"Lutheran." That was all right. Most boys were Protestant, a few were Catholic, and some were *gottgläubig*, "believers in God." That was the new cult, the in-thing to be. It dispensed with the Bible, since that was a Jewish book — and, worse, Jesus was a Jew.

"To what *Jungvolk* [the "Young Folk," for those aged eleven to fourteen, was the pre-Hitler Youth] unit do you belong?" asked Fräulein Reiss.

"I don't belong to the *Jungvolk*," I said.

"But you must," she said, startled, then caught herself. "Yes, I see. You were educated until now on an estate by a private tutor [the curiosity-hostility level in the class rose by several notches]. You must join. Otherwise you cannot attend school. See me after class."

When I presented myself at the end of the lesson, she introduced me to an older boy, two classes above mine, very smart and polished but quite friendly, the leader of a *Jungvolk* unit, and he agreed at once to enrol me. "I have no uniform," I said.

"There is no hurry," he replied. "You can get one later. Our next meeting is on Wednesday."

It was bad. We marched a lot. I had never marched before, didn't keep in step, got kicked and kicked, and was finally told to march at the rear of the column. We sang a lot, just blared it out, catchy Party songs. I did not like the songs and I did not like to sing. I had never taken part in group games. I was the total misfit.

At school, great stress was laid on physical fitness, on team sports, on marching smartly in serried ranks. Had not Hitler himself said that German youth should be hard as Krupp steel and tough as leather? I rode well, but I did not play ball.

The first weeks were miserable. My only joy was the weekends in Kleingraben. Since I could not confide in my mother — she would not be able to help — I had long talks with Konczik. He looked at me with his large, soft horse's eyes, agreed with everything I said, and then we raced across the fields and jumped the widest ditches and I felt good again.

Finally I realized that I had to help myself. There was a small room used for storage at my boarding house. I got that room and made it mine, with shelves full of books and my microscope on the table. I had a talk with my *Jungvolk* leader. I was way behind in many subjects, I explained. If I didn't catch up, I'd fail. Could I be excused from *Jungvolk* duty. He agreed immediately and, I think, gladly. Our friendly, understanding family doctor attested that, due to an accident (I had once fallen off Konczik and cracked a few ribs), I was unfit for sports. The physical education teacher seemed pleased.

I learned which teachers had to be greeted with a smart salute and a loud "Heil Hitler!" and which teachers preferred a polite "Good morning" and no salute. I evaded the class bullies and they lost interest. And I acquired two friends.

Horst, a tall, gangly boy from Berlin, was a born artist and he loved to paint. His idol was the great German Renaissance artist Albrecht Dürer; he tried to create Düreresque images with a modern slant. In school he made flattering sketches for the teachers. Then, to amuse us, he did some quick, cutting caricatures: our biology teacher with his pudgy face became a fat rat with glasses. He produced with equal ease some large, kitschy, but extremely striking and effective propaganda paintings of "Our Führer adored by his Volk" and, as a result, was freed from *Jungvolk* duty.

Helmut was smaller, rounder, quieter, with a gentle face and large glasses. His father, a lawyer, had been severely wounded early in the war and walked with crutches. Helmut's parents invited me often for supper, and I found evenings with them both fascinating and frightening. His mother was friendly, quiet, and, I think, worried. His father detested the Party. He railed against the local *Parteibonzen*, "Party brass," and *Goldfasane*, "Gold pheasants" (so-called because of the yellow-brown Party uniform), grown fat with wealth stolen from the Poles while soldiers died at the front, and he spoke scathingly about Hitler ("that corporal with megalomania"), Göring ("that fat, bemedalled swine"), Goebbels ("that father of the lie"), and other leaders of the Reich.

I had never heard anyone speak like this before. I was partly shocked and partly thrilled, for I knew this was forbidden talk and very dangerous. Above all, I was amazed that he talked like that in front of Helmut and me who were both thirteen, because in my world adults did not talk of adult subjects in the presence of children.

My main problem in school was bad grades. I was way behind in English and all the sciences except biology, and on my Christmas report card Fräulein Reiss wrote a succinct warning that, unless my work improved rapidly, I would fail. My mother looked at me and smiled: "If you make it, you can have a dog," she said. A dog! That was what I wanted most in the world. Staszek had two fox terriers, friendly, happy dogs, and I wanted one for my very own.

My mother paid for tutorials. I crammed, with a magazine picture of a fox terrier pinned to the wall above my desk, and at the end of the term I passed all subjects, except mathematics, with excellent marks.

Two weeks later a crate arrived in Kleingraben with a four-month-old, smooth-haired fox terrier. I called him Hasko, after the Dutch captain in a book I was reading, and he was wonderful, a happy, perky little dog, full of life and joy. He slept on a rug next to my bed and, the moment I awoke, he jumped up, eyes shining, stubby tail wagging, asking "What will we do today?"

There was one problem. Hasko had probably never seen horses before. He thought they were monsters, which — considering his size and their size — was understandable. He looked at Konczik with terror and the first time I mounted became frantic with a mixture of fear and fury, yapped, attacked Konczik, then ran away.

So I dismounted, and for a while all three of us walked together along the hedges that separated the fields. For Hasko, probably kennel-raised, this was a world of endless fascination, filled with a myriad new smells. He learned quickly that he was not allowed to kill anything, not even mice, but if he discovered furry leverets hidden in the hedge and stopped, I would pet and praise him, we'd look at the big-eyed baby hares, and then go on exploring. Slowly Hasko got used to Konczik, and I could ride again. He ran along beside us and life was as perfect as it can be for a boy with his horse and his dog.

When I returned to school in Kalisch in the fall of 1943, I had just turned fourteen and received a letter ordering me to be at the Hitler Youth induction ceremony to be held one Sunday morning (many such events were held on Sunday mornings to interfere with church services) at the Kalisch Cultural Centre.

It was a solemn moment. Some sixty boys, all in brand-new uniforms, stood at attention on the right-hand side of a stage framed by large swastika flags. Top Party men and Hitler Youth leaders sat in the centre. A few gave orders and organized. The hall was full of Hitler Youth, plus parents, relatives, and friends (but none of mine; I had told no one).

We were called to centre stage in alphabetical order, introduced, sworn in, and moved to the left. All applause was to be kept until the end. I knew there was a problem when boys whose names began with D, E, and F were called. When only a few boys remained, an official behind me whispered:

"What is your name?"

"Bruemmer." He checked a list. I wasn't on it.

"Von Bruemmer," I said. He re-checked his list. I still wasn't on it.

He glared at me. "*Verschwinde!* (Vanish!)" he whispered and, when the next boy was called and all eyes were upon him, I slowly backed away and disappeared. I put the uniform away, bicycled to Kleingraben, went riding, and talked with Konczik and Hasko about the day's events.

I had not been sworn in, I had not received the Hitler Youth dagger with the engraved words *Blut und Ehre* ("Blood and

Honour"), but I had to join the Hitler Youth or I could not attend school.

Helmut's father found the perfect solution. He wrote a wonderfully patriotic letter to people in power and asked that his son and some friends, all deeply devoted to Germany's glorious navy, be allowed to form a detachment of Naval Hitler Youth in Kalisch, though he didn't mention that we were several hundred kilometres from the nearest sea. We received an enthusiastic approval and all necessary papers. We met once, formed a unit of three with Horst as our leader, Helmut submitted the required reports and, on paper at least, we had a perfect attendance record.

About a month later, an SS recruiter came to our school, and all boys who had not yet volunteered for military service had to appear before him. Before I went to Kalisch, my mother had told me one thing: "Never sign anything. No one can force you. Just keep saying, 'I cannot sign without my parents' consent.'"

My turn came. I went into the office assigned to him and stood at attention. He began with flattery. I was perfect to join the SS, the elite of the German Reich.

"Sign here!"

"I am sorry, but I cannot sign without my parents' consent."

He switched to humiliation. "Are you a *Muttersöhnchen* [a mother's little boy], who can only do what his mother tells him? You're big now, you're a man. You can decide for yourself! Sign here!"

"I'm sorry, but I cannot sign without my parents' consent."

He tried a dozen approaches and I kept repeating my one phrase.

Finally, in a relaxed sort of let's-get-this-over-with tone, he resorted to lying: "Just sign," he said, "and if your parents object, they can have it erased."

"I'm sorry . . ." I began.

"Get out!" he spat.

In the world at large, millions of men were fighting and millions of people were dying. In Kalisch we felt remote from the war, although there was rationing and people worried about relatives at the front and in the cities that were being bombed. But there was little change in our daily lives.

On weekends and holidays in Kleingraben I returned to the calm serenity of a world ruled by the land and the seasons: ploughing, sowing, growing, reaping. Each spring the hoopoes returned to the nest hole in the old willow and the moorhens built their floating nest on the pond in the park. I watched birds and took notes and Hasko, next to me, tried to sit still, which is a very hard thing for a young fox terrier to do.

Only Arist appeared changed. He spent another furlough in Kleingraben and was quiet and withdrawn. Many of his friends had died. His arm had healed. The left hand now remained slightly bent but he used it with all his former skill. Now *Oberleutnant* ("First Lieutenant"), he would soon rejoin his panzer division fighting in the east. We rode a lot together, Arist on a large roan, the most powerful riding horse in our stable, and he rode with a wild and reckless daring, as if pursued by demons.

IN 1942, GERMAN TROOPS had occupied most of Europe, from arctic Norway to North Africa, from the Caucasus Mountains in the east to the English Channel in the west. Now, in a vast, irregular retreat, the fronts were being moved back, inwards towards Germany.

In 1944, I had no summer holidays. With about two thousand other schoolboys I was sent east, past Litzmannstadt (Lodz), to dig anti-tank trenches, very deep and sharply V-shaped. In theory, like a beetle in a sand trap, once a tank fell into such a trench, it could not crawl out. (In reality, the front collapsed so fast that Russian tanks drove on roads avoiding all the trenches.)

We lived in the barracks of a large camp, surrounded by barbed wire, about twenty boys to each room. We dug and shovelled earth ten hours every day, hurt badly at first, and had big blisters, got used to it, and slowly took some pride in our newly acquired strength. The camp was run by army engineers and adult Hitler Youth leaders.

One evening after work, as we lined up for supper, ten boys were standing on large barrels near the entrance and, as on a medieval pillory, each one wore a "shield of shame," a large cardboard sign that said: "I AM A SHIRKER AND A COWARD."

They had reported in sick. The camp doctor decided they were only lazy and, to set an example, they now stood upon those barrels as we filed past. We were supposed to jeer, and a few did jeer, but it was half-hearted. The boys, their heads bowed, looked too pathetic. The spectacle was not repeated. It didn't have to be. No one reported sick again.

The SS recruiter I had met in Kalisch came to our camp and, among all those boys, he recognized me. Failures probably rankle.

This time he had me. In front of all the boys and the brass he wielded with great skill a very big carrot and a very big stick. The stick was the relentless public humiliation of a fourteen-year-old boy. The carrot was the promise that, if I signed, it would all be finished. I stood at attention, sweating and scared, and kept repeating my one sentence: "I'm sorry, but I cannot sign without my parents' consent."

He changed tack.

"Why do you insist on joining the Wehrmacht?" he asked, referring to an earlier conversation.

"Because my brother is in the Wehrmacht," I replied.

He was hot and angry and, guessing wrongly that Arist might be in the rear, said with a nasty sneer: "I bet he's just as big a coward as you!"

It was a wonderful moment. I looked straight at him and said loudly and clearly: "I do not think so. Otherwise our Führer would not have awarded him the German Cross in Gold." (This was partly true. Arist had indeed been given this high decoration for exceptional bravery, but it had been presented not by

Hitler, who had other things to do, but by Heinz Guderian, the top panzer general.)

There was a long pause. Then the ss man said in a totally different tone of voice: "You must be very proud of your brother."

"I am," I replied.

"Dismissed!"

We were relaxing in our room after work when the door opened and the room senior yelled: "Attention!" It was a high Hitler Youth leader, the camp's second-in-command, and, it was said, a soldier who had been severely wounded.

"At ease!" he said and we relaxed. He asked a few questions. When he came to me, he drew with chalk a sign upon the table, a Hitler Youth badge of rank.

"What rank is this?" he asked. I did not know.

He drew another sign. I guessed. I guessed wrong.

Finally he drew a large, elaborate sign. I could feel the boys trying to tell me something, but I was too flustered to get it.

He pointed to his uniform. It was his rank.

He smiled, quite friendly. "Perhaps you should spend a bit of time learning the Hitler Youth insignia," he said and left.

Two days later, he passed the ditch where I was working. He stopped and motioned to me.

"Come with me," he said.

"Now you're in for it," said some boys from my room.

I followed him. He stopped from time to time to speak to section leaders. Then he walked away to some tall trees and sat down in the shade.

"Sit down," he said. Then he turned to me. "What do you like to do?" he asked.

I tried to think of the correct Party-slogan-type answer. He guessed that and insisted: "Tell me truthfully what you really like to do."

"I like to ride, I like to collect insects, and I like to watch birds," I said, bracing myself for scorn.

But he did not scoff. He asked me many more questions: about my parents, Kleingraben, Arist.

He was silent for a while. Then he said: "From now on you will be my adjutant. There is an empty room across from my quarters. Move into that. Do you have a bicycle?"

"At home," I said. He gave me a two-day pass and railroad money, and I went to Kleingraben and returned with my bike.

He talked. It had been winter on the Russian front. They were attacking, rushing forward, when a bullet hit him. It went right through his upper body, tore through a lung. He was lying in the snow, blood freezing on his body, unable to move, when the Russians counterattacked. He heard the stomping of Russian soldiers, the screech of tank treads that were going to crush him. He fainted. When he woke up, he was in a field station. The fight had shifted again. German stretcher-bearers had found him, but frost had reached his lungs. They were badly damaged and sometimes at night he had violent seizures.

Then came the instructions: I was to sit every night in his room. "In a fit," he said, "I know nothing. So don't touch me. I am strong and might hurt you. Just watch. If I stop breathing for sixty seconds, race with your bike and get the camp doctor.

"You must not talk about this," he insisted. "To anybody." No one, he kept stressing, must know of his seizures.

So, that first night, I sat in his room. He took off the fancy uniform and, in shirt and shorts, went to bed. He talked a bit and soon fell asleep. He was about thirty-five, but to me he seemed old with his sallow skin and sunken cheeks.

The lights remained on all night. I watched him and read. On a whim, on my last trip to Kleingraben, I had grabbed the fattest book I could find, my mother's copy of *War and Peace*, and now I immersed myself in the vast panorama of other worlds and other wars, of the Rostovs and Bolkonskis on their vast estates, of Napoleon riding in triumph over battlefields littered with the dead and dying.

For two nights nothing happened. During the day I bicycled many times to the building where I knew the doctor slept. It took one minute.

The third night he had a seizure. It began, like all subsequent seizures, shortly after midnight. His breathing became irregular. He moaned and tossed. Suddenly he sat up in bed and stared at me with wide glassy eyes. He gasped for breath, and in between the gasps, the frantic fear, the rasping voice: "They're coming!" The spasms became more violent. The tanks were close. The grinding treads. He reached for me. "You're death! You're death!" His voice was hoarse, his face contorted by terror.

The seizure lasted about half an hour. It seemed very long. He collapsed abruptly and lay still. He stopped breathing, and I began to count. Around me, the camp slept and I felt very alone and very scared. After forty seconds he began to breathe again — in small, gurgly gasps at first, then more evenly — and finally he fell into a deep sleep.

I spent three weeks with him. During that time he had about seven seizures, some easier than the first I'd seen, a couple much worse, when those tank treads nearly crushed him. He twisted and shook and tried to run and yet was oddly paralyzed. After the worst attack, the first gurgly breath came only when I had reached fifty-six seconds.

One day he told me he was being transferred. He would leave the next day. I spent a last night with him. I was near the end of *War and Peace*. Napoleon and his army were retreating from Moscow. He had marched into Russia with six hundred thousand men. Fewer than a hundred thousand survived. Winter and war killed the rest.

He came to my room the next morning. He gave me railway money and a six-day pass to take my bicycle back to Kleingraben. He was in his fancy uniform but we did not salute. We shook hands. He smiled a bit. "Thank you," he said and went out.

When I returned from Kleingraben the camp was in quarantine and closed to me. Typhoid fever had broken out. Afraid to be labelled "shirkers," sick boys had worked until they dropped. The disease spread rapidly and many boys died. I went back home.

Hella was there. The grain had been harvested. The fields were bare. Kalina, Hella's coal-black Arab mare, had long since lost her fear of jumping and we raced across the yellow fields of fall, our bodies moulded to the smooth, long, reaching rhythm of the galloping horses. When Konczik and Kalina were tired, we let them rest and graze. We lay in the grass and stared at the sky and the drifting cumulus clouds. There was now a great fear in our world but, like everyone else, we did not want to talk about it.

We went back to school and returned for Christmas. It was a quiet Christmas with a few gifts for the servants and us. After Christmas my mother spoke with us. She told us calmly that we would probably have to flee. I had to leave all my cases with insects, all my books. I could only take my diaries and Hasko. We had to wait until the evacuation order was given.

On January 1, 1945, Soviet troops were still massed east of the Weichsel (Vistula). There, at Stalin's orders, they were waiting passively while, on the west side of the river, in Warsaw, German troops annihilated Polish resistance.

In Kleingraben, two light wagons were readied and loaded with fodder for horses. We packed our suitcases. I took pieces of bread and sugar cubes and said goodbye to Konczik. We had been together for nearly five years. He could tell by my voice that I was sad, snorted softly, and pressed his muzzle against me.

On January 12, 1945, Russian troops launched their great offensive.

By January 18 they had reached Litzmannstadt.

On January 19 we received the order to move.

The house servants, Pan Grabowski, and Staszek stood on the manor steps. We thanked them and said goodbye. Rosa was crying and embraced me. Pan Grabowski and Staszek were upset but formal. Maugosza was very polite but quietly triumphant, for soon, she hoped, the real owners of Kleingraben would return.

We had been told to gather with other refugees near Ostrowo for the westward trek. We never reached it. The roads were clogged with a stream of humans and vehicles pouring west, and we became part of that trek of millions fleeing in fear and desperation.

At night we pulled off the road, fed our horses, and slept at farms or empty manors. While the rest were asleep one of us remained with the wagons and horses at all times, fearing they might be stolen.

It was bitterly cold, and the road was icy. Wagons, carts, people on foot, men on bicycles, it went on and on, this procession of the fleeing, a dark, wavering line creeping through the white land. There were long stops. Carts broke down and were pushed off the road. People cried.

We crawled but rumours flew — rumours of fear and hope. The Russians were close behind us. The Russians had passed to the north. The Russians had been stopped by German troops.

Cossacks on fast, shaggy horses galloped past. They had fought on the German side for an independent Ukraine. Now they were fleeing, for to be caught by Soviet troops meant certain death. They had tried to be liberators. Now they were traitors.

On the fifth day, west of Posen, a great cry flew along the endless throng of the fleeing: "Tanks! Tanks! Get off the road!" Behind us we heard the deep growling of great engines, the crack of shots.

We led the horses off the road and into the field. The long column of tanks advanced, stopped. There were shots and the tanks rolled on. My father and I held one team, Hella and my mother the other. My mother collapsed, hit by a bullet. It had pierced her thigh, but she got up immediately.

Russian soldiers came running. "*Uhr! Gib Uhr*! (Watch! Give watch)" they yelled urgently, waving their guns. We gave them our watches. One waved. "Go back," he called. "Go back. Is finished." And the tanks rolled on, crushing everything that remained on the road.

My father dressed my mother's wound. The bullet had not hit the bone. She could walk. The pain would come later.

Earlier we had passed a small town. Now we travelled slowly back to it, and we found an empty house. My mother lay down. We unloaded the suitcases and the baskets of food, leaving the wagons and horses in the yard. After a while, we heard a noise. People came and drove the horses and wagons away.

For two days nothing more happened. We had enough food. We kept very quiet, and stayed away from the windows. Suddenly the door was ripped open and armed men came in. "Out!" they ordered. We left everything and walked out. Hasko walked out with me. A man kicked him; he yelped and ran back into the house.

They took us to the local jail, really two large empty rooms, one for women, one for men. There were seven or eight men in the room with us, and some straw on the ground. A bucket in the corner was the toilet. In the evening each one of us got a piece of bread and a mug of tea.

In the morning the men, Hella, and I were marched out of town. We were given picks and shovels and ordered to dig a large pit. The ground was frozen, and at first the work went very slowly. My father did not have his nitro pills. He was in severe pain but tried not to show it. A guard noticed his rings. "Give!" he ordered. My father took off his signet ring and gave it to him. "Give!" the man said again and my father took off his wedding ring, kissed it, and gave it to the guard.

In the afternoon, when the pit was large and deep, a truck arrived. It was loaded with dead people, men and women. Hella and I had never seen corpses before and stared in terrified fascination. Frozen solid, they looked grotesque, the skin blue-white, smeared with mud and blood, the faces contorted in the rictus of death. "Don't look," said my father gently and tried to shield us. They threw the bodies into the pit.

More guards came. They talked, they argued, shouted, gave orders. Two guards suddenly came to us and grabbed Hella and me. "Go!" they ordered. We turned to our father.

"Go!" he said urgently. And then he smiled.

Halfway to town we saw our mother coming towards us with a guard, limping a bit but very erect. Hella tried to run to her, but she waved her back and, as we passed, she looked at us and also smiled.

They locked us up again, Hella with the women. I was alone in the room. In the evening, the door opened and a guard came in with a piece of bread and a mug of tea.

The doors were opened early in the morning, and we were marched out. It was a cold, grey, wintry day. Hella and I held on to each other but did not talk. Two guards escorted us, a young guard and a man in his fifties. Both men carried rifles. "Where are we going?" asked one of the women. "To Poznan," said the older guard. There were nine or ten women and Hella and I.

We had walked a couple of kilometres when something raced up behind us. It was Hasko. He had probably run back and forth in town, had picked up our scent, and now he had found me and was wildly, joyfully happy. I knelt in the snow and he whined and licked my hands and face.

"Tell him to go away," said the older guard, his voice hard.

I hugged Hasko, then gave him a shove. "Run!" I said sternly. "Go away! Run!"

He ran a bit, then stopped and ran back. He thought it was some new game.

I slapped him this time and pushed him hard. "Run away!"

He ran, then stopped not far off, puzzled, looking at me. The young guard shot him in the belly. Hasko screamed with pain and fear and tried to drag himself to me.

"Kill him! Please, please, kill him!" Hella and I cried, but the young guard just stood there and laughed. He was enjoying himself.

The older guard took his rifle and fired three quick shots into Hasko, and all that was left of my little dog was a small pile of bloody fur and shattered flesh on the snow.

Poor Hella tried to comfort me, and then something broke. Until that moment we had been rigid, frozen. Now it burst out, the grief, the fear, the despair of children who have lost all they loved, and we held each other and cried.

"They're crazy," said the younger guard. "We shoot their parents and they don't cry. We shoot their dog and they cry. I tell you they're crazy."

The older guard did not respond. He shouldered his rifle. "Let's go," he said. We walked on and on and the day was grey and cold and flocks of crows flew over the wintry fields.

It was nearly dark when we reached Posen. The streets were full of men with guns, some in uniform, others wearing armbands with symbols or inscriptions. There were other groups of prisoners and guards. Men shouted in Russian, Polish, German. Somewhere shots were fired. Someone gave me a hard push with a rifle butt. I stumbled forward and, when I turned around, Hella was gone.

Chapter 4

THE TRAIN TO SLAVERY

IT WAS CHAOS. THE DARK STREETS of Posen, now the Polish town of Poznan, were full of cowed prisoners and nervous, trigger-happy Russian guards. They yelled at us. They hit us with rifle butts, and we ducked and rushed and stopped. We were being herded towards an enclosure surrounded by a barbed-wire fence. We funnelled through a wide gate. Guards yelled orders.

It was a large military camp. Until a few days ago, German soldiers had been quartered here. With others I was pushed into one of the buildings, a large dormitory with double-tiered metal beds. Most still had mattresses on them. Some even had blankets. The shoving and yelling stopped. We had arrived.

I sat on a chair, tired, frightened, confused, and very alone.

"What's the matter, boy?" a voice said near me.

A man stood in front of me, tall and broad, with blond hair, a lean, clean-shaven face, and cold, grey eyes. His name was Karl, and there was something dangerous about the man. People were afraid of him. I would learn that he never talked about his family, his home, his time in the army (he had undoubtedly been in the military, probably the ss, and had changed into civvies). He may have been with one of the special units fighting Soviet partisans and, as a rule, neither the partisans nor the partisan hunters took prisoners. Anyone who surrendered was shot or hanged. So, Karl did not speak about his past and no one ever asked him.

I looked at him for a moment, then told him what had happened.

"Tough," he said, his voice indifferent. "Have you had anything to eat?"

I had not eaten all day, and suddenly I was very hungry. Karl went to a nearby bed and from a large sack took a piece of bread and part of a sausage.

"Eat," he said. "Have you got a bed?"

"No."

He motioned to the man lying on the bed next to his. "The boy will sleep here," he said evenly. "You find another place." The man started to protest, looked at Karl, got up, and left with his blanket. "Leave the blanket," said Karl. He left the blanket.

I lay down fully dressed, but took my boots off. "Keep your boots on," said Karl, "or they'll be stolen." It was February 3, 1945. Only two weeks ago we had left Kleingraben. All around us men were beginning to snore. I was exhausted and slept soundly. "Get up, boy!" It was Karl. For some reason I could never fathom, this cold hard man had sort of adopted me. Perhaps in another life, another world, he had had a young brother.

Guards came in and yelled: "Assemble!" All the men from our dormitory assembled in the yard. We were lined up and counted. Then we were counted again. We waited. It was cold and we had not eaten. Other guards came and counted us.

After a long time uniformed men arrived with papers, inkwells, and pens. We were to be registered.

"Where were you born?" asked Karl.

"In Riga, Latvia."

"Change that to Berlin," he advised. "How old are you?"

"Fifteen."

"Change that to twelve," said Karl. "What's your full name?"

"Friedrich von Bruemmer."

He smiled. "Skip the 'von,'" he said.

One by one we went back into the dormitory to be registered. We were a camp of male German civilians who were to be sent, we later found out, as slaves to the Soviet Union.

There was much confusion, which often led to heated arguments. Many Germans, especially the "Volksdeutsche," Germans born and raised in Poland, spoke Polish just like Poles. Some had changed their names, claimed they were Poles, and tried to merge or vanish as the Russians advanced. They had had to be rooted out, and in the process many real Poles were arrested and were now in our camp.

There were the Polish "collaborators." In theory anyone who had "willingly" worked for the Germans was a collaborator. In practice, willing or unwilling, most Poles in the former Warthegau had worked for, and often with, Germans. Now was a wonderful time for informers, accusers, denouncers. They pointed, and many Poles were arrested. Some were shot, some went to prison, and many ended up in camps, together with German prisoners.

There were real civilians, like me, but there were also soldiers who, hoping for an easier fate than that of a POW, had at the last moment changed into civilian clothes. Some, like Karl, had also changed their identity, as I soon came to realize.

And then there were the *Fremdarbeiter*, "foreign workers," conscript labourers from Holland, France, Belgium, Denmark, and other German-occupied countries, who had worked in factories in the Warthegau. They now claimed loudly that they were "Allies" and should be released. The Russian attitude was "any German can say that" and the vehemently protesting foreigners were roughly pushed back. Some who persisted were beaten. A few were shot.

We were ordered to assemble again in the yard. A commissar (probably an officer of the NKGB, the secret police, later called the KGB) spoke to us in fluent German. "Behave," he said, "and you will be well treated. If you don't obey, you will be terribly punished." That night we finally got a bit of food, a piece of bread and watery soup.

The next day we were divided into small work brigades and marched out of camp under guard to clean up the town of Poznan. The Germans had fled abruptly, leaving most of their possessions. Poles looted the abandoned houses, closely followed by looting Russian soldiers, who sometimes shot the looting Poles.

Russian soldiers had been quartered in the houses, had bivouacked in the gardens, and in an amazingly short time had turned comfortable, even elegant, middle- and upper-class houses into filthy wrecks. These were men who had grown up in one-room log houses, who knew only outhouses. Rumour had it that they tore taps out of walls to install back home, so they would have running water in their *izbas* ("log huts").

To cook their food, the soldiers chopped up anything that would burn: the stolid Biedermeier furniture of most homes, mahogany tables, oak dressers, rosewood panelling. They clogged the toilets, used the bathtubs as toilets or simply shit on the floor. Now the soldiers had marched on and we were supposed to clean the houses.

Karl was very quick. The moment we entered a house, he rushed from room to room searching for portable things over-looked by the looters: cutlery, handkerchiefs, cigarette lighters, any clothes, matches, cuff links, a belt. In one house he found a carpet, rolled it up tightly, and tied it with a rope made of torn sheets. "*Nje moshno!* (You can't)," said the guard when he walked out of the house with his carpet. Karl looked at him calmly and said: "*Moshno.* (I can)." Karl spoke a very simple Russian, only verbs and nouns, no grammar, but he was always understood. The guard shrugged, and Karl added the carpet to his hoard in camp.

It was on one of his lightning raids that Karl, rushing upstairs in a house, nearly collided with a man coming down-stairs. "Cleaned out," said the man and laughed, holding up a

sack with booty. "When I clean, it's clean!" And so we met
Manek, who became our friend and my mentor.

Karl and Manek were totally different. Karl was tall and
straight, Manek smaller, and squat, and he slouched a bit. His
hair was dark brown, his face bland with crafty eyes. Karl was
remote, direct, calm, and cold. Manek was cunning, sneaky, and
cheerful. Karl never laughed. Manek laughed a lot. *Das Leben ist
ja nur ein dummer Witz* (Life's only a stupid joke), he often said.
Karl never mentioned his past. Manek loved to talk about his
past.

Manek had been born in a village in Upper Silesia, the part
the League of Nations gave to Germany in 1921 (the other half
went to Poland). His father was German, his mother Polish, and
he spoke both languages with equal ease.

"My father was the village drunk," Manek said with a laugh.
"And my mother had a kid a year." Manek had been raised
mainly by his Polish grandmother, the village midwife and
healer. An uncle ran a smuggling ring between Germany and
Poland and, when he was eleven, Manek joined the gang as
whistle-blower, to warn of danger.

He didn't finish school. Instead he became an orderly in the
regional hospital and did some smuggling on weekends.

Manek was twenty when the war broke out and he was called
up. How he evaded the draft was one of his favourite stories.
His grandmother, he said, gave him a small bottle filled with a
liquid and detailed instructions. "One hour before the exami-
nation, she told me, drink the liquid and get rid of the bottle.
When they examine you, they will hear an irregular heartbeat.
Play dumb. Just say: Yes, my doctor once told me my heart is
bad, and say you sometimes get dizzy and keel over. It happened
just as my grandmother said, and I was declared unfit for military service."

He continued to work as orderly at the regional hospital and
later he was transferred to a military hospital in German-
controlled Posen. At the last moment, as the Russians advanced,

he faced a dilemma: to become a Pole and risk being shot by Poles as a "collaborator," or stay German and risk being shot by the Russians. He tried a third option. Remembering his grandmother, he concocted an evil brew that made him vomit, crawled into one of the beds, and pretended to be terribly sick. It might have worked, but one of the wounded soldiers denounced him. The Russians beat him and he ended up in our camp. "All that vomiting for nothing," he said and laughed.

Both Karl and Manek were about twenty-five years old.

We cleaned houses in Poznan for a week, scraping shit into buckets and dumping it in the gardens. Some prisoners worked hard and diligently. They were good Germans, and they really tried to clean those houses. Karl, Manek, and I did as little as possible and collected as much as possible from the houses. "Why do we take all this stuff?" I asked.

"Because they will send us to Russia," Karl said matter-of-factly. "And in Russia there is nothing."

Karl was right. One evening, after another supper of bread and watery soup, guards came in and yelled, "Out! Assemble!" The guards carried rifles with bayonets.

"This is it," said Karl. "Take everything." He had two large bags and his carpet. Manek had two bags, and I had one.

The entire camp was assembled and divided into groups of one hundred men each. Guards yelled. They always yelled. "*Dawai! Dawai!* (Get going! Get going!)" and "*Bistray! Bistray!* (Faster! Faster!)." These became the words most hated by Soviet slaves, the leitmotiv to our march of misery.

A long column of prisoners marched through the dark streets of Poznan, armed guards on either side. Some men were already weak, and they stumbled. Laggards were jabbed with bayonets. Behind us we heard shots.

On a siding at Poznan station stood a long train lit by the headlights of military trucks parked nearby. The train consisted of dull red cattle-cars with small barred windows near the top.

Each group of a hundred men was lined up in front of one of these freight cars.

Karl gave rapid instructions. He seemed to know a lot about prison trains. Manek agreed. He took Karl's bags. Karl turned to me: "Stay close, boy," he said. "Be fast and help Manek with the bags."

We were counted one last time and then the order came: "Get in!" Pushing others aside, Karl was first in the car. He jumped up onto a sleeping shelf, rolled out his carpet near the barred window, and reserved space for three. Manek and I followed with the bags. We had the best place.

One hundred men rushed into the car. The weakest came last and got the worst places. The moment the last man was in, guards pushed the heavy sliding door, and it slammed shut with a metallic clank.

One hundred frightened, angry men groped about in the dark. A faint light came through the window. I was about to look out when Karl yanked me down. "Don't," he said. "They may shoot at you."

It was so crowded, we slept spoon-fashion. Sometime during the night a prisoner turned, and in a ripple effect, the entire line of prisoners turned onto their other sides. I slept on the carpet between Karl and Manek. We had taken the blankets from camp and were warm. In the night came the yank and clank of a starting train and then the rhythmic clickety-clack, clickety-clack as the train picked up speed and headed east.

The train stopped in the morning, probably on a siding. The door was pushed open, our gloomy space was flooded with light, and guards came in with buckets of kasha, a greyish gruel, and bread. Each prisoner received a fist-sized chunk of bread and a ladleful of gruel.

Karl, who seemed to have foreseen all that would happen, had made simple pots for us, large cans with wire handles, and into these our gruel was poured. We also had spoons. Most prisoners did not have containers. The gruel was simply ladled into their caps and they licked it out. Later the guards came back with buckets of water and tin mugs. We drank as quickly as possible and filled our pots.

This was to be our once-daily feeding. The door clanked shut and we were again in the gloom. The same guards came every day. Manek quickly got to know them and joshed and joked in his funny Polish–Russian: "Is this your first-class train?" he asked, and they grinned and he got more gruel. I learned to look pathetic and also got an extra scoop. (An eon later, in another life, I went to see the film *Oliver Twist*: I saw myself in little Oliver in the workhouse, holding out his bowl and saying, "Please, sir. I want some more.")

We slept in two layers, one layer on the cold bottom of the car, the others on wooden shelves above them. In the centre of the car was an empty space with a simple stove and pipe, a bucket with coal and some wood. On the side opposite the sliding door was the shit-chute, a sloping board trough that stuck out through a hole in the car, the broader end inside, the narrower end outside. The worst place to sleep was near this chute, especially after many men got diarrhea and those close to the chute got spattered.

Within a few days, the train reached Russia, and when it stopped, there were voices outside, calling. Karl knew exactly what to do. "Pull in the chute," he said. Outside were Russians who wanted to trade with prisoners, their food and tobacco for anything the prisoners had. As Karl had correctly foretold, there was nothing in Russia and consequently everything was needed.

Trading through that shit-rimmed hole was tricky: one heard only voices and saw only hands. Manek did all the bartering for us, and he was good at it. We had those sacks with loot from Poznan and at every stop, Manek exchanged a few items for food and also for tobacco and newspaper sheets, then Russia's premier cigarette rolling and toilet paper, for both Karl and Manek smoked.

Most prisoners had only their clothing, and heavy smokers traded pullovers, shirts, gloves, socks and even jackets if they could be squeezed out of the hole. In return they got small bags of *makhorka*, coarse-cut Russian tobacco. They smoked and shivered and some got the shits. After a week, the first man died. Other prisoners stripped the body and sold the clothing. The naked corpse lay there. It was thrown out at the next stop.

Most of the time we slept or dozed, tired, nearly always hungry, apathetic. But Karl and Manek were active. They walked back and forth in the centre of the car, and they made me walk. Both washed, and they made me wash. In that bag of his, Karl carried a straight razor, soap, and a strop, and he shaved every second day. He showed me how to wash with a minimum of water: take a mouthful of water, spit a bit into cupped hands, use a touch of soap, rub face, neck, ears, and arms, and use the rest of the mouthful to rinse. Rub down with a towel from one of the Poznan houses.

Our train went slowly on and on in a southeastern direction. We passed Kiev and crossed the Dnepr River (Dnieper River) at Dnepropetrovsk. After two weeks, we stopped, the doors were suddenly pushed open, and guards yelled: "Get out!" We had arrived.

Chapter 5

THE COAL MINE OF DONBAS

WE WERE IN THE EASTERN UKRAINE, that vast flat region called the Donets Basin, usually shortened to Donbas, west of the Donets River and north of the Sea of Azov.

What the Ruhr region was to Germany, the Donbas was to imperial Russia and then to the Soviet Union: the densest, most massive, most important industrial concentration in the entire U.S.S.R. It produced more than one-third of all coal mined in the Soviet Union and was dotted with industrial cities, and with steel plants, chemical plants, and immense plants that produced heavy machinery.

This was the industrial heart of the Soviet Union. The factories had been started in the early 1870s by a Welsh industrialist, John Hughes, and the region's main city, now called Donetsk, was first named "Yuzovka," the Ukrainian for Hughes. From 1924 to 1961 it was known as Stalino.

In the late autumn of 1941, the Donbas was conquered by German troops. The retreating Russian armies, obeying Stalin's order to "leave nothing but scorched earth," destroyed as much as possible. Less than two years later, the retreating German armies, obeying Hitler's order to "leave nothing but scorched earth," destroyed as much as possible.

We arrived in a devastated land. Many prison cars had been uncoupled and unloaded en route. At our stop, four cars were opened and fewer than four hundred men slowly crawled out. After lying down most of the time for two weeks, many were unsteady on their feet. They were filthy, bristly-bearded, with the sunken faces and hollow eyes of starving prisoners.

We were lined up, and Russian officers selected men for their camps. It was a slave market. Two young lieutenants appeared to have first choice. One guarded the group of chosen prisoners, while the other walked rapidly along the line, pointing: "*Ti i ti!* (You and you!)" and those selected joined the group. Karl and Manek were immediately chosen. I went with them. *Njet!* said the lieutenant and waved me back. *Brat*, ("Brother"), I said, pointing at Karl, and kept going. He shrugged and rushed on to collect more healthy-looking prisoners. At sixty men he had reached his quota. Other officers divided the dregs.

It was late February. The snow was melting and rivulets of filthy water ran along the rutted road. Everything was covered with coal dust. The snow was grey, the houses grey, the trees were grey. Conical mine dumps dotted the flat land.

We walked slowly, grey, tired men in a grey land, three kilometres to a *banya*, "a bathhouse." Our hair was cut with dull clippers, the blades clotted with blood and crushed lice. All our clothes were to be deloused. "No leather," Karl warned me. "Keep belts and boots out." The intense steam heat of the delousing room killed lice and nits, but also shrivelled leather. A few prisoners lost their boots.

We showered. None of us had washed for a month; for some it was much longer. The hard, grey, sandy soap produced little lather, but like pumice it did rub off the grime. It was wonderful to be clean again.

Clean and deloused we were herded to a nearby camp, a large building surrounded by barbed wire. Most of the six hundred or so inmates already there were ethnic Germans from Romania and Yugoslavia. The food, they said, was bad, the work hard, but the two lieutenants in charge of the camp and most of the guards were friendly.

We newcomers were given three days to recover. The food was as bad as reported: watery soup with cabbage or green tomatoes, a few spoonfuls of kasha, and a chunk of dark, heavy, moist bread. To get bread at the commissary, we were given small pieces of brown paper marked with thirty squares. As we received our daily bread ration, the square for that day was ticked off with a supposedly indelible pencil. Manek instantly spotted the weakness of the system. He smeared our cards gently with soap, we drew our rations, he carefully wiped off the pencil mark with a moist cloth, and later we drew a second ration. It worked fine for a while. Then someone denounced us, and from then on the cards were pierced with a pin.

Karl and Manek became coal miners, the hardest and most dangerous work. Our mine was only seventy metres deep, but the seams of high-quality anthracite coal were narrow and there was ankle-deep water in some of the drifts. Men lay on their backs or sides and hacked out the coal. Others, kneeling, shovelled it into low carts.

The mine cage was not enclosed. It was just an open platform for ten people. Twelve crowded onto it, sometimes fourteen. As the cage rose one day, a man had his arm ripped off, and he died from loss of blood. Another man's head was crushed. After each accident there was talk of enclosing the lift and making it safe, but it remained just talk.

Karl was out of the mine in a week. In his direct way he cornered a top mine man and told him that he was an expert mechanic. They tried him out, and it was true. There wasn't a motor or machine he could not repair. Since most trucks and mining machines were battered and barely functioning, Karl was busy and respected, received special rations, and, on the side and for a fee, repaired the few private vehicles operated by the top men in the mine.

Soon after, Manek, too, was out of the mine. He managed to convince the younger and more credulous of our two lieutenants that he was a real *feldscher*, "a semi-doctor" (this was a German word borrowed in the eighteenth or nineteenth century, when most doctors and their assistants, the *Feldscher*, in imperial Russia were Germans), and should work in the hospital. The regional hospital near the mine was run by an elderly woman doctor. Manek turned on his high-voltage charm and got a nice job.

And Manek, thanks to his grandmother, knew how to heal. When, weeks later, my hands, arms, and chest itched terribly, Manek looked at me and laughed: "You've got scabies." This is a miserable parasitic skin disease caused by microscopic mites and their larvae burrowing and feeding under one's skin.

Manek smeared me with an ointment made of pork fat mixed with powdered sulphur from the hospital and that killed the mites. For a fee, he healed others. Soon he and the woman doctor were running a sort of inconspicuous, after-hours private clinic.

Because I was supposedly so young (according to the records I was only twelve years old instead of fifteen and, since on Karl's advice, I had changed my birthday from June to January, I had only recently turned twelve) I got one of the easiest jobs in the mine. I became a *viburshchik*, "a picker," a word derived from the Russian *vibiratj*, "to pick out."

Every morning after breakfast (a bowl of watery cabbage soup) the prisoners walked under guard the three kilometres to the mine — but control was very lax. The guards who escorted us were either young or old men (the middle group was dead or at the front) and most were lazy. They often asked prisoners to carry their rifles.

The first two kilometres were tough going. By now it was March, and it was thawing in the southeastern Ukraine. Meltwater turned the rich earth into a slippery, sticky mud, so gooey it had stopped German tanks. We trudged along, our boots heavy with mud. The last kilometre we walked on railroad tracks, and that was easier.

Battered trucks dumped the mined coal near the railroad track, and from there prisoners carried the coal in hand barrows to the open railway cars that were being loaded.

The hand barrows were flat rectangular wooden frames with two shafts at each end. Two prisoners at the coal pile loaded the hand barrow. Two prisoners carried it, walking carefully up the bending, slippery plank to the railway car, dumped their load, and went back to get the next one. It took a long time to fill a railroad car.

There were usually two pickers in each railway car. Some were prisoners who were over sixty and considered elderly. A few were Russian women, who looked old and bent and were bundled in *bushlats* (thick, long-sleeved cotton-padded jackets), padded pants, and rubber boots, all coal-smeared and torn.

My picking tool was a simply-made, two-pronged metal rake, a sort of claw and handle. As soon as a load was dumped, I scraped through it, picked out rocks, and threw them over the side.

It was easy. Chunks of coal were rounded and soft. Rocks, though coal-smeared and black, were flat and hard. When struck with the metal claw, coal gave a dull sound, rock a hard clack.

The first day, a ragged, dirty boy stood near the track. He was about ten years old and carried a filthy burlap bag. *Ugol* ("Coal"), he called.

I threw over a piece of coal. He picked it up and, in sign language, asked for bigger pieces. Also in sign language he made the motions of eating. I threw over lots more coal. Whenever a guard or boss came near, the boy whistled and vanished with his sack, and I threw only rocks over the side.

In the evening when we lined up to march back to camp, my coal boy sidled up and gave me a piece of flat maize bread. He would come every day after that.

Nearly every picker had his boy or filthy little girl who collected from us sacks of coal and sold it, for in this land of coal even coal was precious. The guards were supposed to stop this racket, but they usually sat together somewhere, smoked, gossiped, and laughed. From time to time one came over and chased the kids away, and then went back to his chums and the kids returned.

Once or twice inspectors came. The coal kids vanished. The guards looked alert. The bosses told us: "Today all rocks go over the side." The inspectors, relatively well-dressed office-type men, walked cautiously, trying not to get their boots too dirty. They scratched a bit in the coal, found no rocks, and left satisfied. Then our coal kids reappeared, coal chunks flew over the side, and rocks remained in the freight cars.

The main cause for the quantity of rocks with the coal was the Soviet system of quotas or norms. To fulfil Stalin's ambitious economic Five-Year Plans, every worker had a quota, every brigade had a quota, every mine, collective farm, and factory had a quota. They were called "production norms" and ruled much of Soviet life. Quantity was all-important. Quality was a minor concern.

Every man and woman in our mine, prisoner or Russian, was supposed to produce a fixed number of tons of coal each day. If he didn't, he was in trouble. The miner's already slim food ration might be cut. In the worst case a Russian worker who regularly underfulfilled his quota could be accused of being a "parasite," a criminal offence that might get him a ten- to twenty-five-year sentence in a Siberian labour camp, where the average life expectancy was five to six years.

If a worker exceeded his norm, he was praised, received extra food coupons, and might even be named "Hero of Soviet Labour." The most famous super-achiever was Aleksei Grigorievich Stakhanov, a Donbas coal miner, whose team increased its daily output sevenfold. The normal quota was seven tons of coal per man per shift. In August 1935, Stakhanov cut 102 tons in a single shift. Men like him were known as "Stakhanovites." They were rewarded by bosses and Party people and sincerely hated by most workers.

The quota system made no allowance for narrow coal seams, primitive tools, and miserable, dangerous working conditions. Poorly fed Russians and half-starved prisoners could not possibly fulfil the norms. So they increased tonnage by adding rocks to the coal. The bosses, of course, knew this, but to maintain their positions and privileges, tonnage was of vital importance to them as well. At the end of the production line we, the pickers, were supposed to rectify the situation by throwing out the rocks — but because we could get bread for coal, we kept some of the rocks and threw out some of the coal.

(There was another, much trickier and sophisticated system of cheating. It was known as the "paper system" and required brilliant bureaucratic legerdemain, crooked bookkeeping, and a long chain of bribery and corruption. Miners would report "paper tons": they mined five tons and reported ten, and the inflated figures marched up the chain. In a later life, the big boss of a cotton *kolkhoz* ("collective farm") in Uzbekistan explained the system to me in detail, how he delivered tons and tons of "paper cotton" that, somewhere in the Soviet Union, was made into "paper jeans." With men like him, corruption became a polished and immensely profitable science. These were the godparents of today's notorious Russian Mafia.)

One day I passed a workshop at the mine and saw a hammer. I looked around carefully. There was no one nearby. I grabbed the hammer, pushed it under my belt, and hid it in one of the many ruined buildings. In the evening I told my coal boy I had a hammer for sale. (The Russian I had learned so long ago from Stanka in Quellenhof had begun to surface, and I quickly became fairly fluent.) "I tell you tomorrow," he promised.

He waved to me next day, and I waved back. This was our signal to meet after work. Getting away was easy. As we marched to camp I told our guard, "I've got to shit."

"Don't be long," he said, and marched on. I walked behind a building. My coal boy was there, with thirty roubles, enough to buy three small loaves of bread. I showed him the hammer. He examined it carefully, then gave me the money.

I made a detour to a small village market where elderly *babushkas* ("elderly women") covered in woolly shawls sold flat maize bread, real bread, made from good grain, beans, peas, or corn by the glassful, and potatoes, onions, and garlic. After some bargaining and tasting, I bought for fifteen roubles a small loaf of real bread and a bit of honey in a cupped piece of dirty cardboard.

On the way back to camp, I sat down on some rocks beneath a tree and, very slowly, broke off pieces of bread, dipped them in honey, and ate them. It was my most wonderful meal since Kleingraben.

It was now early April and spring, and our camp was awash in nostalgia. Most of the ethnic Germans from Romania and Yugoslavia were farmers, and now they were filled with an intense longing to be home, to be on their land, to sow, to milk the cows, to plant their gardens. Few realized that they no longer had a home. Back "home" their farms had been nationalized, and those that survived their term of slavery would later become refugees.

I did not have a home either. I tried not to think about the past, because it hurt so much. And there was no use thinking about the future, because there didn't seem to be a future. Like Karl and Manek I lived only for the here and now.

It was the birds of spring that bothered me most. Starlings were displaying, courting, singing. Larks rose high into the sky, then spiralled down with their lovely, liquid, trilling song. Swallows were collecting mud and building their nests in abandoned buildings. They all spoke to me of my other life, when I had been free and happy and with the people I loved. Spring is a bad time for prisoners.

$\mathscr{C}hapter\ 6$

ESCAPE

ONE EVENING IN THE MIDDLE of April, Karl took me aside in the prison yard. We stood near the barbed-wire fence.

"Manek and I will escape," he said. "Do you want to come along?"

"*Yes!*"

I was instantly fully alive, wildly excited, and had a lot of questions. Karl explained calmly, succinctly.

We would escape on the first of May, the great Soviet holiday, when all the guards would be drunk. He and Manek had somehow managed to save a thousand roubles. With some of the money they would buy food for about two weeks. We would walk west to Poland, about twenty or thirty kilometres every night. Once in Poland, Manek was sure he could get us to Germany. It might take two or three months. "Don't talk to anyone about this," he cautioned.

The next two weeks were strange! I seemed somewhere between heaven and hell. Heaven was freedom and hope. Hell was fear and foreboding.

West. Every evening near sunset, hundreds of prisoners gathered in the prison yard. It was the time of our last pee before going to sleep, and most men stood near the barbed-wire fence on the west side of camp, pissed, and looked at the setting sun. It was a silent ritual. Somewhere, far in that direction, was home. I stood with the men near the barbed-wire fence, peed, and thought, "Soon I will be free. I will walk west." I looked at the other prisoners, at the dirty, hungry, passive faces and kept thinking, "And none of them know!" It was a marvellously joyful, triumphant feeling.

And then, mostly at night, came the grey spectres of doubt and fear. Our camp was really quite good. True, the two lieutenants, the trusties, and the kitchen staff stole a lot of our food, ate well, and enriched themselves — but it wasn't excessive and, anyway, it was what each one of us would have done given the opportunity. Both lieutenants were young and relatively kind; they never hit prisoners. Most of the guards were friendly, lazy, and lax. Once or twice a week on the way from work to camp, I pulled my "I have to shit" routine, and the guards always agreed. Sometimes I had to see my coal boy. But usually I just wanted to walk back to camp alone, to have a little bit of freedom. The food was bad but, with a few extras, most managed to survive. A few, of course, died. But they were the elderly, the sick. It really was a good camp, and I was afraid to leave.

The guards did get drunk on the first of May but many gathered at the prison from other locations and made a party of it. They wandered about in a mood of drunken chumminess and talked in a slurry-friendly way with any prisoner who came into the yard. Only around three in the morning did some stagger home, and the rest gathered at the prison gate in a drunken cluster.

Manek went out first. A few nights before, he had cut and then loosely retied the bottom strands of barbed wire in a part of the well-lit prison yard that could not be seen from the gate.

I was next. Manek held up the wire from outside, I crawled under with ease, and moments later Karl was outside as well. We had less than two hours until sunrise. Shortly after that, our absence might be noticed. Even making allowance for confusion and hangovers, it would not take the lieutenants, trusties, and guards too long to figure out that we had probably escaped late in the night and could not have walked very far. They would hunt for us close to the mine and camp.

Fortunately, some time before, Manek had found the perfect hiding spot: the most prominent and visible place in all the land. He had climbed the high, now disused, conical mine dump to look around and chart our initial route. At the very top, he had found two shallow pits, about seven feet long, two feet deep, and wide enough for two or three men lying close together. Perhaps they had been made by children at play. Perhaps they were the result of natural subsidence. Karl agreed that that was the one place no one would look for us.

We walked quickly to one of the house ruins near the mine, where Manek and Karl had hidden three bags with food and our few belongings, including Karl's straight razor and strop. We climbed the hill, trying not to dislodge stones that would clatter down the steep slope. Then we ate some bread, drank some water, and lay down in the two pits. Soon after, the sky began to glow and the sun rose.

Our hiding place, visible from miles around, was only two kilometres from our camp, and not far from the coal mine. From time to time we heard snatches of excited voices. Manek wanted to have a cautious look, but Karl said firmly: "Lie still and be still!" We lay and listened, and the sun moved very slowly across the sky. After a while, I slept.

It was strange to wake up and not be in prison or working at the mine. We waited until dark, cautiously slid down the hill, and walked west, avoiding roads where guards might wait in ambush.

Manek, the former smuggler, felt at home in the dark. I had always liked the dark, had good night vision, and as a child on fall nights in Quellenhof had loved to walk alone in the forest and listen to the sounds of nature. Karl, as always, was coolly competent. He directed our march, guided by the stars, keeping Polaris, the North Star, on our right.

The earth was dry, the walking easy. We skirted villages and houses. Dogs, fortunately for us, were rare then in the Soviet Union. Food was too precious to share with dogs.

We walked from darkness to dawn, then looked for a day-time hiding place. That, in this flat and treeless land, was always a problem. The first morning we were lucky. Near dawn we came upon a sort of prairie slough, a small pond surrounded by a broad belt of reeds. We walked a few yards into the reeds, trampled down a sleeping area, got water from the pond, ate, lay down upon our beds of reeds, and slept.

After the initial thrill, that marvellous euphoric feeling of being free, our nightly marches became routine. One night, near a river, we blundered into a swamp, tried to back out, fell into ditches, and were surrounded by a great chorus of frogs. We changed direction so often that even Karl got flustered, and Manek took over. He slowly led us away from frogs and water onto higher ground. We came upon a road, broad and paved, obviously a major highway, and walked west.

Two or three trucks travelled by night on the road but we could hear and see them far away, lay quietly in the ditch beside the road until they passed, and walked on. The road came to a bridge and, like all major bridges in the Soviet Union, it was guarded. Manek walked ahead to reconnoitre.

He was back in a few minutes and conferred with Karl in whispers. Karl nodded. Following Manek, we walked at the base of the road berm to the bridge, then crawled upwards to the level of the road and the beginning of the bridge.

On the other side of the road, less than twenty yards from us, three men sat near a small fire and talked. Their rifles lay next to them on the ground. "Wait!" Manek whispered.

After half an hour or so, the fire had burned down to a small heap of glowing embers. One of the guards stood up, walked to a large pile of cornstalks, took an armful, threw it onto the embers, and sat down again. For a while nothing happened.

Then a few dry leaves caught fire and suddenly the flames rushed up. The guards sat in a circle of light so bright we could see their faces clearly. All stared at the soaring flames.

Manek moved. Crawling flat on the ground, he got onto the bridge and kept moving. Karl and I followed. Blinded by flames, the guards could see nothing in the dark beyond the fire. We felt terribly visible, and waited tensely for that sudden yell, only feeling secure when we were back in the protective darkness of the night.

We walked west like that for seven nights and all was well and wonderful until it rained. The downpour began about midnight. The dry earth of a country road turned into clinging mud. It rained harder and harder and became much colder. An icy wind swept over the land.

At dawn we found a small stand of willows not far from the road and hid there. We were soaking wet, and our bread was soggy. The wind became stronger and colder. The rain continued. We lay on the wet earth and shivered.

In the early afternoon, Manek had had it. He was shrewd, resourceful, and crafty, but he lacked Karl's stoic stamina. "Let's go!" he said. "It's too damn cold!" I prayed Karl would agree. Always thin, I had lost more weight during the train trip and in camp, and was now shivering uncontrollably. But Karl said, "No." We must wait for darkness.

Two hours later Manek got up, wet, miserable, and angry. "I'm going," he said. "There hasn't been a truck or person on that road all day. Not in this weather. You want to stay, stay. I'm going!"

Karl looked at him, then shrugged. "All right," he said. "Let's go."

We had not walked long when a truck approached. It was too late to hide — there was no place to hide. We walked on trying to look like wet peasants trudging home. That time we were lucky.

An hour later, long before the saving darkness, another truck came from behind. Men with guns stood on it. *Stoi!* ("stop!") they yelled.

Manek lied and bluffed, but it was no use. We were obviously escaped prisoners. We got onto the truck and they drove to a small town. They searched us but did not find the money Karl and Manek had hidden in the lining of their caps. Then they took our bags away and locked us up. We were their only prisoners. At night they gave us some of our bread and water.

Manek, a bit subdued, suggested we should say we didn't know the name of the camp from which we had escaped. "If we're sent back," he warned, "they'll put us underground and let us slave until we die. I'll do the talking." Karl agreed.

In the morning there was a lot of shouting outside our jail. People called. Church bells were ringing in the distance. The sun was shining. It was a lovely morning.

Our cell door was opened. Several men with guns stood near the door. "Out!" one said.

They marched us around the building into a yard that ended in a dirty, crumbling wall that once had been whitewashed.

"Stand there," the senior man ordered. "Face the wall!"

They were going to shoot us. Manek mumbled. I think he was praying. Karl, next to me, appeared totally unmoved. He stared at the wall with a slightly ironic smile on his face.

Behind us, there were shouted commands.

I tried to think, to pray. Fragments of thought and images zigzagged through my mind. I felt a strange emptiness and tensed, waiting for the blows of the bullets.

From a crack in the sun-warmed wall a beetle emerged and walked up the wall. I recognized it, remembered the species.

"Fire!" came the command. And then dry clicks, and the men behind us laughed.

It had been a joke. The rifles were not loaded. (As it turned out, these were militiamen. Although we did not know it of course, they had very little power, and had no right to shoot prisoners or anyone else. That was the prerogative of the secret police, the NKGB.)

That morning it had been on the radio that the war was over. Germany had surrendered, and they felt like celebrating, doing something patriotic. Someone had said: "Let's shoot the Krauts!"

In the end, they had settled for this mock execution, and were a bit disappointed that Karl seemed merely amused. I felt the tenseness ooze out of me, and became soft and shaky. "Did you shit your pants?" they asked.

They gave us tobacco and a newspaper sheet. Manek tried to roll a cigarette, but his hands shook so badly he kept spilling tobacco. Karl rolled his cigarette smoothly, his hands perfectly steady, lit it, and smoked.

"Germany kaput!"

"Hitler kaput!"

"Hitler had only one testicle," said one of the militiamen. "They said so on the radio." The subject seemed to fascinate them. Did we know about it, they asked. We didn't; in Hitler's Germany one did not talk about Hitler's testicles. (John Toland in his massive biography *Adolf Hitler*, quoting medical reports, states with certainty that, in the number of testicles at least, Hitler "was normal.")

Some women arrived with bread and milk and we ate with our guards in the courtyard. They were warm and friendly and laughed. They had a lot of questions and Manek, now recovered, had all the answers.

"How old are you?" one man asked me.

"Twelve," I said.

"Poor kid," he said with genuine compassion, and poured another cup of milk. He was one of the men who, a few minutes earlier, had lined me up for "execution."

We remained in that jail for two more days, the militiamen continued to be friendly, and we continued to eat with them in the courtyard. Finally, they loaded us and our bags (they had not taken anything) onto the truck, four men with rifles came with us, and we drove back east.

After a few hours we reached a great, sprawling complex of factory buildings, which covered many acres. At the gate a factory guard squeezed into the front seat to direct our driver. We stopped in front of an office building. They led us into the building, the militiamen reported to a lieutenant sitting behind a desk, and then, with a friendly nod to us, they left.

Chapter 7

THE DEATH CAMP AND ITS CAPTAIN

THERE WAS SOMETHING STRANGE about the lieutenant behind the desk. He appeared to be extremely nervous. He shuffled papers. He had an oddly vacant face. Perhaps he was drunk. We soon learned he was often drunk. Later we understood.

Officially he was second-in-command of the prison camp within the factory complex, but we prisoners rarely saw him. He knew, of course, the horror of this camp, the disease and starvation, the torture and death, but there was nothing he could do about it. So he stayed outside, sat in the office, registered prisoners, and got reports from Franz, the head trusty. He was a decent man and he was part of evil, and he wanted no part in it.

He hardly glanced at us. He asked questions, Manek answered, and he filled out registration forms printed on greyish paper. When he came to my age and Manek said "Twelve," he looked up startled, stared at me, and for an instant there was a pathetic look of pity in his eyes. Then he looked down again and continued to fill out forms.

He went with us to the gate of the prison and told one of the guards to fetch Franz. Franz, the head trusty, was — after the captain — the man most feared in camp. He was stocky, and strong, with dark hair, a flabby face, and shifty eyes. He was a

German from Serbia, and spoke several languages: German, a German dialect, Serb, Russian, Hungarian, Romanian, and perhaps others. Most of the other trusties were from his region in Serbia and all were his cronies. He appeared massive and well-fed.

He picked us up at the prison gate. "What's in those bags?" he asked. "Food," Karl said evenly. For a moment I thought Franz would confiscate the bags, but he looked at Karl and changed his mind.

"Once you go to work," he said with a smirk, "those bags will be stolen."

He looked at Karl again. "Do you have money?" he asked.

"Yes," said Karl.

"Pay me two roubles a day and I will guard your bags," Franz said.

"Ten roubles a week," Karl said. "For all three bags."

The two men stared at each other, then Franz shrugged. "All right. Ten roubles a week."

He took us into the main prison building. It was huge: three stories high, with an inside entirely of metal. It had once been a large factory building, with many machines working on several levels. The factory had been destroyed twice during the war: once by retreating Russian armies, later by retreating German armies. Now all the machinery had been removed, the building had been repaired, and it housed about two thousand prisoners. All the floors were of iron sheets, welded together, the stairs were of iron, the rafters of iron, the roof of metal. Bare light bulbs dangled from wires. They burned day and night.

The stench was horrible, the sour-putrid smell of sweat and filth, shit, stale urine, and death. The dirt-caked windows were high in the wall, and could not be opened.

Franz led us to a special section on the second floor, where prisoners slept who paid him protection money. There were a few bare metal beds, but most prisoners slept on the metal floor. A man sat in the corner. He was evidently terrified of Franz.

"You watch their bags," Franz told him.

"Yes," said the prisoner. "I'll watch. I always watch." He cringed and tried to smile ingratiatingly. He was one of Franz's creatures.

Franz left. We cleared a space for three on the metal floor and put our bags down. Most men were already at work. The great metal building was nearly empty. Here and there, curled up or sprawling, lay the dying and the dead.

Supper was at seven. The kitchen and mess hall were in a large, single-storey building behind the metal dormitory. Near the mess-hall entrance, at the barbed-wire fence, a pile of naked corpses lay rotting in the sun.

We got our food on battered tin plates or bowls as we entered, then sat down on benches at trestle-supported tables of wooden planks that filled the hall. The tables, the benches, the floor, were all crusted with filth. Occasionally one of the kitchen staff spread sawdust on the mess-hall floor.

We received three meals a day and the food rarely varied. Breakfast: watery cabbage soup and two or three spoonfuls of kasha, the thin grey gruel we were used to. Lunch: more cabbage soup and kasha. Supper: the same. Sometimes there was a film of fat on the cabbage soup. Some prisoners, the stokers, transport workers, and others assigned to extremely heavy work, received double rations.

In addition, each prisoner received every morning a piece of bread. It was our main food, and it was bad. It was dark, soggy, and heavy, made of poor-quality grain — probably spoiled during transport and storage — potato flour and, some said, sawdust. Wise prisoners, men with an iron discipline like Karl, cut their bread into slices and dried and toasted them on the stovepipes in camp, but most prisoners ate their bread immediately. We were always hungry.

Every day after supper, the trusties lined us up in the prison yard in blocks of one hundred prisoners, twenty across, five deep, for easy counting. Plus those on shift work in the factory.

Plus those in the kitchen. Plus the trusties themselves. Plus the dead and dying in the building. Plus the corpses on the pile near the kitchen. It went on and on. The men, haggard, hungry, tired, stood stolid and passive and waited, and the trusties counted and added and argued.

In our first week some time between eight and nine in the evening, the captain came, and Franz made his report. In the prison yard, neatly lined up, stood the blocks of prisoners. Several trusties stood in the yard facing the prisoners. Four powerful trusties stood near the prison door.

The captain was a dapper little man, with knee-high leather boots polished to a high gloss, a neat uniform, clean and well-pressed. He had a flat face, dark hair, dark eyes that gleamed when he was excited, and small white hands. He often wore gloves of soft leather. He limped a bit when he walked.

After receiving Franz's report, he turned to us and stared, then strutted back and forth and cursed the prisoners. "*Prakljatii njemtsi!* (Damned Germans!)." That was the main theme. *Prakljatii njemtsi!* He said it over and over again. He walked faster and faster, his limp was more pronounced, and his voice rose and became shrill as he grew more and more excited.

Suddenly he stopped and shouted something to the trusties. They were ready. The four men near the door went into the building, and moments later we heard terrified screams.

The four burly trusties came out of the building, dragging a desperately struggling, screaming, emaciated man. "No!" he screamed. "Oh no! Please, please, no!" They forced him to his knees.

The captain picked up a heavy iron rod that was leaning against the building. He turned to the kneeling prisoner who still screamed and raised his arms in supplication. Then the captain swung the iron rod high and smashed it down upon the upstretched arms of the prisoner. The screaming became shriller, the frightful screech of agony. The captain beat and beat and there were the dull thuds on battered flesh and broken bones. He hit the prisoner's face and smashed his nose. He knocked out one eye. He broke his shoulders, his ribs. But he did not hit the head. Finally, sweat was pouring down his face, he was panting, and his eyes stared wildly. The man collapsed and lay, a whimpering pile of broken flesh and bone.

Suddenly the captain stopped. He threw down the iron rod. Flushed and sweaty he marched back and forth, his limp now very evident. Gradually he relaxed. He kicked the dying man, then stopped and told a trusty to wipe the blood off his boots. He turned and walked out of the camp.

We were dismissed. The smashed man was dragged back into the *Karzer*. He died that night.

Manek and I were horrified. Karl, who may have seen people beaten to death, was coldly disgusted. Nearly all the other prisoners appeared indifferent. "*Passiert paar mal die Woche* (Happens a few times a week)," one of them explained to us newcomers. They had seen it before. They would see it again. The show was over. They could go to sleep. One of the trusties picked up the iron rod and leaned it against the building.

Karzer in German is an old-fashioned, harmless word. In past centuries many universities had a *Karzer*, where rowdy or drunken students were locked up for a day or two. The Russians took over the word a long time ago and, in their language, it now means a simple jail or lock-up. In our camp, however, the *Karzer* was a gruesome place: a small, barred room, where men waited for days — sometimes weeks — to be tortured to death by the captain. Some went mad. We could hear them scream at night.

Sometimes when he was in a chipper mood, the captain ordered Franz to unlock the *Karzer*. Then he would step in and stare at the cowering prisoners. He would point. "You're next!" He would hesitate. "Or maybe you!" he would say, pointing at another prisoner.

That was one of his amusements. Another was his standard joke. He sometimes came to camp while we were lining up for supper outside the mess hall, next to that pile of twisted, bloated shapes that, not long ago, had been human beings. He would strut back and forth, his boots gleaming, and lecture us on being *njekulturnie* ("uncultured") and lazy.

Then his voice would became friendly.

"Cheer up," he would say. "Soon you will go home."

He would stare at us and smile.

"Really! It's the truth. I'm telling you the real truth. Soon you will go home!"

He would pause for effect, then point at the pile of rotting corpses.

"You see! They have already gone home!" and he would laugh delightedly. It was his favourite joke. He told it about once a week.

Generally, though, the captain did not bother much with the camp. The lieutenant in the office did the paperwork, and Franz and the trusties ran the camp.

They lined up the prisoners for evening roll call and in the morning for the work brigades. They assisted the captain in his orgiastic killings, but they never killed. They might slap a prisoner, but even that was rare. We feared them because they had power, and we envied them because they had plentiful food. They slept on beds with thick paillasses, in separate rooms that were off-limits to other prisoners. They were fat and safe and smug.

Beneath them in the camp hierarchy came the kitchen staff. They, too, were Franz's cronies, but they had no power and fewer privileges. They cooked bad food for their fellow prisoners and good, rich meals for the trusties and themselves. They also lived in separate rooms.

Finally, there were Franz's creatures, a dozen or so prisoners who were the domestic slaves of Franz and his fellow trusties. They made the rounds every morning, dragged out the corpses of those who had died during the night, and threw them out onto the pile by the kitchen. They emptied the shit barrels near the door that we used at night when the dormitory was locked. They washed the floors in the private rooms of trusties and kitchen staff. For this they did not have to go to work in the factory and they got some extra food. They lazed about and cowered and did the trusties' bidding.

About half the prisoners in camp were ethnic Germans from eastern Europe, peasants who desperately wanted to be home on their farms. They had escaped from other camps, sometimes en masse. A few were from Germany. The rest were Hungarians, Romanians, Bulgarians, Moldavians, Croats, Serbs, and a multitude of other nationalities, some of the millions of civilians rounded up and sent east as slaves, first by the Soviet army and then by the NKGB. In early spring, a steady flow of prisoners had reached this camp. Now only a few arrived, and finally none. As prisoners died, the camp population declined from its peak of about two thousand prisoners, which it was at when we arrived in mid-May 1945. All worked in the large, heavily guarded chemical factory.

Our camp was a prison within a prison. The factory complex was surrounded by a high wall, topped by many strands of inward-sloping barbed wire. There were towers with armed guards at frequent intervals. Powerful lights lit the factory wall at night.

The complex had only two gates. One, flanked by guard towers, admitted freight trains that were searched by a few guards when they came in and by many guards when they left the factory.

The other gate, through which we had been driven into the complex by the militiamen, was for all vehicles — and all, upon leaving, were carefully searched by guards. Next to the gate was a large room, where many guards frisked all workers leaving the factory, either quickly and superficially, or very thoroughly when the cold-faced chief of security was present. It was said of him that he was a man without pity.

In one corner of this guard-sealed, prison-like complex was our camp: the two main buildings, the large yard, the open pits with rows of shit-covered planks across them that were our latrines. All of this was also enclosed by a high, triple-stranded barbed-wire fence. There was only one gate, watched by armed guards, through which we prisoners went to work each day.

Chapter 8

THE FACTORY

THE MORNING AFTER WE ARRIVED in camp, I was assigned to a large work brigade with the odd name *obshe zavodskoye* (the "all-over-the-factory" brigade). Our work brigade, made up of about two hundred prisoners and perhaps another two hundred Russians, looked after all the pipes, plumbing, and drainage of this huge chemical plant.

Led to work in the morning by the brigade leader, a prisoner with power and privileges, we assembled at the large office and warehouse of our unit. There the Russians reported for work, were assigned tasks, received and signed for the tools they needed, and then scattered all over the factory, wherever piping had to be installed or repaired.

The head of the entire division was the *nachalnik*, "the top boss," a tall, sparse man, very erect and austere, with a narrow face and sallow skin. He was always serious. No one ever saw him laugh or smile. He was a senior Communist Party man, had been highly decorated, and on special occasions wore a row of medals. He never spoke to prisoners and had very little to do with us. He had a private office and secretaries, and senior workers and foremen went there to report. They took their caps off before they entered.

The man who dealt with the daily running of this complex division was called the *Meister*. (This German word had arrived in Russia at the time of Peter the Great, who, in his monumental effort to *modernize* and *westernize* his ancient eastern realm, brought thousands of foreigners to Russia, many of them German master artisans. *Schiffsbaumeister*, "master ship builder," or *Oberküchenmeister*, "head cook," were titles then used in the Russia of Peter the Great. Those fancy titles have vanished, but *Meister* became a Russian word for an expert senior foreman.)

Our *Meister* was in his early forties but looked much older, with short-cut greying hair and the muscular, compact body of the Russian peasant. He was a quiet man, but decisive, and not even the senior engineers knew the complex factory-wide system of pipes and drains as well as he did. One of his many duties was to assign work to prisoners.

Since the *Meister* was under pressure from higher-ups, who, in turn, were under pressure from those even higher, to fulfil factory norms and quotas that obviously could not be fulfilled if vital pipes broke or drains were plugged, it was his difficult task, for he was essentially a kind man, to get the maximum amount of labour out of starving prisoners without being too cruel.

The Russians of our division worked as pipe fitters, welders, or on other jobs, singly, or as small teams. The prisoners worked in large groups. For instance, one group of twenty or thirty men bent pipes, which was hard and difficult work.

The pipe benders worked outdoors in a large open area. The pipe to be bent, about twenty feet long and from two to ten inches in diameter, was laid on the ground and one end was closed with a heavy wooden bung. Then the pipe was lifted and leaned against a tower of wooden scaffolding.

Several prisoners dried fine-grained sand, perhaps from a Black Sea beach, in a huge pan above a fire. Other prisoners poured the dried sand through a fine-meshed sieve. The dried, sieved sand was hoisted in buckets to the top of the tower, and prisoners poured it through a broad metal funnel into the upright pipe.

On ladders along the pipe stood prisoners with short, stout metal rods. They beat against the pipe, creating vibrations, so that the sand within would settle densely and tightly.

When, after a long time, the pipe had been filled with sand, its top was closed with another bung, and the steel pipe, heavy to begin with and now, full of sand, extremely heavy, was cautiously lowered to the ground. Once a rope slipped, and the pipe fell and killed two prisoners. Worse in the eyes of the supervisor, the bung came out, much of the sand was spilled, and it took hours to replace it.

The sand-filled pipe was carried to an outdoor forge and the section to be bent was heated until it glowed dull red. Upon command, the pipe was rushed to a large metal table with inset steel posts, placed between these posts and bent. Since it was filled with sand, the steel pipe bent smoothly, without cracking or crinkling. It also cooled rapidly and each time it would bend only a little bit. Then it had to be carried to the forge and reheated.

Speed was important. The prisoners were weak, the pipe heavy, a portion of it was red-hot, and the foremen yelled those familiar words, "*Dawai! Dawai!* (Get going! Get going!)" and "*Bistray! Bistray!* (Faster! Faster!)." It took a long time to bend a pipe.

I worked with the ditch diggers. Twice destroyed during the war, the factory was now being hurriedly rebuilt. Large areas were still in ruins, the yards overgrown with plants, the broken buildings home to starlings and swallows. Many other buildings had already been rebuilt or repaired, machinery had been installed, and they were now in production. Everywhere old drains had to be dug up, repaired, or replaced and then reburied. Other trenches had to be dug for new drains, new pipes, new sewers, new sumps.

It was hard, filthy work, and sometimes dangerous. Deep trenches were rarely cribbed, because planks were rare and more precious than prisoners. A few times trenches did collapse and prisoners were injured or killed. When that happened, there was talk of cribbing, but it remained talk.

Much worse for us was the fact that some of the factory effluent was caustic. All who worked in such drainage areas, even prisoners, were supposed to wear rubber boots, and we did get issued boots, but they were old and cracked and most of them leaked. The corrosive fluid burned our feet, wounds developed and then became larger and deeper. Prisoners could no longer walk and work and they died of starvation.

At noon, the entire factory stopped for lunch. All Russian workers went to their mess halls (senior personnel might leave the factory and eat at home), where they received food according to a rating system and extra food if they had *talons*, food coupons issued in part as reward for outstanding labour and in part as reward for knowing the right people or being useful to the right people.

All prisoners went back to camp, slurped their cabbage soup, ate the bit of kasha, and lay down to rest. At one o'clock we walked back to the factory.

In the evening, after work, Russians and prisoners returned all tools, boots, and other items that had been issued to them at the division warehouse. That could be a lengthy procedure. If anything were missing, be it only a screwdriver, it was a major problem and potentially an extremely dangerous one.

Theft in the Soviet Union was not just theft. It was "sabotage," for the "theft of state property" was a serious crime, an offence against the socialist state that could be punished by death. The usual punishment was a ten- to twenty-five-year sentence in a slave-labour camp.

Because it was so risky, common theft by common workers was probably rare at our factory. Prisoners who stole faced an even more horrible risk. If they were caught, they were locked up in the *Karzer* to await torture and death.

Russians and prisoners worked six days a week, ten hours a day. Our division, by its very nature, often had to deal with emergencies: broken pipes, clogged drains, flooded buildings, and furious managers all over the factory. Everything had been hurriedly built, often with poor-quality material. Since norms had to be met, engineers and workers improvised, resulting in weirdly twisted Rube Goldberg pipe systems in many factory buildings.

Since I spoke Russian, the *Meister* sometimes sent me along with Russian emergency teams. I liked that. Many prisoners were, despite the miserable and insufficient food, still obsessed with Teutonic *Tüchtigkeit*, that nearly compulsive drive to do all things thoroughly and well. Not only did they drive themselves, they also drove fellow prisoners, and this trait was encouraged and used by Russian foremen to get the most out of prisoners before they died.

The Russian workers, generally, did not believe in doing anything either thoroughly or well. For our team, the important thing was to somehow fix the problem, repair the leak, pump out the sump, weld the pipe. I was usually the "go-boy"—all day I heard "fetch this," "get that," "hold this," "hold that," as I turned on taps or closed them, climbed high on ladders and held lights.

It was easy work. The men were usually kind, they did a half-assed job, but, for the time being, the problem was solved. We worked very long hours. The Russians got extra pay and food coupons. I, too, got *talons* for which the night staff at the kitchen gave me a bowlful of kasha and even poured some oil over it.

Sunday was our day of rest. The captain did not come to camp on Sundays. We ate breakfast, slept until noon, ate lunch, and then about half the prisoners slept on or dozed. The more energetic ones washed and deloused.

All prisoners were crawling with lice. Only the trusties and the kitchen staff, as one of their many privileges, regularly went to the *banya*, a bathhouse outside the factory, washed, and steamed their clothes to kill the lice. We took off piece after piece of clothing, examined each one carefully, crushed any lice between our thumbnails and also crushed the nits, the tiny, elliptical, white louse eggs sticking to our clothing.

About a thousand prisoners in our camp spent two hours or so every Sunday afternoon crushing lice and nits. The other thousand just lay there, glad to rest, too apathetic and exhausted to care, and a grey, crawling mass of blood-sucking lice covered the insides of their clothing and their bodies.

Chapter 9

SURVIVAL

OF MY FORMER LIFE, only two things remained: a good-quality tweed jacket that had once belonged to Heddy and a pair of boots, hand-made by a Polish cobbler in Kleingraben, that, despite hard use, was still in good condition. In the Soviet Union both were valuable. Factory workers paid well for good-quality prisoners' clothing, either to wear — for most were desperately short of clothing — or to resell to others outside the factory at a good profit. Since no "theft of state property" was involved, such clothing could safely be taken out of the factory.

When we arrived at the camp, I slept wearing both the jacket and boots. As it got warmer, I used the jacket as pillow and kept the boots next to my body. One morning both were gone. I slept between Karl and Manek. It had to be one of them. Or both. They said they had seen nothing, heard nothing. "Those bastards!" said Karl.

They were my only friends, the only people I trusted. I suddenly felt desperately lonely. Perhaps in a death camp, one has no friends. I tied rags around my feet and went to work. That night I joined the vultures.

Every day between ten and twenty prisoners died. Most died at night, usually between midnight and three o'clock in the morning. Near every dying man sat some fellow prisoners, waiting for his death so they could get his clothing. These men were called the vultures.

Some were vultures every night, others intermittently. All followed a few basic rules. No prisoner was stripped until he was really dead. Men in need of clothing for themselves took precedence over fellow vultures who planned to sell the dead man's clothes.

Immediately after evening roll call, I made the rounds. Like other vultures, I was guided by the quality of the dying person's clothing and the imminence of death. I joined a small group of experienced vultures near a dying man with fairly good boots of about my size. "Boots?" I asked. They were spoken for — but by a seller. Since I needed them for myself, I had first rights. I sat down and we waited.

We rarely talked and we did not like it if the dying talked. Most lay still, their eyes closed, their breathing shallow. Others watched us, their eyes staring. They knew why we sat there, what we were waiting for. A few talked — of home, of a wife, of parents, of children. They begged us to give messages to people they loved. We tried to shush them. "Sure, sure. We'll tell. Be quiet now."

I fell asleep that first night. Sometime in the night a fellow vulture nudged me. "He's dead," he said quietly. That, too, was part of the vulture ethic. One did not take spoken-for clothing that "belonged" to a vulture who had fallen asleep.

We stripped the corpse. I pulled the boots off his feet. Others took pants, shirt, jacket, a pullover, underwear. In the morning Franz's creatures would search the body once more, in case the vultures had overlooked a cross, a hidden ring, some memento that could be sold, then dragged it out of the building and threw it on the pile near the kitchen.

A WEEK LATER, I nearly joined the dying, and Karl and Manek saved my life. Like many prisoners, I suffered from diarrhea, probably caused by the sour-cabbage soup and the bread made from spoiled grain. That changed abruptly to dysentery, the top killer in our camp. I was wracked by terrible cramps. My body first ejected spurts of liquid feces, then came mucus mixed with blood. It was a vile, filthy way to die, one I saw daily. It weakened me so quickly that, by morning, I could not go to work.

I knew that if I didn't work, I would die. One of the camp rules, perhaps a Marxist maxim, was that a prisoner who did not go to work did not get any food. The combination of disease and starvation killed quickly.

At that moment I didn't care. I was too exhausted, too weak, in too much pain. All I wanted was to lie still, to rest, to sleep. Dying would end the struggle. It would be a permanent rest, and death appeared tempting and easy.

"Get up!" said Karl. I moaned that I couldn't. He yanked me up. "Stay here and you die," he said. He looked at me, his face cold and hard. "Pull yourself together! Don't give up, boy! Don't ever give up!"

Karl marched me into the yard, and I dragged myself to work. By the time we reached the brigade office, I could barely stand. My pants were wet with shit and blood and mucus.

The *Meister* assigned work to all the groups, then detailed me to work with an electric welder, a Russian, who was repairing pipes. He was an older man and kind. "Just sit and rest," he said. I spent much of the day at a nearby outhouse. Whenever I came back, the welder waved his hand. "Just rest," he kept saying.

During the day, Manek had been busy. He had gone to the timber yard and got oak bark. He cut the bark into narrow strips and boiled them in water on a prison stove. He had collected yarrow in a destroyed part of the factory that was overgrown with plants, and he boiled it in another can. He also had small chunks of charcoal.

Karl had bought bread, real bread, and had fetched my supper kasha ration from the kitchen. That was against the rules, but no one liked to argue with Karl.

When, after walking very slowly back from work, I arrived in camp, Karl and Manek took over. Manek made me chew charcoal and drink cup after cup of the brown-black, extremely bitter oak-bark decoction. Karl toasted slices of good bread on the stovepipe. I ate the kasha and the bread and drank the yarrow infusion.

That night the violent spasms stopped. I slept. In the morning I was still weak and exhausted, but no longer in pain. I ate more bread, Karl brought my breakfast kasha, and, at Manek's urging, I drank a lot of his bitter oak-bark brew and yellowish yarrow tea. "Whenever people in our village had the shits real bad," Manek said, "my grandmother made them yarrow tea. And oak-bark's the thing for dysentery. Stops the bleeding."

I went to work, again with the kindly welder who kept saying, "Just rest."

Within four days Manek had cured my dysentery. I was still very weak, but also pleased. Everywhere men were dying of dysentery, and I had pulled through — thanks, of course, to Karl's ruthless bullying and to Manek, who knew how to heal.

Still, it was my first victory. So many others died. I lived. I was going to go on living. "I will not die!" I kept repeating that. Into my mind floated a few lines from a rather schmaltzy song I had heard in an earlier life in a long-ago world:

Es geht alles vorüber, es geht alles vorbei
Nach jedem Dezember kommt wieder ein Mai.
(All things pass and end someday,
After every December there will come a May.)

That became my mantra. I would not die. I would live. There would be a May.

In a really bad prison camp the all-important thing is to survive each day, to lie down at night and say to yourself, "I have survived another day."

But there should also be hope, for those who are without hope usually die. That's why I kept repeating my mantra, "there will come a May." It was my promise of survival and hope. I also learned from Karl and Manek, who were masters in the art of survival.

The year 1945 was one of hunger in the Soviet Union. The *kolkhozy*, the great collective farms, never efficient, had been devastated by the advancing and retreating armies of Germany and the Soviet Union. Millions of hungry soldiers had marched across the land, eating, destroying, scorching the earth. Millions of Russian farm workers had died in the war.

Food rations for Russian workers in 1945 were barely adequate for the work demanded from them. Food rations for prisoners were less than adequate for the work demanded from them.

Our starvation rations were further cut by a chain of corruption and greed. The captain, we later learned, sold much of the prisoners' food. He stole from the living and he stole from the dead. By simply not reporting deaths, he kept drawing rations for "dead souls," and then sold the food.

The trusties also stole food and sold it. The kitchen staff sold food. All of them ate well, and some were flabby with fat. The prisoners died of starvation, disease, and despair.

Among the first to die were the peasants, heavy, hard-working men from all over eastern Europe. They had worked hard on their farms. Now they worked hard in the factory. And while they lasted, in the evenings and on Sundays, they sat together and talked about food. Endlessly.

Their powerful bulks shrank. Their skin hung loose. And still they talked of food. What they had eaten at home. How much they had eaten at home. They talked in detail about their favourite meals. About the meat. Lots of meat! And the sauce! Such wonderful rich, fat sauce. And dessert. The great cakes. How many eggs went into the making of the cake. How much butter. They talked a lot about butter. Then came the Sunday meals. The holiday meals. When one man stopped reminiscing, another started. They talked of food and wasted away. Haunted by constant hunger and the memories of plentiful food and wonderful meals, they lost the will to live.

Disease destroyed them, starvation edema and dysentery. Now too weak to work, they did not get any food. They no longer went to the latrines. They lay huddled on the iron floor, blood and mucus oozing out of them, stinking, covered by flies.

We just ignored them. They were the living dead. No one knew them. No one cared. The trusties made the rounds each morning and kicked them. "Go to work!" They did not respond. They had given up. At night the vultures sat near them and waited for them to die.

A few prisoners occasionally caught my attention. There was an elderly man from Breslau in Silesia (he was probably in his fifties, but anyone over fifty was considered elderly, and few of them survived). In his former life he had owned a pet shop.

He loved to talk about his pets, especially about the canaries. He was very proud of his canaries, they sang so beautifully. He kept cages with top singers close together, and they inspired each other. "In the morning the entire shop was full of singing," he said. "It was like a canary choir."

He was a soft, gentle man, and he did not last long. He got dysentery and lost the strength to work and the will to live. One evening he called to me. He knew I loved animals and wanted to talk. He talked about the pets he loved, about his canaries, about the kittens he raised, about his own cats.

As he talked of his cats by name, he began to talk to them, his voice became fainter, but there was a smile on his face and he slid softly into death. Next day he was another bloated corpse on the pile by the kitchen. His death hurt me and I cried, one of the very few times I did cry in camp. I never again became fond of another prisoner. Like others, I wrapped myself in the cold, grey, protective mantle of indifference.

One day, shortly after I had survived my first bout of dysentery, the *Meister* gave me a large old burlap sack and told me to collect fodder for his cow.

Like many Russians, the *Meister* had a small garden, some chickens, and a pig. He also had a cow. In the evening after work, he or his wife took the cow out to graze along the roads.

The factory was vast. Many buildings were in ruins. Large areas were empty and now rank with weeds and grasses (that's where Manek collected his healing herbs), and having grown up with cows in Quellenhof, I knew the grasses that were good for them.

In the sack was half a bottle of milk and a small piece of bread.

I hid in a ruined building, uncorked the bottle, and slowly, very slowly, sip by sip, drank that wonderful rich milk and ate small pieces of real bread with it. Only the starving know the total bliss of food. I made it last as long as I could, safe in that ruined building.

Then I collected grass. At the end of the day, the sack was pressed full, so heavy I could barely carry it. I put it near the office. The *Meister* saw me, came out of the office and checked the bag. "*Molodiets* ("Smart Kid"), he praised. I thanked him for the milk and bread. He nodded and smiled.

From then on, during that summer and fall of 1945, I collected food about once a week for that blessed cow, drank half a litre of her wonderful milk, and ate a bit of extra bread.

It was marvellous, it helped stave off starvation, but it was not enough. Only more food could save me. And stealing and smuggling would get me money to buy more food.

But thieves and smugglers, if caught and turned in by guards, were locked up in the *Karzer*. There they waited until trusties dragged them out so the captain could slowly beat them to death with his heavy iron rod.

Chapter 10

TO STEAL AND NOT BE CAUGHT

OUR PRISON WAS STRICTLY GUARDED, and so was the factory. Yet it was fairly easy to steal and, if prisoners wanted to, they could easily escape. The security system, theoretically strict, was full of loopholes.

Morning and evening security was thorough, lunchtime security was lax. We left in the morning in orderly, counted brigade groups, and returned in the evening in orderly groups that were again counted by the trusties. At lunchtime the prisoners streamed back to camp, ate, rested, and went back to work, and no one checked their coming or their going. It was therefore easy for a prisoner to spend the one-hour lunch period in the factory.

Work stopped in the factory. Only a few essential services continued. The Russian workers walked to their mess hall to eat, talk, and rest. Most buildings were empty for that one hour.

Prisoners who stayed in the factory could also leave the factory grounds. The factory guards' job was to prevent theft, not to stop prisoners from leaving, and for me it was particularly easy, because I was so young.

"Where are you going?" one of the guards at the factory gate would ask.

"To the bazaar," I replied, pointing to the small market not far from the gate.

"All right. But don't be long," the guard said, frisked me, and let me go. Since the greatly feared head of security usually went home for lunch, the search would be quick and superficial.

The reason few prisoners escaped, despite this lax security, and most did not steal or smuggle, was our fear of the *Karzer*. Every week we watched the captain torture two or three prisoners to death, and these were men who had been caught stealing or smuggling, men who had tried to escape.

By mid-June I knew the factory well. Since my "all-over-the-factory" brigade installed and repaired pipes, I had been in many buildings. When I finally decided that I had to steal to get enough food to survive, my first target was the paper sacks that were filled in several buildings with the chemicals our factory produced.

These were heavy-duty, two-ply bags, made of strong brown paper, which lay in neat piles next to the machines that filled them. Outside the factory these bags were worth fifteen roubles each, the price of one-and-half loaves of good bread, since paper then was rare and precious in the Soviet Union.

I planned my first theft carefully. I knew the building, knew where the sacks were stacked. If I took one, it would not be missed.

I spent the lunch hour in the factory. When the Russian workers had gone to eat, I walked into the building. I looked around. All was still. There was no one. I walked to the pile of sacks, took one, and was beginning to fold it when a voice behind me said, "Stealing sacks, are you!"

A Russian man stood in the shadows near the door. I must have looked like a caged rabbit facing an approaching snake, paralyzed by the fear of a terrible death, for he said immediately: "Don't be afraid. I will not tell."

He was a man in his fifties, with greying hair and a broad, friendly face. He smiled.

"First time you steal?" he asked.

"Yes," I said.

"Then you must learn to do it better," he said with a soft laugh. "I will tell you."

He walked to the door and checked that no one was coming.

"Be natural," he said. "Walk assured. Don't slink. Have a reason to be in the building. Case it first. Know it well. Enter it when you are sure all have gone to lunch and yell loudly 'Misha' or any other name. Several times. If someone answers, say you're looking for Misha, then go and don't come back for a while.

"If no one answers, take a paper sack, fold it carefully. Put it tightly under your belt and jacket, so it doesn't show.

"Then walk out. Relaxed. Busy. Going somewhere. Learn to be invisible, never attract attention, and always have an answer ready why you are in a certain place."

He watched me fold and hide the bag. He looked out the door. No one was near. He smiled again. "Now go," he said. "*Ostoroshno* (Be careful)."

I met him from time to time in the factory. He always smiled, a nice, warm smile, then looked away, pretending he didn't see me, that I was invisible.

Much later, I asked the *Meister* about this man who had given me my first lesson in theft. "He's very nice," I said, without telling the *Meister* how we had first met.

"He had a son," the *Meister* said, "older than you. About sixteen or so. During the war, partisans blew up a German car. The Germans rounded up hostages and shot them. One of them was his son."

Stealing was risky. Smuggling was risky. Only one person smuggled with near impunity, the man we called *Scheiss-Heini*, "Shit-Heini." His real name was Heinz. He was about twenty-five years old, and had probably been a soldier who changed into civvies and had been scooped up with other civilians as slave labour.

Shit-Heini was from a poor section of Berlin. He had escaped from a first camp, wandered westward, was caught, ended up in our camp, and, before we arrived, had somehow managed to get the best job in the factory: he emptied the cesspits beneath the many factory latrines.

He had a horse, and a cart that carried a big oblong barrel with a large opening at the top and a hole and bung at the rear bottom end. He drove up to a privy, removed the board behind it, and ladled the contents of the cesspit into the barrel with a small bucket firmly attached to a long pole.

He worked methodically, sloshing urine and excrement into the barrel and all over the barrel, the cart, and himself. He was covered in shit. He rarely washed himself. He never washed his clothes. Even the hardened guards at the factory gate hated to search him or his cart and barrel.

When the feared head of security was present, a tall, stern man who, people said, was utterly ruthless, everyone was thoroughly searched except Shit-Heini. He filled the barrel to the very top, threw an old burlap sack over the opening, and, as he drove, it would slosh and dribble. At the gate the guards pretended to search him. The head of security never interfered, and Shit-Heini would drive out. He unloaded his cargo into a broad and deep war-time trench or, for a small fee, fertilized gardens and fields with it.

He would stop briefly at a certain house, drop off all smuggled goods, and receive money for the last load. His fence, an elderly woman, was totally honest — so was Shit-Heini.

He never stole anything himself. He smuggled the loot of thieves like me, and the proceeds were split fifty-fifty. He probably also did contract smuggling for some of the Russians. If he did, he was smart enough not to talk about it.

Small items, like my paper sacks, he carried on his body beneath a skin-tight smuggler's vest that I later copied. Large items, like saws, hammers, axes, and containers with screws or nails, he dumped into the barrel and fished them out when the barrel was empty. Neither he nor his fence were fussy. Shit was his armour and he walked in an aura of protective stench. In our crowded, stinking dormitory building, Shit-Heini had a corner to himself.

In a camp full of starving prisoners, Shit-Heini lived well. He rarely bothered to eat in our mess hall. He had lots of good bread and butter for breakfast. He bought cans with meat "Made in America," the ultimate prison luxury.

He once bought a large can of "American butter." On the label it said "Peanut Butter." "Peanut" didn't mean anything to him, but the German and English words for butter are identical: Butter—"butter." He paid a lot of money for what he assumed was real butter, and then was horrified when the can contained what looked to him like axle grease.

He came to me. "Can you read that?" he asked. "What is that stuff? Can one eat it?"

My school English, learned in Kalisch, was limited and not very practical — too much poetry and nothing about peanuts. Also, I had never seen a peanut, eaten a peanut, or heard of peanuts, but I worked my way slowly through the text on the label and figured out what it probably was.

"It's nut butter," I explained. "Made from American nuts. Very rich in fat." "Fat" was a magic word in camp; we all craved fat. Shit-Heini was fairly happy and rewarded me with a slice of real bread covered with peanut butter.

Like other "successful" prisoners, Shit-Heini paid protection money to Franz, and his possessions were guarded against theft while he was away working.

With the money from the sale of my first paper bag I went out of the factory to the nearby bazaar and bought, after some haggling, half a loaf of bread and, as a special treat, two sugar cubes. One I ate immediately. The other I kept, and all that day I looked forward to eating it, slowly — deliciously slowly — at night.

From then on, my thoughts circled around theft and food. I learned the art of stealing. Success meant food and life. Failure could mean torture and death. As in an earlier life I had once spent hours watching birds, so I now spent a lot of time observing people and their routines in the great factory. Each theft was carefully reconnoitred and planned, then carried out quickly, yet without rushing.

Scheming, planning, doing. Stealing became a constant preoccupation and kept me from the brooding and despair that, with starvation and disease, killed most men in camp.

WHEN WE HAD ARRIVED at the camp, both Karl and Manek, since they were strong, had been assigned to one of the toughest work brigades: "Transport," the loading and unloading of freight trains that were shunted in and out of the factory.

Karl soon cornered a senior factory engineer and told him, in his limited noun-verb Russian, that he was a top-notch lathe operator. They tried him and, sure enough, he really was an excellent lathe operator. Since he never spoke of his past, we never found out where he had acquired so many different skills.

From then on, Karl worked with Russians in a large machine shop, and came and went as he pleased. In addition to his factory work, he made, from stolen steel, excellent knives (including one each for Manek and me) and various tools that Shit-Heini smuggled and sold for him.

Karl also made an especially beautiful knife and presented it to the senior engineer who had got him the job. Word spread. Soon Karl received regular orders for fancy knives and tools from rich factory bosses, who paid him well. It was quiet, risk-free, and lucrative and Karl ate well.

Manek remained with "Transport." At first his work was hard. But Manek soon slithered sideways into a much easier job. He became assistant to a Russian "checker," who verified freight-car loads. There must have been more to it, for after a while Manek had a lot of money.

Manek, who until then had often laughed and liked to boast and brag and tell tales of his crooked past, became very secretive. None of us knew how he earned that money. But we could guess.

Manek and Russian associates probably stole, most likely with the connivance of some of the factory elite and the senior guards, large quantities of goods, using the freight cars to smuggle the loot out of the factory. In a factory crawling with informers, it must have been risky. But they planned well, bribed well, lived well.

Chapter 11

THE GATE OF FATE

I LIKED TATYANA. She was a tall, nearly mannish, Russian woman and one of the best workers of our "all-over-the-factory" brigade. I worked with her from time to time on emergency jobs, fixing broken pipes and drains.

Tatyana was a war widow, one of millions in the Soviet Union. More than twenty million Russians had been killed in the Second World War, and most of them were young men, the cannon fodder of the war. Now there were young widows all over the Soviet Union. Few would find another husband, for the young men were dead.

Tatyana was about thirty years old and had been married for eight years. Her husband had been killed in the fall of 1944, less than a year before, "somewhere near Leningrad." She did not know where he had died or where he had been buried.

She had two children, a girl of seven and a boy of five, and they were the total joy of her life. Her parents had died when she was young, and she had few friends and no relatives. All her love was concentrated on her children.

Whenever we worked together, I asked after her children, and Tatyana's broad, peasant face, normally serious and plain, lit up. She was so proud of them. They were wonderful children.

And so clever. The little girl wrote well and was one of the best students in her class. And the little boy! He said this and he said that! She loved the children with all the love that was in her kind and lonely heart.

One day, a major drain broke. Tatyana, some other Russians of the brigade, and a group of prisoners dug down to get at the broken pipe, but water kept gushing up. No one knew where to turn it off. While one group was trying to reach the broken drain and repair it, Tatyana and others dug a trench to reroute the water so it would not flood a factory building.

I helped Tatyana to build a sort of dam out of old planks to block the water, me holding the planks while she nailed them together. She desperately wanted to get the job done, for we were already late and her children would be at home waiting for her.

When we were finished, she rushed to the warehouse to return the hammer and then ran home to her children.

During the next few days I did not see Tatyana. "Is she sick?" I asked the *Meister*.

"No," he said. "She has been arrested."

"Why?" I asked.

"For theft," he said, his face passive.

Later I heard a few more details. After she had returned the hammer to the warehouse, she had hurried to the gate to go home. The chief of security worked late that day, and he was still at the gate when she arrived and the guards searched her more carefully. In the big pocket of her old working jacket they found handfuls of nails. She had forgotten to return them.

The chief of security ordered her arrest. She was charged with "theft of state property," a serious crime in the Soviet Union.

"Ten years," the *Meister* said, his face carefully blank. Ten years in a slave labour camp in Siberia.

"And her children?" I asked.

"They have been sent to a Soviet orphanage," he said and turned away.

IN JUNE I BEGAN TO STEAL. In July, after carefully studying the guards at the gate and their habits, I added smuggling. The guards frisked prisoners and Russians alike, thoroughly if the head of security was there or just a few pats if he had gone for lunch, but there were certain body areas they rarely touched: armpits, crotch, and upper back, the area between the shoulder blades.

I made myself a copy of Shit-Heini's skin-tight smuggler's vest. Then, with string, tied a carefully folded paper sack securely onto my back between the shoulder blades. My vest came down over it, and over that I wore a large, loose, padded jacket that I had stripped off a dead prisoner.

The guards knew me, had searched me many times, and the search was superficial. I tried to be relaxed. At the market I quietly told a woman I knew that I had a paper sack and asked her where I could sell it. She told me to go to a certain house.

I knew the house. The village was just outside the factory, and whenever I had the time, I rushed to the nearest village houses, knocked on doors, and begged for bread. Since all women in the Soviet Union worked except the wives of upper-class Communists, there were usually only grandmotherly *babushkas* at home. With my shaven head, sunken cheeks, and skeletal body, I looked like a pathetic starving child.

These women had very little and I was not the only beggar, yet they were kind and often gave me a bit of food or, with a nearly embarrassed smile, said: "I have nothing. But come again. Maybe I'll have something next time."

In the house to which I was sent lived a stout old peasant woman, her daughter-in-law who worked in the factory, and her granddaughter, Vanushka, a lively, tow-headed child of seven. The old woman's son had died in the war. She was always kind. Once, when she had no food and I left, she felt so bad that she sent Vanushka racing after me, all excited and happy, to give me two carrots.

Now I told her I had a paper sack for sale. I took it from its hiding place. "Smart," she said approvingly. We settled on fifteen roubles for the sack — the standard price. Yes, she said, she would buy more sacks and anything else I could bring out of the factory.

All went well until, one day, when her grandmother was not home, Vanushka came with me to try and sell the sack somewhere else. The first two houses were closed. The third had no money.

The fourth house we tried was quite large. We knocked, entered, and there, having lunch, was the feared head of factory security, the man of whom it was said that he had no pity. Before I could stop her and humbly beg for bread, Vanushka prattled excitedly that "he has a paper sack for sale."

I was terrified. A prisoner caught smuggling could be tortured to death by the captain. The man looked at me, his eyes hard and cold.

"Let me see it," he said. Earlier I had taken it from its hiding place and now held it up my sleeve. I gave it to him.

The security chief examined the sack carefully.

"How much?" he asked.

"Fifteen roubles," I said.

He walked to a dresser, opened a drawer, took out fifteen roubles, and gave them to me. I said, "Thank you," and Vanushka and I left, the girl babbling happily and I very shaken.

I didn't smuggle anything else for a while. I walked through the gate "clean" when I knew the chief of security was on duty. The guards searched me thoroughly, as they always did in his presence, but as usual they did not touch the area between my shoulder blades. Their chief glanced at me briefly, uncaring, indifferent. He said nothing.

I told my *babushka* fence what had happened, and of my fears. She just laughed. "He was off duty. He needed paper. You had paper. So he bought it. That's all!"

A few things could be safely smuggled. One of them was lighters made privately —*nalewo*, "on the left," as the saying went — in the factory.

In 1945, matches were rare and precious in the Soviet Union. Smokers used spills of paper or wood lit at stoves to light their cigarettes made of the rough tobacco called *makhorka* rolled in newspaper. The main use of Soviet newspapers then was as toilet paper and cigarette paper. Those who could afford to buy them, prisoners or Russians, had lighters similar to those used before the invention of matches in England in 1826.

These flint, steel, and wick lighters were produced by Karl and me, and I smuggled them out of the factory. The finger-thick wick was made from the cotton wadding I pulled out of dead prisoners' padded jackets. The wick of each lighter was enclosed in a small metal protective tube made from pipe that I stole and that Karl cut into sections.

I also provided the steels. Files made especially good steels. I stole the files, and Karl cut them into sections and polished the edges. Flints I collected at one of the factory gravel piles.

The cotton wick worked best if it had ash on its burned end. One skilful stroke of steel against flint sent a shower of sparks against the wick. They clung to the ash and could be cautiously blown into a glow. Experts got a light with every stroke. After a cigarette was lit, the wick was pulled back into the tube, the glow died, the ash remained.

(In a future life, when I spent thirty years with Inuit in the Arctic, they showed me how they had made fire before the white man came bringing matches. One method was similar to that we used in Russia in 1945. They struck "fire stones," pyrite rocks, together and caught the sparks on the slightly oiled bolls of arctic cottongrass and blew them into flame.)

Smuggling a lighter was not a problem. I carried the lighter in the pocket of my large jacket, and it was all right. I could have a lighter. Everyone could have a lighter. That it was made in the factory with stolen material, and that each time I left the factory I carried another lighter, was of no interest to anyone. A handful of nails could have got me killed. The lighters were all right.

In mid-August, as a special treat, we got fish to eat — tiny fish encrusted in salt. The camp had probably received a huge load of them. At supper each prisoner got two ladles full of the tiny fish. Manek warned immediately in a loud voice: "Don't eat them!"

But nearly all the starving prisoners ate them. They begged for more and they got more. And next day they received even larger helpings.

Following Manek's advice, however, Karl and I took all the fish we could get, leached most of the salt out of them with repeated changes of water, and then boiled them together with beans bought at the market.

The prisoners who ate large quantities of these little fish, became desperately thirsty. They drank a lot of water, and their legs began to swell.

Until then, dysentery had been the top killer in our camp. Now, in addition, starvation edema, or dropsy, destroyed the prisoners. Their legs became like columns, grotesquely swollen. The skin became taut and glossy, and when pressed, it did not bounce back. The indentation in the nearly violet-coloured skin remained for a long time.

The legs, easily cut, were full of suppurating wounds. Flies laid their eggs in the wounds, and soon they were crawling with maggots. The prisoners, drained by hunger, diarrhea, and despair, did not go to work, were no longer fed, and died in agony.

Manek knew how to heal edema. He dug up dandelion roots, cut them into pieces, and made a potent, extremely bitter, decoction from them. That and dandelion tea acted as powerful diuretics, and the prisoners who followed his regimen pissed out the accumulated fluid and survived.

Manek covered festering wounds with poultices of camomile that grew in abundance in the factory. He grew mould on pieces of bread, made a mould paste, smeared it on the wounds, and usually they healed.

He gave free advice, but he healed only those who could pay. Essentially, the health and fate of other prisoners made no difference to him. If they died, they died.

We were all like that. We knew each other by first names, knew the nationality of other prisoners, but we did not make friends. We worked together, talked a bit. Some lived. Some died. There was indifference and anonymity among the living, and there was anonymity in death.

Ten to twenty prisoners died every day and no one bothered to inquire who they were. The camp crew hauled the stripped corpses out of the building and threw them onto the pile near the kitchen to rot in the summer sun. Once or twice a week a truck came, and the corpses were loaded onto the truck and covered with a tarp that hid the gruesome sight but not the stench. They were driven out of the factory gate, dumped into a deep war-time trench, and covered with rocks and earth. The trench was an anonymous mass grave for the anonymous dead, for persons who were now among the millions listed as "missing."

Chapter 12

FROZEN POTATOES

IT COULD HAVE BEEN the perfect job.

At one time in its past, our factory had produced phosphorus, and vast amounts of it had soaked into the earth. Now prisoners dug up this evil, poisonous soil, shovelled it onto a horse-drawn cart, and Klaus, another prisoner, and I took the load out of the factory to a dump a couple of kilometres away.

It was an easy job, full of opportunities. But Klaus, unfortunately, was totally wrong for it. He was from Transylvania in Romania, a stolid young farmer, hard-working, conscientious, honest, simple.

The problems started the moment we left the factory. I wanted to go begging. "No, no!" Klaus said anxiously. "We don't have time. We must unload and then get back for another load."

One day the *Meister* took me aside. "You and Klaus will stay during lunchtime," he said. "I'll tell you what to do."

When all had gone, the *Meister* drove the cart to the pile of smouldering earth. He went into the building and returned with a heavy, oblong parcel sewn into a burlap bag.

He placed the parcel into the centre of the cart, where a plank sagged a bit, covered it with rocks, then earth, then more rocks, and finally we loaded the cart with the phosphorus-soaked earth, which burst into flames and white smoke when exposed to air.

"You will take this to the dump," the *Meister* ordered. "Unload it with all the other smoking earth, and be sure the parcel is well covered." Klaus didn't speak Russian. I told him what we had to do. He was frightened and said so.

The search at the gate was superficial. The chief of security had gone for lunch, and his underlings did not like to search the poisonous earth. They frisked us briefly and we could go.

When we reached the dump, we found a group of gypsies there searching for things that could be used or sold.

The moment we arrived, Klaus said: "We must unload!"

"Not while the gypsies are here," I insisted. "We'll just sit and relax, look lazy, and wait."

But Klaus could not be lazy or look lazy. He fidgeted, stared at the gypsies, and got all excited.

"This is bad!" he exclaimed. "We must unload and go back!" He jumped onto the cart, shovelled out earth and rocks, dropped the parcel, and then carefully cleaned the cart. I covered the parcel with smouldering earth. Then Klaus insisted we go back. "We must get the next load!"

The *Meister* was badly upset when I mentioned the gypsies. "You should have stayed there," he said angrily. "This is very dangerous. Take out another load of earth and stay until the gypsies are gone."

When we arrived at the dump, the gypsies had gone and so had the parcel.

The *Meister* was scared and angry. He told me to stay behind after work. When all had left, Russians and prisoners, he took me into the office of the *nachalnik*, the top boss of the "all-over-the-factory" brigade, a senior and highly decorated Communist Party man. I knew him, of course, but I had never spoken to him. An austere, reserved man, he rarely spoke to prisoners.

"Sit down," he said when the *Meister* and I entered his office. We were alone. His secretaries had left. "Now tell me exactly what happened." He was quiet but tense as I repeated the entire story.

"Are you sure they were gypsies?" he asked.

"Yes," I said. "The women were dressed the gypsy way, with very long skirts."

He was silent for a while. "I think it will be all right," he said to the *Meister*.

To me he gave fifty roubles, enough money to buy several loaves of bread.

"Don't speak about this to anyone," he said. "And tell that *durak* ["that fool"] to keep quiet."

They had tried me and found me wanting. I never got another chance at a "big deal." I also never found out what had been in the parcel. Something extremely valuable, no doubt, for both the *Meister* and the *nachalnik* to take such a risk. But I did not dare to ask the *Meister*.

I was sent to other jobs and continued my small-time theft and smuggling. Klaus, like nearly all the other honest farmers in our camp, eventually died from overwork and starvation.

BY MID-SEPTEMBER about a thousand prisoners had died since our arrival in mid-May. This now seemed to worry the captain. His boots were still polished to a high gloss, but there was less bounce in his strut as he marched back and forth in front of the greatly diminished groups of prisoners in the yard. However, he still worked himself into a frenzy of hate and excitement and, when it had reached a certain pitch, he shouted and the trusties dragged another screaming prisoner from the *Karzer* into the yard so the captain could beat him to pulp with his heavy iron rod.

In May, June, July, and August he killed two or three prisoners like that each week, but now that half the camp population was dead, he allowed himself only one torture session a week.

In October it suddenly became very cold. One Sunday, early in the morning, there was an abrupt commotion and about one hundred prisoners were rounded up to help harvest potatoes on a *kolkhoz* ("collective farm"). Karl and Manek had vanished instantly. I had been sound asleep, was too slow, and was herded with the other prisoners onto three waiting trucks.

It was still dark and bitterly cold. During the warm summer months the prisoners had sold most of their clothes, as well as those they had stripped from corpses. Many now wore only pants and jackets made of burlap, thin, porous, and often torn, which provided little protection. In comparison, I was warmly dressed. Because bulky clothing was good for smuggling, I had a large padded jacket and two pairs of torn but ample pants, one worn over the other.

We huddled in the back of the trucks, keeping as low as possible to escape the cutting wind. The trip lasted only one and a half hours, but when we got to the *kolkhoz* most of the emaciated prisoners were shaking uncontrollably and could barely talk.

They drove us directly to the fields, where tractor-pulled ploughs were turning over frozen earth and exposing masses of frozen potatoes.

The *kolkhozniki* had harvested their own potatoes in good time, before the frost. But they also had a state harvest norm to fulfil. If they did not meet it, they were in deep trouble. The potatoes we harvested had, when cut, that typical shiny, glassy appearance of frozen potatoes. Such potatoes rot. It was a totally useless harvest.

But only the quota mattered and the *kolkhozniki* and the prisoners gathered potatoes all day. Men emptied the large baskets into trucks. The trucks drove them to town. The harvest was weighed, recorded, and sent by train to Russian cities desperately in need of food, even though these were frozen potatoes that would turn into a stinking, rotting mush.

The *kolkhozniki* were not unkind. They made fires on the fields and roasted potatoes in the coals — for themselves and for the prisoners. At lunchtime we all got a marvellous hot soup, with bits of pork in it.

But our rest was short. The ploughs kept turning up the frozen potatoes, and men, women, children, and prisoners gathered the useless harvest.

We worked until dusk. It was only a few kilometres to the *kolkhoz* buildings, but we were exhausted, famished, cold and it seemed miles away. We were hoping for a good hot meal and a fast trip back to camp.

It was nearly dark when we reached the *kolkhoz* buildings. There were problems, there was confusion, there were loud arguments. The prisoners stood close together in a miserable huddle. The guards shouted, people yelled.

Our truck drivers, I gathered from snatches of talk, had partied all day, were drunk, did not feel like driving, and wanted to drink some more. Our guards wanted to join them. The *kolkhoz* had lots of *samogon* ("home brew") and after the long, cold day the *kolkhozniki* also wanted to drink.

The problem was what to do with the prisoners.

"They must have food," someone said.

"They've eaten potatoes all day," said someone else.

Finally something was decided and we were told to move. "*Dawai! Dawai!* (Get going!)" I kept at the very edge of the group. As we passed the corner of a building, I ducked sideways and vanished into the dark.

Later I learned that the prisoners were driven into an unheated metal tractor shed and locked up for the night. That problem solved, *kolkhozniki* and guards had supper and then joined the drunken drivers for an evening of heavy drinking.

I waited in the dark until things quietened down, then cautiously, keeping to the darkest areas, searched for the pigsty, where I hoped to find warmth and food. Guided by the instincts of a country kid, I found the building, opened the door, and moved from the cutting cold outside into the lovely warm funk of pig shit and swill.

The pigs had been fed and grunted contentedly in the dark. In the corners of several troughs I found swill that contained pieces of boiled potatoes, ate well, collected more potatoes for the morning, found the water tap, drank, washed my hands, located the pile of straw that is part of most pigsties, crawled in, covered myself with straw, and, warm and full of food, fell asleep nearly instantly.

I awoke at dawn. The pigs' grunting was no longer so sleepily contented. Now it was the impatient grunting of pigs thinking about food and feeding. The troughs had been sucked empty, and I gratefully ate the potatoes I had taken out the night before. It was time to move. Pigs are fed early, and there was no place to hide in the sty.

I had passed a nearby barn the evening before. It was clear and bitterly cold outside. I walked to the barn, crawled into the hay, and, fairly warm, dozed and listened to the farm noises. People came and fed the eager, screaming pigs. Then it was quiet again.

Suddenly there was a great commotion. People called, yelled, ran. I struggled from my nest in the hay and looked outside. Many people were running. I joined them. No one noticed me.

An excited crowd stood near the tractor shed. "Oh my God! Oh my God!" several people said loudly. Inside the shed lay a large pile of prisoners. Most were dead. Emaciated, famished, clothed in thin burlap rags, they had frozen to death during the long night. Those still alive could neither talk nor move.

Kolkhozniki, guards, and drivers were horrified. They were not cruel people, just thoughtless. They had been tired last night. They wanted to eat and drink *samogon*. The prisoners had to be locked up somewhere. The shed seemed like a good idea. No one had expected this.

Now they were genuinely upset — many were also worried. They had asked for and had received one hundred live prisoners. Now most of them were dead. There might be questioning. There could be trouble.

The guards sorted the still living from the dead, and the *kolkhozniki* carried them carefully from the icy shed into the overheated *kolkhoz* meeting–dining room.

"Give them vodka," some said. Others suggested hot tea, hot soup, hot anything.

The prisoners looked ghastly. Their skin was a dirty bluish-white, their eyes stared, they twitched and, after a while, began to have terrible spasms. Their thin bodies shook violently. They babbled, and spit ran out of their mouths.

Someone finally thought of calling the *kolkhoz* nurse. A strong woman in her forties, she too had had lots to drink the night before. Now she assessed the situation and then took over. The fascinated children were chased out and told to go home. Some men and women helped. The rest were told to stand in a corner and shut up.

About then, someone noticed me.

"Where have you been?" he asked.

"In the pigsty." I said.

Nu wot, molodiets! There's a smart kid, he said.

An older woman took me in charge. She fed me marvellous food, good bread with rendered pig fat and hot soup, urged me to eat more and, when I was totally full, took me to her home and put me to bed. "Sleep," she said and left. It was my best meal in months, my first sleep in a real bed since Kleingraben. It was pure bliss.

My woman returned in the afternoon with more food and with news. Several more prisoners had died. The corpses were now being loaded onto a truck and taken back to camp. The nurse had said the survivors should not be moved for a couple of days.

The *kolkhozniki*, now feeling guilty, wanted to feed the prisoners massive meals and give them lots of vodka. The nurse forbade both. The prisoners got several small meals a day. They rallied.

My elderly woman fed me well. In the evenings we talked. Her husband had died in the war, but her son and both daughters had survived. All worked on the *kolkhoz*, and one evening they came with their children. They brought food.

They were a bit awkward at first, not quite sure how to behave with a German prisoner. But my old lady made me tell again how I had spent the night with the pigs and had eaten potatoes from the troughs, and they laughed. We drank tea and it was cozy and friendly.

After four days, the nurse said we could go back to camp. My elderly woman gave me a bag full of food, then kissed me, Russian-fashion, on both cheeks and said softly: "May God protect you!"

This time we travelled in a covered truck. It wasn't warm, but it sheltered us from the wind. About thirty prisoners had survived, and they were pleased. They talked in detail about the wonderful food they had eaten. "Real bacon!" they said with awe. It had been a good time. The dead were not mentioned.

After four days of comfort and good food, it was hard to be in camp again, with its stench, the dying, the twisted corpses, the sour, watery cabbage soup, the dark, moist lumps of bread.

For some, things were better. Since a thousand prisoners had died, the survivors had much more space. Already, in July, Karl, Manek, and I had moved to a special area.

From the second floor of the building, a few metal steps led to a structure that looked like a large iron balcony high above an open space over the first floor. When our dormitory had been a factory building, some machine had probably stood there.

We had cleaned the area and lugged up three metal beds. Manek had a talk with Franz, paid some money, and we got well-stuffed paillasses. It was much better than sleeping on the metal floor.

Karl built himself a sort of cobbler's bench there. This was his newest venture. One of the top bosses in his part of the factory had bought a beautiful pair of boots that had once probably belonged to a German officer. Now the boots were scuffed and torn, and he wore them to work. When one sole came loose, he tied it on with string.

Karl noticed this and told him: "Get me leather, good thread, and a chunk of wax, and I'll repair your boots." He got all he asked for. Tools and lasts he made in the machine shop. He worked on the boots in camp, slowly, methodically, with great skill and care. When he was finished the boots were nearly as good as new.

The boss was delighted, paid well, and must have bragged, because soon other highly placed people came to Karl with shoes and boots that needed repairing. Then someone asked whether, given leather, Karl could make new boots. Karl said yes. The new boots were perfect.

The demand became so great, Karl needed more time. The Important People spoke to his factory boss. From then on Karl went to work in the factory only to make tools for himself or for sale. He had become the well-paid cobbler to the regional elite.

Surprisingly, the abrupt death of seventy prisoners at the *kolkhoz* seemed to upset the captain. We were issued padded winter clothing. We received more food; the sick received food. Scuttlebutt had it that even the doomed prisoners in the *Karzer* received additional food.

In truth, the men in the *Karzer* were no longer doomed to torture and death. Only they did not know that. The captain had stopped beating prisoners to death. He had a new diversion.

One evening, the captain came to roll call with a dog. Its leash was a rope with a noose around the animal's neck. In his other hand the captain carried a stick.

The dog, a German shepherd, walked close to its master, cowed and cringing, its back arched, the tail between its legs. The captain marched back and forth and ranted: we were uncultured, lazy, dirty, stupid. "*Prakljatii njemtsi!* (Damned Germans!)," he shouted, his voice getting shrill.

We knew the sound. Soon he would reach his climax and then he would bludgeon one of the screaming prisoners from the *Karzer* to death. We had heard it before. We had seen it before. We didn't care. We stood there, quiet, cold, bored, apathetic: "Let's get it over with and then we can go to sleep."

The captain made an abrupt turn. The dog, caught by surprise, walked on and pulled him. His anger instantly turned to frenzy. He slashed at the dog with his stick. When the screaming animal tried to run, he pulled it back and slashed and slashed. In desperation, the dog lunged at him. The captain lifted it half off the ground, the noose tightened around its neck, and he beat the hanging body.

The captain did not kill the dog nor did he break its bones as he used to do with prisoners. He just tried to inflict a maximum amount of pain.

He slowly strangled the dog, and kept beating it, shouting abrupt sentences: "You want to bite me! I feed you! And you bite me! I'll teach you!" and the blows continued.

Suddenly he let go. The dog collapsed and lay there, gasping, whimpering. He kicked the dog but it did not respond. He leaned over and patted its head. "Now you are a good dog," he said.

He marched back and forth for a while. Then he picked up the rope. "Let's go," he said, and the dog got up and slunk out of camp after its master.

Chapter 13

THE BENEVOLENT RULE OF
THE SECRET POLICE

THE TYPHUS EPIDEMIC began in early November. Most prisoners were crawling with lice, which spread the fatal disease. The men were weak. They had little resistance and the death rate soared. Some days more than fifty prisoners died.

Then something extraordinary happened. Many Russians, terrified of typhus and of contact with prisoners, refused to come to work. That must have alarmed the authorities.

One morning, after the trusties had lined up all the prisoners who were able to stand, two Russian officers came into our camp, a major and a lieutenant. Both belonged to the NKGB, later called KGB, the often-renamed and always-feared Soviet secret police.

The major spoke briefly. We were in quarantine. No one was allowed to leave camp. He and the lieutenant were now in charge. Dismissed.

We never saw our captain again.

The second-in-command, the poor haunted lieutenant who wished only to see no evil and have no part in evil, the man we had only rarely seen in camp, also vanished completely.

The NKGB major ordered Franz to open the *Karzer*. He stepped inside, then recoiled, his face shocked. "*Oi boshe!* (Oh my God!)," he exclaimed in a low voice.

None of us had ever looked into the *Karzer*. We didn't want to see the *Karzer*, know the *Karzer*, think about the *Karzer*. We knew it was hell and it was near, and any one of us could end up in it to await torture and death. We never thought about the men in the *Karzer*. We never talked about them. When our captain was in one of his moods, and the trusties dragged one of the prisoners out of the *Karzer* and into the yard so that the captain could beat him to death, it had become a show. Maybe, to protect ourselves, we no longer thought of the *Karzer* inmates as humans. Now we looked at them as people in London once looked at caged lunatics in the Bedlam insane asylum.

There was a shit bucket in the corner of the *Karzer*, but some prisoners no longer bothered to use it. Some were simply too weak to use it. The room was thickly encrusted with excrement, blood, urine. The stench was foul, miasmic. The floor was slippery with shit.

There were eight prisoners remaining in the *Karzer*. They received the same rations as we did, and in body they looked like other prisoners, emaciated, filthy, dressed in rags. But now, for the first time, we looked at their faces. The faces that stared back at us were terrible, faces of fear and madness.

The major turned to Franz. "Tell them," he said, "they can come out. Nothing bad will happen to them any more." Franz translated into German, Hungarian, Romanian. The prisoners did not respond. They lay or squatted there and stared.

The major understood. "Leave the door open," he ordered. "Give them time."

Under new rule, change came quickly to our camp. All prisoners went to the *banya*. Our heads were shaved and we washed with a semi-liquid greenish soap. Our clothes were steamed to kill lice and nits.

While we were there, the camp was sealed and fumigated. All rags, paper, and our treasured paillasses were collected and burned. All this they repeated day after day until they were certain all vermin, fleas, bedbugs, and especially lice had been eliminated.

Our food rations improved. We received kasha with oil on it. The bread improved. "They took out the sawdust," said the prisoners.

The camp was cleaned. All corpses were removed and buried. The buildings were scrubbed. The *Karzer* was washed out with boiling water. The entire building smelled of carbolic soap.

Once our officers were certain that there were no more lice, we got new mattresses. I went with other prisoners and the lieutenant to fetch burlap mattress covers from a warehouse.

On the way back, near a factory building I knew well, I said: "Comrade Lieutenant, I've got the shits. I've got to go!"

"All right," he said. "But come straight back to camp."

I stole two mattress covers and hid them. (Later, when the quarantine was lifted, I retrieved them, smuggled them out of the factory, and my *babushka* fence paid forty roubles each for them.) When I returned to camp, I quickly threw my load onto the pile. When they were counted, some were missing. But more prisoners had died, so it didn't matter.

Once the camp was clean, the prisoners clean, the mattress covers filled with fresh straw, and a new cesspit dug, the doctors came, and the major and lieutenant began the interrogations.

We undressed and were paraded, one by one, in front of two women doctors. When, much later, I saw pictures of the survivors of Auschwitz, Dachau, and other concentration camps, I saw myself and the other prisoners at our camp in them: the shaven heads, the sunken cheeks, the hollow eyes, the stick-figure bodies, just mottled skin over bone, the buttocks gone, just flat behinds and the dull, passive stare of humans that have been destroyed by the absolute power of evil.

Among all those hairy men lined up to be seen by the doctors, I was embarrassed by my hairless young-boy body.

The doctors looked at me with interest. "A typical example of arrested puberty due to malnutrition," one said. The other consulted a list. "Not really," she said. "He's only twelve." (I was really sixteen.)

She told me to step on the scales: "Seventy-one pounds," she read out. She smiled a bit. "Never mind," she said, "you will go home."

The major and the lieutenant summoned us to the camp office and questioned us at length: "When did you arrive in camp? How many prisoners were there in camp? Tell me the names and nationality of all the ones you remember. Did the captain kill prisoners? How did he kill prisoners? How often did he kill prisoners? Did anyone else kill prisoners?"

They had many questions and we had few accurate answers. We were perfectly willing to answer questions, but we simply had no satisfactory answers. The interrogations got nowhere, because we had become so indifferent to the deaths of others.

"But you must know how many men were in your brigade when you arrived in May," the major insisted.

"I think about two hundred," I said.

"Tell me their names," he ordered, pen poised.

"Well, there was a Heinrich. He was from Pomerania . . ." I started.

"What was his last name?" the major asked.

"I don't know."

And so it went. In May there had been about two hundred men in my brigade. Now twenty-four were left, and several of them had typhus and would probably die. All the others had died. They had just vanished, nameless, faceless. I remembered a few vaguely, but most of them not at all.

In December, when the typhus epidemic had run its course, about two hundred prisoners were left of the two thousand who had been in camp in May. Karl, Manek, and I were among the survivors.

Although we did not see our captain again, we heard many rumours about his fate. Prisons are always rife with rumours. Every prisoner knows at least one new rumour every day.

Our captain, it was said, had been arrested and charged with several serious crimes. One charge was "Waste of State Property." We were, after all, slaves, and belonged to the state. He had deprived the state of our labour by destroying so many prisoners. He was also charged with the torture and killing of prisoners for his own amusement. That was forbidden. In the Soviet Union the torture and killing of prisoners was the duty and prerogative of the secret police.

Another serious charge was "Corruption and Theft." Both were common, entrenched, and endemic in the Soviet Union, as they had been before in czarist Russia. But the captain had been caught, and that could be fatal.

As prisoners died, he had destroyed their records, but continued to draw food rations for the dead, including oil, occasionally fish, and sometimes even meat. All that he sold. The "dead souls" had made him rich.

Unless he had good connections and very powerful friends, the captain probably got the standard Soviet Union sentence: twenty-five years of slave labour in Siberia. For most, that was a protracted death sentence.

Apart from questioning us, the NKGB major remained distant and aloof. The young secret-police lieutenant, on the other hand, was friendly and gregarious. He often spent his evenings in camp, talking with prisoners who spoke Russian.

He watched Karl at work. "Will you make a pair of boots for me?" he asked.

"Yes," said Karl. "If you bring good leather and if you pay."

The lieutenant laughed. "I'll pay," he promised. "I'll pay well."

A few days later he brought a small ball of real cobbler's twine, a chunk of cobbler's wax, and a bag full of superb leather. "The best," he said proudly, and Karl agreed.

The lieutenant smoked cigarettes. American cigarettes. There was a picture of a camel on the package. Such cigarettes cost one rouble each, and a package was worth as much as two loaves of bread. He sat on our "balcony" in the evenings, watching as Karl made his boots, and chatted with Manek and me.

On our part, the talk was general and cautious. We never trusted anyone, least of all an NKGB lieutenant, be he ever so nice and friendly. Among the many rules of survival in the Soviet Union, one of the most important was *ostoroshnost*, "caution."

To avoid contact with Russians, we were set to work in three all-prisoner brigades. My group took one of the ruined buildings apart, cleaned the bricks, collected metal pipes and wood, and loaded debris into trucks with hand barrows so it could be taken to the dump outside the factory.

It was a make-work project to get us out of camp. We chopped up retrieved wood and made a fire in a sheltered corner of the building. Someone wheedled tea and some sugar from the kitchen staff. We did a bit of work. Then guards, prisoners, and the Russian truck drivers sat around the fire, drank tea, talked, dozed, were lazy.

Christmas was good and bad. We got extra rations, and we did not go to work. We had much to be grateful for. We had spent seven months in hell and had survived.

But some prisoners celebrated Christmas. A few prayed. They sang Christmas songs, familiar songs, especially *Stille Nacht, Heilige Nacht* "(Silent Night, Holy Night)," melodies that had been part of a happy life, so long ago, when I celebrated Christmas with a family I loved.

One thing I quickly learned in prison: you don't think about the past and you don't dream about the future. You live for the day. All that matters is to survive this day. To work as little as possible and not be punished. To steal and not be caught. To smuggle and get some extra food. To lie down at night and say: I have survived another day.

There was no love in camp. There was no hate in camp. Only cold, grey indifference. It was our armour, and the Christmas melodies cracked it and it hurt terribly. For the first time in months I thought about my parents, about Heddy, Hella, and Arist, about love and Christmases together. I lay on my metal bed, pulled the padded jacket over my head, and cried, in loneliness and despair, until I fell asleep.

THE NEW YEAR, 1946 brought us a new captain and me a perfect job.

Early in January, the trusties told us to assemble, and the NKGB major spoke briefly. There had been no new typhus cases in three weeks; the epidemic was over. He and the lieutenant would leave. A new captain would be in charge of the camp.

Then the young lieutenant stepped forward. He wore the boots Karl had made for him. They were superb, the best work of a fine craftsman. He had been pleased and very generous, and had paid Karl well. In addition, he had brought a bag with amazing gifts, things from another world, unknown to prisoners and ordinary Russians alike, most of it made in the United States: chocolate, a large case of tobacco and real cigarette paper, cans of fish, cans of meat, cans of butter, real butter, a large can of ham, things available only to the Soviet super-elite and to the secret police. "*Dla was!* (For you!)" the young lieutenant had said, motioning to Karl, Manek, and me.

Now the lieutenant spoke to the assembled prisoners — in fluent German — and every prisoner guiltily tried to remember what he had said in the lieutenant's presence that he shouldn't have said.

The next day we lined up again and the "new captain" came. He was a man in his forties, the stocky Russian-peasant type, with short-cropped hair already greying at the temples.

He spoke briefly. He himself had been, he said, a prisoner — in a German camp, a very bad camp. He knew we had suffered. He promised to be strict but fair.

Later, Russians in the factory told me more about our new captain. He had been wounded and taken prisoner early in the war, when German armies raced east in 1941. He suffered brutality and starvation in a German prison camp in Russia, had managed to escape, joined Soviet partisans, and later rejoined the Soviet army.

Thanks to this, he escaped the horrible fate of most Russian POWs of the Second World War. In one of his most cruel orders of the war, Stalin decreed that "in Hitler's camps there are no Russian prisoners of war, only Russian traitors, and we shall do away with them when the war is over."

Stalin kept his word. When it came to mass murder he always kept his word. All Russian prisoners, many of whom had suffered terribly in German camps, were, immediately after "liberation" by Soviet troops, sent to even worse camps in Siberia. Those in western Europe were handed over to Stalin by the Allies — the Americans, British, and French — for torture and slow murder in slave-labour camps.

Our new captain had been maltreated and starved by Germans, and now, having power over German prisoners, might have been revengeful and brutal. He wasn't. His own suffering had bred not hate but compassion.

When, sometime later, a guard hit a prisoner, the prisoner, a hot-tempered Hungarian, hit back. There was a row, and the prisoner was overpowered and dragged back to camp. Under the "old captain" (as we called our former commander) he would have been thrown into the *Karzer* to await torture and death.

The new captain merely asked: "Who hit first?"

All agreed it was the guard.

"No one is allowed to hit prisoners," said the captain. The Hungarian was released. The incident was over. Our new captain was a fair and decent man.

It was not easy for the captain to remain fair and decent, however, for the prisoners he had inherited were, generally speaking, a tough, shrewd, nasty lot. The good ones had all died:

those doleful peasants who talked only of food; the gentle souls who tried to help others; those dutiful people (mostly German) who believed in "good work" and, poorly fed, worked themselves to death.

The scum survived: the graft-fattened trusties, the thieves, the crooks, the shirkers, the smugglers, the swindlers, and a few, like Karl, who had special skills. They may have been the fittest, but they were not the nicest.

Chapter 14

THE MEISTER'S STORY

AFTER THE QUARANTINE WAS lifted, we returned to our various brigades. Of my group that had once numbered about two hundred, only eighteen were left. Many now worked as assistants to Russians.

One day in early January, the *Meister* told me he had a good job for me. About a kilometre from the factory in a little valley and next to a creek was a pumping station that had to be heated in winter. A Russian had had the job, but he was careless, got drunk, forgot to lock the station, had twice been caught by the *nachalnik*, the top boss of our brigade, and now had a tough job in the factory.

The *Meister* said he had suggested me for the job and, a bit reluctantly, the *nachalnik* had agreed.

"Now listen, Fedja," said the *Meister*. "You will go there every day. Don't steal anything at the pumping station. Always lock the door when you leave. The *nachalnik* may check in the morning. So be sure to be there in the morning. Make a good fire and keep the place clean." He stopped, then added in a low voice, "And when you steal and smuggle be very careful." He knew my *babushka* fence and was well-informed.

From then on I went to the brigade office every morning after breakfast, collected a large wheelbarrow, walked with it to the great carpentry building, and — with permission — loaded the wheelbarrow with wood shavings and chips and bits of wood to start the fire. Sacks of coal were at the pumphouse. If unobserved, I stole tools. The very first day a senior man in the carpentry building took me aside and we worked out a plan for smuggling.

Resting from time to time, I trundled with my wheelbarrow to the factory gate, and the guards searched it and me. They knew I was smuggling. Maybe they even knew what I was smuggling. But since it was so blatant and, in a way, nearly legal, they always let me pass. On my body I smuggled stolen paper sacks, light bulbs, rubber for shoe soles, and small tools. In the wheelbarrow, visible to all, I smuggled wood.

I pushed the wheelbarrow to the pumphouse, took shavings and wood chips, and lit the fire in the stove. Once it was burning well, I piled on coal and adjusted the vents.

Then I went outside, made sure no one could see me, and, following instructions given to me by the senior man in the carpentry shop, removed a large, flat stone at the base of the building, put all the good wood pieces into the space behind it, and replaced the stone.

In a small house on the other side of the valley lived a *babushka*, who could see the road and the path to the pumphouse from her window. Around noon, when the *nachalnik* and the *Meister* had come and gone, and no one was near, she came with an old sack, collected the wood, gave me money, and went home.

It wasn't much money, since three were involved, the carpenter, the *babushka*, and I, but it was a nice steady income. The carpenter pre-cut top-quality planks into pieces that could pass for scraps. I mixed them with real scraps and shavings, and the guards let me pass. The carpenter retrieved the good wood from the *babushka*, joined pieces in his home shop, and made beautiful furniture for wealthy Communists.

I cleaned the pumphouse carefully, and afterwards kept it spotless. I always locked the door. And I never wandered far. I walked a bit in the valley or sat outside the pumphouse on a little bench I had made and watched the few birds of winter.

The *Meister* came occasionally and we sat together and talked. It was then that he told me how he had been arrested in 1938 by the NKVD, the secret police.

Foreign prisoners were then probably the only safe people to whom a Russian could talk freely. Anyone else might be, or might turn, police informer: your husband, your wife, your children, your best friends.

Denunciation was the patriotic duty of every citizen. Failure to denounce "criminal remarks" was in itself a serious crime that could get you ten years in a Siberian slave labour camp. Or twenty-five years.

Therefore, on those quiet winter days on the bench in front of the pumphouse, where no one could overhear us, the *Meister*, that clever, gentle, decent man stuck in a world of evil, liked to talk to me, for he could not speak to anyone else.

When he was young, he had been an ardent Communist. An idealist. A believer. If the *kulaks*, "the rich peasants," resisted collectivization of their farms for the greater good of all and of Communism, then they had to be eliminated.

But then came the "Great Terror" of 1937–1938. Stalin had already murdered millions. Now he turned upon the faithful, the men who had founded the Soviet Union, the Old Communists, his comrades-in-arms, who had helped him to reach the pinnacle of absolute power.

The great men of Communism were arrested and tortured into confessions. "Who else?" And they named names. And more were arrested and tortured until they confessed and named more names. Waves of arrests and executions spread over the entire land.

His icons had been desecrated and the *Meister* was outraged, the way only believers can be outraged. One evening, at home with his family and some friends, he had got drunk and had muttered angrily that it was Stalin who was the real criminal.

The next night they knocked on his door. At 3 a.m., the time of the secret police, the time when their victim's resistance was lowest, his confusion and fear greatest. He was sentenced to ten years' slave labour.

Then, at the height of the war, he and millions of other convicts were drafted into "punishment battalions" to be used as cannon fodder. Poorly armed and poorly clad, these expendable men spearheaded Soviet charges, attacking in wave after wave, to be cut down by German guns. When the Germans ran out of ammunition and, softened by artillery fire, began to waver, Soviet soldiers attacked, sometimes shielded by walls of corpses.

Most convicts died. The *Meister* was severely wounded. But the Russian front advanced, and he was carried to a field hospital, where he slowly recovered. In the fall of 1944 he was granted amnesty. He returned to his family and resumed work in the factory.

Did he know who had denounced him, I asked.

No, he didn't know. "And I don't want to know," he said with a sad smile.

It was probably one of his children.

"They encouraged the children to tell what parents talked about at home," the *Meister* said.

"Who did that?" I asked.

He shrugged. "The teachers. The Young Pioneer leaders. They made the children feel important if they denounced their parents. They praised them. They promised not to tell the parents. But, of course, they reported to the secret police."

He shrugged again, resigned. "That's our life," he said and walked back to the factory.

In the evening I would carefully adjust the fire for the night, lock the door, and walk to the little bazaar outside the factory gate. I would leave the wheelbarrow in safekeeping with one of the market women, walk up to the house of my *babushka* fence, sell her things I had smuggled out of the factory, drink tea and chat with her and Vanushka, and then walk back to the market to buy food.

It would have been easy to escape. I left both the guarded camp and guarded factory every day because my job was outside the factory. Each night I returned to prison. And so did all the other prisoners.

At the time of the "old captain," few escaped because we were terrified of his sadistic murders of escaped prisoners who had been recaptured.

Under the "new captain" we did not escape because now, compared to the past, our lives were really quite good. Where would we be sent if we escaped and were recaptured?

Also — and this was a major deterrent to escape — rumour had it that we would soon be released. The Poles would be sent home. The Hungarians would be sent home. The sick would be sent home. All would be sent home. Rumours swirled and changed, but the leitmotiv remained: "soon" we would be sent home. "*Skoro domoi!*" said the Russians.

I spoke with Karl and Manek about escaping. Both nixed the idea, in part, perhaps, because they were among the wealthiest prisoners in camp.

"No," Manek said firmly. "Not this year. They are releasing prisoners from other camps. I know that is true. I think we, too, will be released this year. The war ended a year ago.

"If we're not released," Manek continued, "we'll go next year. By train. I know how to do it. It'll take a lot of money, but it can be done. But this year we stay here."

So, lulled by safety and relative comfort, and soothed by hope, no one escaped.

IN APRIL MOST DAYS and nights were warm and the pumphouse no longer had to be heated, so I became assistant to a welder in the factory. He was an excellent welder who knew exactly how to make quick, bad work look like good work.

During the lunch hour I roamed the factory, scouted, and stole. I enjoyed stealing. I liked the planning. I liked the thrill of stealing — and I loved the rewards of stealing, the extra food I could buy. I was then probably the most daring and skilful thief in our factory. Small-time and always alone. "Big-time" theft I left to Manek and his Russian partners.

Spring came, my second spring in prison. The trees turned green. Birds were flitting in and out of dead factory buildings. And suddenly, desperately, I wanted out.

I went to the camp office and told the captain: "I want a *propusk*, (pass) to spend an entire day away from camp."

"Will you escape?" he asked.

"No," I said. "I will be back in the evening."

He looked at me. "Word of honour?"

"Yes," I said. "Word of honour."

He picked up paper and wrote out a *laissez-passer* for twelve hours.

I walked out of the factory and was free. For twelve hours. No one asked me for my pass. No one paid any attention.

I took a tram into town, and I walked past militiamen. They ignored me. I ambled towards the market. A big market. There was hardly any food in the state stores, but at the market, women, and some men, sold the produce from their private plots, and there was plenty of food.

There, too, I noticed with professional interest, many things were openly for sale that had evidently been stolen from "my" factory and many other factories. I knew that my *babushka* fence made periodic trips to this large market to sell the things I brought her.

I bought bread. Good bread. I bought a can of American meat. I bought fruit. I bought chocolate. It was luxury, pure luxury and it was marvellous.

I walked back to camp through open country. It was a lovely spring day. I stopped at a reed-rimmed pond. The grass near it was dense and lush.

I lay on the grass and slowly ate the wonderful food. I was lazy. I was alone. I was free. For six more hours.

A pair of moorhens were building their nest on the pond. They called and they worked. A pair had always nested on the pond in the Kleingraben park. I had spent hours there watching them — in another life. It seemed infinitely remote, unreal.

These birds were real. The male, eager but sloppy, dumped beaks-ful of water weeds on the growing nest. The female, fussy, tucked at the edges of the nest to make it neat.

It was warm in the sun. There was a buzz of bees, the low, monotonous music of grasshoppers. I lay on the grass and dozed, then fell deeply asleep. I awoke with a start and, for a moment, was disoriented. Where was I? Then it all flooded back. The moorhens were still busy with their nest.

It was dark when I returned to prison. The captain was in his office. I knocked. "Come in," he said, looking up from his desk.

"You're back," he said. "What did you do?"

"I went to town, to the market," I said. "Later I walked out onto the land, to a pond, lay on the grass, and watched birds build their nest."

The captain was silent for a while. Then he smiled.

"Yes," he said. "Yes. I understand."

Chapter 15

WORKING WITH ALEKSEI

THERE WAS A DESPERATE HOUSING shortage in the Soviet Union after the war. Building houses for the masses had never been one of Stalin's priorities. During the war the "leave nothing but scorched earth" orders of Stalin and Hitler had been faithfully and efficiently carried out, first by the retreating Soviet armies in 1941 and 1942, then by the retreating German armies in 1943 and 1944.

They burned villages and flattened cities. When the war ended, people lived packed together in the remaining houses and apartments, in cellars, in shacks. To alleviate the situation in our area, an apartment block was to be built outside the factory. A few prisoners were detailed to work with Russians on the project.

Leaving the factory in a group made stealing and smuggling difficult. We ate lunch at the workplace. A mobile canteen came with food for the prisoners. I could no longer roam the factory. It limited my stealing and my income.

There were, however, other possibilities to earn some extra money. With two other prisoners I mixed mortar with shovels in a large, flat-bottomed wooden trough. Good mortar is made with one volume of cement, plus two volumes of sand, together with some lime. Our recipe was simple. We used less cement and more sand and sold the surplus cement.

Since our Russian foreman was running this scheme (and several others), it was easy and safe. We left about a quarter of the cement in each sack. At the end of the shift, someone came, collected the "discarded" bags, and each of us received some money.

There was a ready market for cement. While we were building shoddy apartments for the workers, the factory elite, the bosses, and top Party people were building their own houses. This was legal. They leased land from the state and then applied for building materials.

That's when the real difficulties began. They might get, to start with, a few roof shingles and some fairly brittle linoleum for the kitchen floor. They might even get some bricks. But they did not get cement.

The right, and legal, way was long and strewn with problems: applications to be approved or denied, a vast amount of paper to be filled out, the bureaucratic quagmire, the eternal shortage of everything.

But there was also "the left way," *nalevo*, as the Russians said. It cost a lot more, but was quick. It siphoned off materials from government building projects and channelled them, for a hefty fee, to the Communist elite to build their new houses.

The apartment building we helped to construct was doomed to instant aging. Mortar made with too little cement and too much sand weathers quickly, water dissolves it, frost cracks it, wind abrades it. But that was not our problem.

In the summer of 1946, the *Meister* told me to work with Aleksei, a man who belonged to our brigade. I knew Aleksei. He was easy to recognize. His hair, face, and clothes were the rusty-brown colour of furnace ash, for he cleaned the giant furnaces that were the heart of the factory.

The building with the twenty or so furnaces was one of the largest in our factory. I rarely went there. It was a miserable place and there was nothing there I could steal. It was immense, dark, hot, noisy, full of smoke, the glow of slag, the roaring furnaces.

The stokers, always half-naked, shovelled coal into the furnaces, their coal-dusted bodies gleaming with sweat. The coal was bad, mixed with stones that had not been picked out when the trains were loaded at the coal mine. As a former *viburshchik*, "a stone picker," at a Soviet coal mine, who had left the rocks and sold the coal, I knew a lot about this problem.

Each furnace had two fire-tubes that carried heat through the immense boiler, creating steam in the boiler, the driving force of much of our factory.

Slowly a boiler's efficiency decreased as ash clogged the fire-tubes. A thick layer of non-conductive scale coated the interior of the boiler.

Then the furnace was shut down and the water was drained from the boiler. Furnace and boiler were allowed to cool off for four days. After that, Aleksei had to remove the ash, rebuild fire-damaged brickwork, crawl into the giant boiler and chip the scale off its curving metal walls. The job, I had heard, was exceedingly hot, filthy, and dangerous.

Aleksei was twenty-five years old, slim, strong, and energetic. It was said that he was an ardent Communist, and Russians and prisoners were cautious in his presence. He also had the reputation of an achiever, a top worker. His picture was on the board that featured people who overfilled norms and quotas. These were people I tried to avoid.

But Aleksei had asked specifically for me, because, he had told the *Meister*, I was very thin, the right shape for crawling into the ash-clogged innards of the furnace. (In Dickensian England, chimneys were often cleaned by thin little boys.)

My first day, Aleksei broke a hole into the rear brick wall that enclosed the boiler and furnace and cautiously crawled into the ash pit at the end of the boiler. I handed him a light bulb on a long electric cord, our only illumination in that hot and dusty darkness.

"Come," he called.

It was very hot and dry. The ash was soft, light, and nearly hip-deep in the pit. There was a draft from the open door of the furnace, which blew through the furnace tube and on through corridor-like flues. They led up into the great smokestack that towered above the factory and spewed smoke, soot, and ash over the factory and the land.

Aleksei crawled into the furnace tube from the rear and scraped ash backwards with a half-moon-shaped board. As he advanced, I followed, pushing the ash further back and out of the tube. There was only a speck of light in front, the open furnace door, and, behind us, the faint glow of the light bulb. We worked mainly by feel, like two moles in a dark, ash-filled tunnel, but the ash was light, the work easy.

After an hour, Aleksei said: "That's enough."

We crawled backwards, shoving ash out of the tube into the ash-filled pit at its end.

Aleksei hung the light bulb from a nail near the hole in the brick wall and settled back in the soft ash. "Now we rest," he said.

We talked. After an hour, there was a shout and a head appeared in the hole. It was a boss. "Don't move," Aleksei whispered to me.

He jerked forward, stirring up a dense cloud of ash.

"How is it going?" asked the boss. The light blinded him. He could see nothing. The dense dust made him cough.

"It's very bad, Ivan Sergeivich," said Aleksei. "The furnace was on too long. Much of the brickwork is broken. The ash is deep. It is very bad." He coughed loudly. "We will have to work extra time, and even then it will take ten days. If the boiler has to be descaled, that's another ten days."

The boss made unhappy noises. "Try to do it faster," he said. "You don't have to remove all the ash. We can't have the furnace shut down for twenty days."

"It will be very hard," said Aleksei. "But you know you can rely on me."

"How's the boy?" asked the boss.

"He's good," said Aleksei. "He's so thin he can get into places where even I can't go. Right now he's cleaning that bad corner that leads to the next chamber. And you know, Ivan Sergeivich, what a shit-place that is. Hot, and the ash is waist-deep."

"Yes," said the boss. "I know. You will try and speed things up." The head vanished.

Aleksei crawled back. "The stupid bastard knows nothing," he said and laughed. "That fat pig. The hole in the wall is too small for him. He cannot crawl through it. And now he's scared. The furnace was on too long. If, because of that, it now has to be shut down for twenty days, he's in deep trouble. It looks very bad on his report."

He stretched out. "Now we sleep until lunchtime," he said.

Life with Aleksei was good. Slowly, over weeks, he told me his story.

He had joined the army at the outbreak of the war, a young, eager, *Komsomol* (Communist Youth League) trained Soviet patriot.

He had been driven back and forth by the war, had seen death and heroism, the suffering of the common soldier, the power and brutality of the political commissars. He learned to survive, to appear loyal, eager, subservient. By the time they reached Germany, he was a sergeant. Germany was the ultimate shock. Even devastated and pillaged, it was still so obviously richer than the Soviet Union that Aleksei realized all he had been told had been just propaganda, just lies.

"They lied to us, Fedja," he exclaimed, still bitter. "They lied to us at school. They lied to us at Young Pioneers. They lied to us at the *Komsomol*. It was all lies!"

He lost the dreams and the faith he had once cherished. But he was too smart to let it show. He stayed chummy with the

Party big shots, knew the informers, spouted the appropriate slogans, and took from the Germans all that was valuable and easy to carry.

After the war, he was given work in the factory. He married. He had a small apartment, but was starting to build a house. His war loot would pay for the house, he said.

He attended all important meetings; he knew all the important people. He was politically active. And when the man who cleaned the furnaces needed an assistant, Aleksei volunteered for what everyone considered one of the most evil jobs in the factory. It was also one of the best-paid jobs in the factory.

His older partner had taught him everything about industrial furnace and boiler cleaning. He had also been his mentor in the field of expert cheating: how to do little and still impress the bosses; how to inflate reports; how to hint at catastrophic damage and then, when the top men were scared, report that you had repaired the damage.

Now the old man had retired, and Aleksei decided a prisoner would make a good partner. He had picked me because I spoke Russian, the *Meister* had told him that I was a crook and could therefore be trusted, and it was one job where it really was important to be thin, tough, and flexible.

"They never come in here," Aleksei said with a laugh. "They know it's hot and dark, and I've told them it's terribly dangerous. So they only know what I report. I lie and they give me extra pay, extra food."

He was cynical. There were "they," and "they" had power and privileges. And then there were the workers, the Soviet serfs, and they had nothing. Aleksei was determined to join "them."

"Two more years and I'll get a Party job, and then all this is finished," he said and threw up a handful of ash.

"Some day I'll be the *glawnii direktor* (the supreme director) of the factory," he laughed.

The *Meister* knew of his duplicity, but no one else — not even his wife. But he felt a need to talk, and a foreign prisoner was perhaps the safest person.

"You know, Fedja," he said, "you prisoners are the only free people in the Soviet Union. You are already in prison, so you no longer have to be afraid. We are afraid. We are afraid to be caught, to be denounced, to go to prison. It's nearly always twenty-five years. We know *they* [the NKGB] come for you at night. You hear a noise at night and you're afraid. All are afraid. I have many friends, but I do not trust one of them. We all live with fear. Even *He* is afraid. *He* sits in *His* Kremlin and looks at them and thinks 'Which one is going to kill me?' And then *He* kills first!"

Aleksei always spoke of Stalin as *On*, "He," as of some evil, omnipotent deity whose name must never be pronounced.

At Party meetings, at all meetings, Stalin, of course, had to be praised and loudly worshipped. Pictures of the Soviet Holy Trinity — Marx, Lenin, Stalin — hung in every office, every mess hall, every meeting place, and the picture of Stalin was usually the largest. All wisdom, all power, was ascribed to him. In private people rarely spoke his name, for it inspired awe, some real worship, but, most of all, immense fear.

Aleksei and I talked a lot and we did some work. We hauled hundreds of buckets of ash out of the furnace tubes and the ash pits. We unscrewed the massive bolts that held the small, circular cover at the top of the boiler and removed the cover. Nearly naked, we lowered ourselves into the dark, hot, moist interior of the boiler, its walls covered with a finger-thick layer of brownish scale.

The longer a furnace was on, the less efficient it became. But that was not nearly as obvious as the abrupt loss of power when one of the furnaces was shut down.

So the bosses let furnaces burn far too long. That destroyed the brickwork near the front of the fire-tube. Ash accumulated in the tubes, the pits, the flues. That cut the draft and decreased the heat that reached the surrounding boiler.

In the boiler, the non-conductive scale layer became thicker and thicker. When the boiler had finally reached a degree of inefficiency that could no longer be ignored — usually much less than 50 percent of capacity — the bosses finally ordered it shut down, and Aleksei was told to clean it "as fast as possible."

"It is stupid but it is good for us," Aleksei said, pleased. The stupidity of bosses was one of his favourite themes, closely followed by the cupidity of bosses. He planned to soon be one of them.

Since the key words were "as fast as possible," we replaced only a portion of the fire-destroyed brickwork. We removed some of the ash. We chiselled the thick scale off the boiler walls, sheets of it clattered down, I filled buckets with it, and Aleksei hoisted them out of the boiler and spread the tartar-like stuff in artful heaps to make a little look like a lot.

We worked about four hours a day. The rest of the time we rested, talked, slept. Then, after work, Aleksei made his grossly exaggerated report. He was good at it. He knew the catchy slogans (he read the Party newspaper with care). He flattered the bosses who held power. Since his outstanding reports also reflected favourably on them, they were happy to accept them and record them. He always came out of the office with *talons*, "coupons for extra food," for himself and for me. We also were allowed to shower every day.

Every time Aleksei opened the rear of a furnace and crawled in, he reported, truthfully, that it would take at least 20 days and might even take more than a month to clean it. That estimate was recorded. But he was urged and begged to make it faster.

Between lengthy talks and rests, we did a superficial, half-assed job. After twelve days, Aleksei bricked up the hole at the rear of the furnace and immured within our sins of omission.

He then reported that the furnace had been cleaned — and eight days ahead of schedule. It was an amazing feat. "Heroic," was the Soviet in-word at the time. It was an "heroic feat."

The bosses were delighted. Aleksei was praised. His picture was on the board of "hero workers." Very big people hinted at a promotion. His house was nearing completion. Aleksei was the exemplary and successful new Soviet man, and as assistant to a "hero worker," I was entitled to double rations at our camp kitchen.

During the lunch hour I visited various factory buildings looking for things to steal. Paper sacks were still my staple. There were lots of them, they were easy to take, they were not missed, and they were light and compact to smuggle.

Light bulbs were more difficult to remove, for they were not screwed into sockets but were soldered to the wires, and these had to be carefully cut. But a light bulb was worth two loaves of bread and was fairly easy to smuggle, as a sort of extra scrotum between my legs.

Rubber mats in front of high-voltage switches were easy to steal and were valuable for use as shoe soles.

All tools were needed. Small ones I smuggled myself. Shit-Heini, still the top smuggler in camp, took the large ones out for me and we shared the money.

There was one item I greatly desired, but to steal it would be dangerous and difficult: the foot-wide, inch-thick drive belt of a factory machine would make high-price boot soles.

I drifted in and out of buildings. If people are used to a presence, they no longer see it. A dirty kid in oversized ragged clothing got no attention at all.

I found out which machines were regularly turned off during lunchtime. Were there guards in the building? What was their routine? How dark was it? I loved dark places.

Finally, after a week of careful, unobtrusive study, I settled on one belt. I watched the building from afar. When all the workers had left for lunch, I walked into the building, shouted, and waited.

No one was there. I had honed the knife Karl had made for me to razor sharpness. The belt was taut and heavy and easy to cut, but as the last strands parted, the machinery groaned loudly, and I was badly scared.

I cut off a twelve-foot section, wrapped it around my midriff, tightened it with a rope belt, put my tight-fitting smuggler's vest over it. Over that came a loose pullover and finally my large ragged jacket.

I walked to the door. No one was there. I waited, checked all the doors of nearby buildings. Then I walked out, quickly, purposefully, keeping near buildings, crossed the road, zigzagged back to the furnace building, and hid the belt in a hole behind loose bricks.

Next day we were talking of this and that and suddenly Aleksei said: "Fedja, listen, I think it was you who stole part of a drive belt yesterday. Be very careful. You stopped that part of the factory for three hours while they tried to get a new belt. The people got shit, and they made them work extra hours. The boss got shit, and he's been after the guards to catch the person who did it. They are very angry. Don't smuggle it yourself. It is too dangerous. Be careful."

Luckily, I didn't have to smuggle the belt out of the factory. Cut into sections, that drive belt provided durable soles for the boots Karl was making for the big bosses. They paid well for such excellent soles. If they were aware that they were made from a missing drive belt, they did not mention it. They just walked out of the factory with their new boots.

Summer passed; fall began. Prison and factory were my only life. I was neither happy nor unhappy. The horrors of camp under the "old captain" seemed long, long ago. Now life was fairly good. I had lots to eat and had gained weight.

Stealing had become an engrossing passion: I loved the planning, the thrill, the pleasure of "a job well done," the reward of extra food, nice food. I was good at it, took pride in it, and was never caught.

One evening in mid-September, while I was eating my supper *kasha*, a trusty came into the mess hall and called: "Bruemmer. You're wanted at the office. Right away."

"You're going home," some prisoners said.

I shrugged. I did not believe that. But I worried: had one of my bigger thefts been observed and reported?

But it was true. "You're going home," said the captain. He smiled and seemed pleased.

Seven men from our camp were being released. Six had been classified as "sick" by the doctors. They had barely survived the old captain's rule, and had never recovered. I was officially only thirteen years old and was classified as a "child." From its millions of slaves, the Soviet Union was releasing children and the sick. Karl's advice, so long ago in Poznan, to make myself three years younger, had always helped me. Now it released me from prison.

The captain filled out the forms. "Get your things and come back to the office," he said. "You have half an hour."

Manek was not in camp. He and his Russian partners were probably planning something. Manek was the only prisoner who sometimes left prison for several days and nights and nothing was ever said.

Karl sat at his bench, working, smoking expensive cigarettes. He had heard the news.

"*Also, auf nach Berlin!* (So, off to Berlin)," he said with his cynical smile. He did not say, "You're going home." He knew I had no home. A world away, an age ago, at the worst time of my life, when I was crushed by sorrow, fear, and loneliness in Poznan, a voice had said: "What's the matter, boy?" and I had met Karl.

He had been my guide, my friend, a sort of older brother. He had saved my life. We had been close together for twenty months, yet I knew nothing about him, not even his real name. He was still as cold and remote as on the first day we met.

I put my few things into a bag. It was time to say goodbye. Karl got up and for one instant his face softened. "I'm glad you made it," he said. We shook hands. He sat down at his bench. The cynical smile was back. "*Mach's gut, Junge!* (Take care, boy)," he said, and resumed working. Not once in twenty months had he ever called me by name. It was always "boy."

We got onto the back of a truck. The captain sat next to the driver. We drove slowly through the factory, and stopped at the gate. The guards searched us. I knew most guards. The one who was supposed to frisk me just gave me a friendly pat. "*Domoi* (Home)," he said and laughed. He didn't have to search me. For once I was "clean." We got back onto the truck and drove out of the factory.

Just beyond the gate, in the yellowish circle of light of a street lamp, some men were talking. One of them was the *Meister*. I banged on the cab roof of the truck. The driver stopped.

"What is it?" asked the captain.

"I want to say goodbye to someone."

"All right. But be quick."

I jumped off the truck. The *Meister* had seen me. "You're going home," he said, that warm, kind smile on his face. I tried to thank him. He, too, had helped me to survive. We shook hands. "All the best," he said.

I climbed back onto the truck and it started. We waved to each other. The truck picked up speed, and the *Meister* and the factory vanished.

Chapter 16

SLOW TRAIN TO FREEDOM

AT THE STATION CHAOS REIGNED. Our train was long, forty dull-red cattle cars. Prisoners were coming from many camps. Most were sick. Some were crippled and hobbled on simple, home-made wooden crutches.

The seven men from our camp were assigned a car. We were lucky, and were the first ones in. Thanks to Karl, I knew the best place: the upper wooden platform near the window.

Our captain came to check. We said goodbye. He was good and decent to the end. "I handed over ample rations for you," he told me. He stressed the "ample," and I caught the hint.

The loading and counting of prisoners lasted all night. Guards still yelled, but no one hit prisoners, no one shot lagging prisoners. Guards were not afraid that we would escape. We came to the Soviet Union packed in one hundred to each locked cattle car. Now there were only sixty prisoners to each car, and when, at dawn, the train finally started, the doors remained open.

During the morning, the train stopped on a siding. The convoy captain gave orders. Guards, spaced at intervals, repeated them. The train would stop each day. We were to defecate and piss on the tracks underneath the train. We would receive our rations once a day. We were never to go far away from the train. Ten minutes before starting, the locomotive would whistle twice, and once more one minute before starting. All prisoners were to return to their assigned cars. If anyone were very sick, it must be reported. If anyone died, the death must be reported. Corpses were not to be thrown out of the train during the trip.

The guards came with rations: a piece of bread, a bit of sugar, a bowl of soup.

The first three cars behind the locomotive were filled with women prisoners. Some were elderly; most were sick. Some were young women with babies.

Since Marxist–Leninist doctrine proclaimed the equality of the sexes, it was only natural that there should also be women slaves in the Soviet Union. Millions of them. Most were Russian women, sent to slave-labour camps, occasionally for real offences, mostly on trumped-up charges, often the victims of anonymous denouncers.

In addition, women from all over eastern Europe had been sent to work in Russia, mostly Germans and ethnic Germans, but also women from all the lands "liberated" by Soviet armies.

A young women with a baby walked back and forth along our standing train.

"Where was your camp?" I asked.

"Somewhere east of Stalino," she said.

"What did you do?"

"Worked in a big factory," she said. "Built tractors. We did the same work as the men."

"Bad?"

"Yes. Hard work. Poor food. Some died. Many were sick. The sick are now being sent home. And women with babies."

"How come all the babies?" I wanted to know.

She laughed. "About a year ago, a rumour went through camp that women who had babies would be sent home."

The guards, all men, were happy to help. She shrugged. "It worked!" She rocked her baby a bit. *"Mein Andenken an Russland* (My souvenir of Russia)," she said with a fond smile.

Towards the rear of the train were the cars for the guards and the convoy officer, the kitchen car, the car with provisions, and, at the very end of the train, four cars with Poles, a few sick, most healthy, who were being repatriated.

Our train stopped often, sometimes for hours, for we were a very low priority. At one stop I wandered back to talk with the Poles, a bit leery in case they would yell at me for being German. I needn't have worried.

"Where did you learn Polish?" they asked.

"I was in Kalisz during the war," I explained.

That was fine. They did not like Germans, but now they really hated the Russians — with a passionate, visceral hatred.

This was new to me. In my two camps, people did not hate the Russians. The "old captain," a mad sadist, we hated and feared. The "new captain," who was a decent man, we liked. Some prisoners still harboured a Teutonic disdain for Russians, but most of them liked to work with Russians and adopted their myriad ways of cautious shirking and shoddy work. There was no friendship between Russians and prisoners. But there was no hatred.

The Poles hated the Russians. Loudly. That's probably why they were in the last four cars.

"The sons of bitches! Those whoresons! Dogs' blood and cholera!" The lovely Polish curses just rolled out. "They came to liberate us! They came to free us! They stole half of Poland! And they made us work in their damned mines!"

They were Polish coal miners, and they had been sent to the coal mines of the Donbas. Officially this came under the heading of "fraternal relations" between socialist states: little brother Poland helping "big brother" Russia with much-needed expert coal miners. In practice they were conscript labourers, rounded up and sent to the Soviet Union.

They had received the same food rations as Russian miners and had been paid for their work. But the Russians had treated them as prisoners. They had lived in a guarded prison and had marched to and from work under armed guard. They had complained and were roughly told to shut up. They had tried to stage a strike and some were badly beaten.

It all rankled. Historically, Russians and Poles had never liked each other. Now new hatreds were added to the old ones, and the men in our four "Polish cars" just sizzled with hate.

On top of this, they had found out that the convoy captain and the guards were selling our provisions. "That's why our soup is just water and our piece of bread is so small," they said. They were furious and made such a fuss, they got extra rations. They also had money and bought food at our frequent stops. Our Russian convoy guards avoided the Poles.

At every stop, as if by magic, a crowd of Russian women appeared. All carried baskets with food for sale. The Poles and I had quite a lot of money, and consequently had enough food. But for many, especially the sick, the diminishing daily rations were a hardship. Soon, the first prisoners began to die on the train that was supposed to take them home.

We travelled slowly in a northwesterly direction. The land stretched to the horizon, flat, fertile, infinite. This was the famous *chernozem*, the rich, black earth of the Ukraine, once the breadbasket of imperial Russia. Now much of the land lay fallow, neglected, and bread was precious. At some stations lay large piles of grain, potatoes, sugar beets, all guarded by men with guns.

After four days we reached Dnepropetrovsk. A narrow, single-track bridge spanned the Dnepr River. Giant pieces of the former bridge, a victim of war, lay grotesquely twisted in the river. Ragged children herded goats along the river banks.

We passed many factories, some still in ruins, others already working, huge smokestacks rising above furnace buildings. Less than a week ago, I had crawled around inside such a furnace, working with Aleksei. It already seemed unreal and very long ago.

The devastation of war was everywhere: ruined houses, broken trees, dead tanks, rusting trucks, a giant graveyard of partly burned railroad cars. Among them, bullet-riddled but still elegant, was a fancy coach with large gold letters: *Reichskommissar Ukraine* (Reich's Governor Ukraine).

Two days past Dnepropetrovsk, we were shunted again for many hours onto a siding while more urgent trains used the main line. I sat in the open door of our car.

The convoy captain walked by.

"How's it going?" he asked jovially.

"*Ploche!* (Bad)," I said loudly.

He stopped. "Why?" he asked.

I complained about the bad food, about not having enough food. We had been supplied with ample rations, I said. Our camp commander, a captain, had told me that. I carried on and on, my voice high and shrill (it hadn't changed yet, due to starvation-delayed puberty). He tried to shush me, but I just spoke louder.

"Shut up and come with me," he ordered.

We walked together to the provisions car. He unlocked it and we climbed in. It was like Ali Baba's cave: full of treasure. Stacks of cans. Sacks with food. The convoy captain took an empty sack, put in loaves of bread and half a dozen cans with meat.

"Here," he said with a sort of sour grin, half-amused and half-annoyed. "From now on, be quiet. Don't talk about this to anyone," and he waved at the freight car full of food.

OUR TRAIN NOW TRAVELLED— still slowly — through the broad belt of land that had been part of Poland until September 1939. The Soviet army conquered it after Hitler and Stalin, at that time friends and allies, had agreed to invade and divide Poland. After the war, of course, the Soviet Union would keep its portion of Poland, and compensate Poland by giving it a broad belt of Germany, right up to the Oder and Neisse rivers.

After ten days or so, we arrived in the historic city of Brest–Litovsk on the river Bug. Until 1915, it had belonged to imperial Russia. In the First World War, it was conquered and occupied by German troops, and on March 3, 1918, representatives of imperial Germany signed here with Leon Trotsky, commissar for foreign affairs of the brand-new Soviet Union, the peace treaty between their countries.

From 1920, when the Polish Marshal Jozef Pilsudski defeated the invading Soviet army near Warsaw, Brest–Litovsk was Polish. In 1946, when our train reached it, it belonged to the Soviet Union. Today it is the city of Brest and belongs to the Republic of Belarus.

In late September 1946, when our train came to a halt, the city was still called Brest–Litovsk and it was then home to what was probably the world's largest pile of loot. There were acres and acres of loot.

Our train — three cars with women, mostly sick, four cars with Poles, all angry, and thirty cars with Germans, mostly ill and some close to dying — pulled in on Russia's wide-gauge (5-foot or 1.524-metre) track. Across from our train on the European-gauge (4-foot 8½-inch or 1.435-metre) track stood a long train with loot. All of us were ordered to leave our train, and we assembled in a nearby meadow.

"You will unload the cars on the other track and transfer the contents into the freight cars in which you have arrived," said the convoy captain. "Then you will go home. The guards will assemble all able-bodied prisoners into work brigades."

I was fairly "able-bodied," but no longer willing.

"Watch my bag," I told a crippled prisoner, "and I'll give you some bread later." I backed away, vanished behind some huge crates with machinery, and watched cautiously from a safe distance.

There was a nasty fuss. Since nearly all the eighteen hundred German prisoners were sick, crippled, or dying, that left as "able-bodied" persons in our convoy only the Polish miners and the young German women with babies. The train they were supposed to unload was full of crated machines. Many, it turned out, weighed a ton or more and had to be reloaded into the train in which we had arrived. All this had to be done by hand, and neither the women nor the Poles were keen on the job. Prisoners yelled. Guards yelled. The Poles cursed loudly.

The convoy captain promised workers double rations, but that didn't help. There were angry shouts: "What have you done with our food?" All this, I realized, would probably take several days. Prison life had taught me much, including the shirker's maxim: "Keep a low profile and, if possible, vanish. If you're not there, they can't recruit you."

I left them with their problems and wandered away through an amazing land of loot.

Officially this came under the heading of "war reparations." In practice it looked as if the Russians were sending much of eastern Germany, the area they controlled, to Russia: office equipment, farm equipment, entire factories, cars, trucks, rolling stock, tractors, furniture, store shelves, railroad tracks, giant wooden spools with cable, telephone poles, toilets, and probably kitchen sinks.

The major problem was that those at the sending end of this gigantic relocation program were much more efficient than those at the receiving end.

Somewhere in Germany a huge factory had been dismantled and crated, to be reassembled, like an immense jigsaw puzzle, somewhere in Russia. Over a period of several weeks, the factory, now in thousands of neatly numbered crates, had been loaded into many freight cars and sent to Russia. At Brest–Litovsk all the freight cars had to be unloaded and their cargo sent on in Russian-gauge freight cars.

When the freight cars were finally unloaded at the new factory site somewhere in Russia, it had been discovered that a thousand crates of absolutely vital machinery had gone astray. While the missing crates were being traced, the crates that had arrived sat in the open. The wood slowly rotted, the machinery rusted.

Some of the missing crates had gone to the wrong factory locations, adding to the confusion there. Thousands, probably tens of thousands, perhaps hundreds of thousands of the other such "missing crates" now rested in that immense land of loot at Brest–Litovsk and slowly decayed.

Rows of former German army trucks stood on flat tires close together between the crates. I opened a truck door. It creaked loudly. I stretched out on the front seat and slept.

It was early afternoon when I awoke, a bit disoriented at first, and then hungry and, above all, very thirsty.

The vast area filled with war-reparations material was enclosed by a high barbed-wire fence, along which armed guards patrolled. Not far from the fence was a large, barrack-type building. At one corner stood a barrel that was full of rainwater.

I was just about to dip my cupped hands into the water when a burly man in a uniform plus dirty-white apron came out of the building.

"What are you doing?" he asked, his voice loud and gruff.

"I'm only getting water. I'm very thirsty," I said meekly.

He softened immediately. "Don't drink that water. It's bad. I'll get you tea."

In this building, it turned out, some of the guards lived. It was also their mess hall, and the big, burly man was the cook. A table and bench stood outside the building.

"Sit down," he said when he returned with a large glass of very sweet tea.

"Who are you?" he asked. "What are you doing here?"

I explained.

"Why aren't you working? Unloading those cars?"

I hesitated for an instant, then decided to be honest. It sometimes pays. "I've worked enough for Russia," I said.

He laughed. "*Nu wot, molodiets!* (There's a smart kid!)."

"Have you eaten?" No, I said, and hoped.

He brought me a huge bowl of rich barley gruel with lots of meat. "Eat as much as you want," he said. "The rest take along for tonight. Where are you going?" he asked.

"To Germany."

He grinned. "You don't have to go to Germany. Germany is here!" he said and waved his arms.

"What are they going to do with all this stuff?" I wanted to know.

"I don't know. They don't know. Nobody knows," he laughed, now very friendly. "It'll just sit there and rot and we'll guard it. *Nitshewo* (Never mind), it's a good job!"

He put the surplus gruel into a large can with a wire handle. "Come again tomorrow. After lunch. Then the men either work or sleep."

I meandered back, past endless crates, past metal-grey filing cabinets marked *Auswärtiges Amt* ("Foreign Office"). I took a look inside. The cabinets were empty.

The Poles were still working.

We spent four days in Brest–Litovsk. I slept on the front seat of the truck, and my cook-friend fed me well. He talked about his family, his home. He showed me snapshots of his girlfriend. She looked nice and roundish, like someone who would be happy married to a cook. On the last day, he filled my can with stew and gave me a sack with bread and sausages.

The Poles had worked hard but carelessly. Some crates had been damaged. The crates had arrived neatly stacked, but the Poles had transferred them pell-mell into the Russian cars. As a result, there was no room for about a hundred crates. Trucks came and added them to the acres of other crates to rot in peace on the industrial graveyard of Brest–Litovsk.

The next morning we moved into our new cars in the same order as before. Guards counted us, then counted us again. So far, about forty prisoners had died.

The train moved slowly across the River Bug, as we passed from the Soviet Union into Poland. Several German prisoners said loudly: "*Auf Nimmerwiedersehen!* (May I never see you again!)." Twenty-eight years would elapse before, in a very different life, I would return to the Soviet Union.

Compared with the Soviet Union, Poland looked rich and neat. The villages were clean. The well-kept gardens had just been harvested. We no longer saw children dressed in rags. Large piles of newly harvested potatoes lay near some of the stations, and none were guarded.

Our train stopped on a siding. Now Polish women with baskets of food materialized. One had white bread and sausages.

"How much?" I asked, pointing at the sausages.

"*Dwadziescia marek* (Twenty marks)," she said, then added in German "*gute Wurst*" ("good sausage").

I was stunned. Most German prisoners who understood were stunned. "Marek" meant marks, reichsmarks, the currency of Hitler's Germany! It seemed bizarre, unreal. Like being told in today's Athens that the *staters* of ancient Greece can still be used.

For nearly two years we had lived in total isolation from the rest of the world. The only two pieces of real information I had heard in all that time was that Germany had surrendered and that Hitler was dead. The rest was rumours.

And now the first Polish woman I met offered to sell me *gute Wurst* and asked to be paid in reichsmarks. It was very confusing. Prisoners who emerge into the world after long isolation tend to be very confused people. They remember the past but cannot understand the present, because the linking years are missing. We were then in late September of 1946. I had not yet heard of the atom bomb or that two of them had flattened the Japanese cities of Hiroshima and Nagasaki in August 1945.

Oddly enough, quite a few German prisoners had reichs-marks. The money had not been confiscated at the time of their arrest and deportation. Since most people hate to throw away money, however valueless it probably is, they still had their marks, and now, feeling suddenly miraculously rich, used them to buy bread, hard-boiled eggs, and sausages.

We stopped in Praga on the east bank of the Vistula River. Beyond lay the ruins of what had once been the beautiful city of Warsaw.

It was a bad place to wait. There are two places which to Poles symbolize Soviet perfidy: one is the forest of Katyn, now in Belarus, where, in the spring of 1940, the Soviets shot, on Stalin's orders, twenty thousand Polish prisoners, including five thousand senior army officers.

The other place is Praga. In August 1944, inspired by the nearness of the mighty Soviet army, Poles began the Warsaw Uprising. They fought the Germans house by house, cellar by cellar. They fought for sixty-three days, and when it was over, two hundred thousand Poles were dead and old Warsaw no longer existed.

All this time, on Stalin's orders, the Soviet army, massed a few kilometres away in the Warsaw suburb of Praga, watched complacently the mutual slaughter of Germans and Poles and did nothing. It suited Stalin to perfection. The Germans were killing the very Poles who, in future, would have opposed his planned creation of a subservient Polish puppet state.

Four months later, on January 17, 1945, when the Polish fighters were dead and the German armies exhausted, Soviet soldiers crossed the Vistula River and "liberated" the ruins of Warsaw.

All Poles knew the story. Our Poles knew the story. They stood in an angry cluster, looked across the river at the dead city that had once been the pride of Poland, and hated both Germans and Russians. But the Germans were now defeated, and many were fellow prisoners. The Russians were victors, with a victor's arrogance, and the Poles just loathed them.

That's probably why we sat half a day in Praga. The Soviet authorities may have considered it unwise to release our fuming Poles into Warsaw in broad daylight. Besides, it was a Soviet secret-police tradition to load and unload prisoners at night.

The next night we passed through Poznan. There, nearly two years ago, my prison journey to the Soviet Union had begun. Now I was still very young in appearance but oddly old in soul. I had seen too much death.

In Poznan, too, on Karl's advice, I had changed my persona: I had altered my name, my age, my place of birth.

Now I had to change my place of birth again. After speaking to a few Berliners on our transport, it was quite clear to me that in Germany I could not pass myself off as a native of Berlin.

Berliners speak *Berlinisch*, or as they used to say, *Berlinerisch*. I speak Baltic German, a sort of High German dialect with an eastern lilt. Since Baltic Germans lived isolated from Germany for seven hundred years, they retained some ancient words that other Germans find either incomprehensible or very quaint. Over the centuries they also adopted more than a thousand words and expressions from the languages of their neighbours: from Polish, Swedish, Russian, Latvian, Estonian, and Yiddish. And that's not how they speak in Berlin!

Baltic German lost its home and roots in 1939 when the Baltic Germans left Latvia and Estonia. Today it is a dying dialect. Perhaps some five hundred people still speak it. All are past seventy years of age, and I am one of them.

Since it seemed like a poor idea to start life in Germany as an obviously bogus Berliner, I kept my new birth date (which made me thirteen years old, rather than seventeen) but changed my place of birth from Berlin to Kalisz, Poland.

The next night our train crossed the Oder River and we passed from Poland into Germany or, more correctly, the Soviet

Zone of Occupation, generally known as the Russian Zone. Our journey had lasted more than three weeks. About fifty prisoners had died on their way home. The train stopped. We had arrived in Frankfurt an der Oder.

Chapter 17

BERLIN, 1946

WE HAD ARRIVED IN THE LAND of *Tüchtigkeit*, of German efficiency, a now poor but still well-organized world. After Russia,
it was quite a shock.

In the Soviet Union workers often behaved like sour serfs. In
the entire Soviet empire, there was only one employer, the State,
immense, faceless, threatening. It set ambitious work norms and
quotas, rewarded workers meagrely and could punish them
ruthlessly. On February 9, 1946, Stalin had announced a new
five-year plan mandating production increases of more than 50
percent.

The greatest weakness of the system, as I had seen myself,
was that it worshipped quantity and revelled in soaring statis-
tics, but paid little attention to quality. The workers, who were
punished if they did good work but not enough of it, learned
like Aleksei how to produce bad work but lots of it. The rot of
inefficiency and shoddiness pervaded the Soviet Union and
would eventually destroy it.

Many of the prisoners who had survived slavery in the Soviet
Union had absorbed the "sour serf" ethic of Russian workers.
With their dull "I don't give a shit" attitude, the prisoners were
like oxen: if prodded, they moved, but slowly, reluctantly.

Now, coming from the Soviet Union in the last days of September 1946, we prisoners were greeted in Frankfurt an der Oder by the first blasts of Teutonic efficiency.

German guards took over. Men with stretchers came and removed the dead, the dying, and the very sick. The women were led away by female guards.

The men who could walk moved slowly to a large assembly yard, enclosed by barbed wire. Beyond it was a paved road, and on the other side were neat brick houses, their roofs covered with mellow red tiles. Women, nicely dressed, were working in the gardens.

On the road, students walked to school. They, too, were nicely dressed. They carried satchels. They talked and laughed and joked. Some were my age, but seemed so very young. In the same way, I walked to school in Kalisch only two years ago.

The students did not look at us; they probably did not even notice us. Prison transports arrived here every day. The picture was familiar: the barbed-wire fence and, behind it, groups of men in rags, with short, bristly hair, bearded, filthy, clutching sacks, dull, grey, docile. The students did not look at us, for we were less than human, from another world.

The guards divided us into companies of about thirty men. I now belonged to the 34th Company.

The orders began:

"34th Company! Receive rations!" (We got bread and a bit of sugar.)

"34th Company! Shower! Clothes will be deloused!"

"34th Company! Receive clothing!" You took what you got. I got a good pair of pants and a jacket that had once belonged to a man more than twice my size.

"34th Company! Register!" A bored clerk recorded the data of my invented — but hopefully safe — persona: Name: Friedrich Bruemmer (no "von"); Born: January 27, 1933 (instead of June 26, 1929); Place of Birth: Kalisz, Poland (instead of Riga, Latvia); Profession: student; Parents' profession: both teachers,

both dead; Relatives: no known relatives. It was all exactly as
Karl had once advised me: "When you lie, keep it short and keep
it simple!"

The orders continued. 34th Company this! 34th Company
that! Get soap. Get more rations (bread and a bit of sugar). Get
shoes. I got a pair of clumpy canvas shoes with wooden soles.

The old army drill started again. We shuffled on and on —
all day — clutching the precious bags that contained our few
belongings.

In the evening they marched us out of town to a quarantine
camp. We were assigned to barracks. The first activity storm was
over. We could rest.

All inmates in this camp were Germans and ethnic Germans,
nearly all victims of the greatest "ethnic cleansing" program of
modern times, perhaps of all time.

In 1939, Hitler and Stalin, then friends and allies, began the
Second World War by invading and dividing Poland. The Soviet
Union annexed roughly one hundred and eighty thousand
square kilometres of pre-war Polish territory. After the war, the
Soviet Union kept this land and compensated Poland by shifting
it about two hundred miles westward and giving it one hundred
thousand square kilometres of Germany.

The twelve million Germans who lived in this region were
expelled. As the Toronto historian Margaret MacMillan noted
in her book *Paris 1919*: "The Second World War and its after-
math showed yet another solution [to the minority problem]—
the expulsion and murder of unwanted minorities. Some twelve
million Germans went westward. . . ."

Their farms, their estates, their businesses, their houses, all
they owned was confiscated. If they were lucky, they were able
to take a couple of suitcases with clothes and a few photo
albums, and then they were kicked out to join the vast army of
refugees fleeing west.

These were the Germans from East Prussia, West Prussia,
Pomerania, and Silesia, plus ethnic Germans from Poland.

Millions more were expelled from Romania, Hungary, Yugoslavia, Czechoslovakia. It was an immense exodus, wave after wave of the dispossessed, all heading west into war-destroyed Germany.

They were called *die Koffermenschen*, "the suitcase people," for all they had left in the world was in one or two suitcases. They walked with them, sat on them in the drafty halls of bombed-out railway stations, and slept near them.

For millions of people, those suitcases were a last remnant of "home," a home they would never see again, for they were now homeless. They clung to those suitcases in bad times, and later in better times. (In 1949, I too acquired such a suitcase, pressed cardboard with glossy, cheap plastic corners. I still have it. It sits on a wooden shelf in the basement of our house in Montreal.)

For millions of these wretched refugees it was not a straight flight from east to west, from the region they had once called home to East Germany or West Germany. For them, there was a terrible and often fatal detour: the slave-labour camps of the Soviet Union.

Stalin had an insatiable need for slaves, for cheap, expendable labour. Each year at least a million prisoners died in his slave-labour camps. They had to be replaced. Most replacements were Russians, arrested, as required, on trumped-up charges by the NKGB.

After the war, during that gigantic program of ethnic cleansing that swept eastern Europe, the very old, the very young, and women with small children were expelled to Germany (or Austria). Men and women between seventeen and sixty years of age, millions and millions of them, were sent to slave-labour camps in the Soviet Union to have the life squeezed out of them. The dead were buried in mass graves in the Soviet Union. The strong and healthy remained. Some were not released until the mid-1950s (Stalin died in 1953). The sick, the halt, the lame were gradually released since they were of no further use to the Soviet Union.

Some of them, about sixteen hundred, were with me in the quarantine camp in Frankfurt an der Oder.

Doctors came. Tuberculosis was rampant among returned prisoners, and all of us were X-rayed and examined. Doctors and nurses stopped in surprise and horror at the bed of my neighbour.

His name was Johann. Once he had owned a large, beautiful farm in East Prussia. The Soviet Army overran East Prussia before he could flee, and he was sent to the Donbas and had worked underground in a coal mine not very far from the mine where I had worked.

During one shift, while moving blasted coal and rock, his pick hit an unexploded stick of dynamite. He had been leaning forward, and the explosion hit his upper body and his head.

It tore off his ears, tore out his eyes, shattered his face.

His face was now a huge, bloated mass, coloured deep blue by powder burns. The eye sockets were empty and blood-red, the nose a reddish hole. He had no lips. His mouth was a bloody gash with teeth.

It was a nightmare face. He sort of knew it was bad but did not realize how bad. A Russian doctor had patched him up a bit and, having no further use for him, they sent him "home."

Being his bed neighbour, I got stuck with Johann. He had been given a stick, but he was not yet used to being blind, and he had also been moved around a lot in recent days. I guided him to the toilet, to the mess hall, and back to his bed. He was pathetically grateful, and quickly became frantically dependent on me.

The moment he heard me move, he called: "Where are you going?"

"Out."

"Don't leave me!" he pleaded. "Please don't leave me!"

"I'll be back," I assured him. "I won't leave you."

It was annoying. For nearly two years now I had learned to depend on no one, physically or emotionally. And no one depended on me. It suited me. I did not hate anyone. I did not love anyone. I did not trust anyone. I had the standard prisoner mentality.

I did not want to be bothered looking after this blind man with his decayed-corpse face. And I did not want to listen to more of his stories, for they were explicit and awful, and I had heard too many of them.

The farm in East Prussia had been in his family for many generations. Each generation had added, and improved, and when Johann took it over before the war, it was a prosperous, beautiful farm, with rich land, huge orchards, a lot of cattle and horses.

He was then about forty years old. He had married his teenage sweetheart, they had had three children, and life had been wonderful.

When the war started, he was drafted, wounded in France (he still walked with a limp), and returned to the farm.

In 1944, Soviet armies came closer and closer.

"We should have left," he said in that sad, hollow voice I had heard so often before. "But they told us to stay. They would tell us when to go. We were not allowed to leave before they told us to go." And farmers hate to leave their land.

Then it was too late. The collapse came abruptly. He and his family remained on the farm. Soviet soldiers came to rape his wife. Sometimes ten a day. They often forced him to watch. It seemed to give them special pleasure.

"There was nothing I could do," he said and stared at me with those bloody eye sockets. "There was nothing I could do." He kept repeating that. Sometimes he cried, and tears dribbled out of those blood-red holes that had once held eyes.

The soldiers came day after day. Some kept returning, to rape again. A few brought candy for the children.

Then Johann was arrested, taken to Russia, lost his eyes, his face, and now he was here, and I was stuck with the man.

"Where do you think my family is?" he kept asking.

"I don't know."

"You will help me find my family," he begged.

"Let's see where they take us, and then I will speak to the camp authorities. Maybe they can help you."

"Please don't leave me!"

"Don't worry. I won't leave you."

I got used to his face but, wearied of his talk, his clinging, I sat outside in the fall sun. There were some benches, and I watched flocks of waxwings feed in the rowan trees.

Technically, we were no longer prisoners. But we were not free either. The camp was surrounded by barbed wire and there were guards.

"What are you doing? You should be in the building," said one of the guards in that bullying voice guards like to use.

"I'm watching birds," I said.

"Why?"

"Because I like watching birds. These are waxwings and they tell me there will be an early winter and it will be very cold."

He stared. "You're kidding me!" he said, half-curious, half-suspicious.

"No. These are subarctic birds. When they come south this early it means it's cold in their regions and there's not enough food. And that's usually a sure sign of a cold winter here."

"Say, that's fascinating," he said, now quite friendly. "You're with that blind man, aren't you?"

"I'm not," I said, annoyed. "He just sleeps in the bed next to mine and I help him a bit."

In addition to doctors, Communist Party people came to welcome us to "Free Germany," now ruled (more or less) by the Sozialistische Einheitspartei Deutschlands (SED), the Socialist Unity Party of Germany, led by the wonderful comrades (and Stalin-blessed Communists) Wilhelm Pieck, Otto Grotewohl, and Walter Ulbricht.

They spoke feelingly about the wonderful, fraternal Soviet Union, which had freed Germany from the terrible yoke of Nazi tyranny. Luckily, they kept it short and they didn't stay long, because even the most devoted Party people realized they were speaking to a very unreceptive audience. They left stacks of Party propaganda leaflets, which we used as toilet paper — not as a political statement, but because we needed toilet paper.

Once again our heads were shaved, since there were head lice in our camp.

The doctors sorted out the worst cases of TB and other potentially dangerous and contagious diseases, and after a ten-day quarantine period, we were marched back to the station. I was stuck with Johann.

"Please, Friedel. Please don't leave me!" he kept begging.

This time we got into a real passenger train. Most windows were broken and boarded up, but there were seats. Travelling with Johann had a few advantages, for we were given good seats. The others squeezed in wherever there was space. Most sat on the ground. People stared in horror at Johann, then looked away. The train took us to Rüdersdorf, a small town near Berlin famous for its limestone quarries.

They marched us to a huge *Umsiedlerlager*, "a relocation camp." There a small staff of very dedicated social workers tried to find relatives for those in search of relatives; homes for the homeless; jobs for the jobless; solutions for people without hope.

I found myself miscast in the role of saintly escort to this living horror. I resented him. I had begun to feel sorry for him, and I did not want to be sorry for him or anyone else. I was not sorry for myself. But I was stuck with Johann. He slept again in the bed next to mine.

"Don't leave me," he cried. "Please help me!"

Desperation made me pushy. Within two days I was in the office of Herr Jonke, the busy man in charge of the camp.

I told him briefly about Johann. He went into another office and returned with Fräulein Teppert, a grey-haired, harassed, overworked social worker.

We went together to my barracks and she saw Johann. "*Ach, du lieber Gott!* (Oh, dear God!)" she whispered, shocked. Johann had heard us. The explosion had not destroyed his inner ears. His hearing was acute.

"Where have you been?" he asked, his voice anxious. "I've got to piss. Please don't leave me."

I took him to the toilet and then back to his bed.

"I'm going out," I said. "Don't worry. I'll be back soon."

Fräulein Teppert and I went out. "How terrible," she said. "Are you related?"

I explained. I gave her a condensed version of Johann's terrible life, rapes and all.

"I will deal with this immediately," Fräulein Teppert promised. "What about you? Where are you going?"

"I don't know," I said. "I have no home."

She glanced at me. In my narrow pants, wooden-soled canvas shoes, worker's cap, and super-large man's jacket that floated about me and down to my knees, I must have looked pathetically Chaplinesque.

"How old are you?" she asked.

"Thirteen."

"How long were you in the Soviet Union?"

"Nearly two years."

"Was it bad?" she asked softly.

"Yes," I said evenly, factually. "In my camp of two thousand prisoners only two hundred survived."

"My God," she whispered, shocked. "What happened?"

I shrugged. "Starvation. Hard work. Dysentery. Typhus." I didn't mention the captain and his torture sessions.

Fräulein Teppert straightened. "You will hear from me," she promised. "Soon."

Four days later, Johann and I were called to the camp office. Johann walked holding my arm. I warned him of steps and obstacles. I was quite used to him by now.

They led us into a sort of simple conference room. Herr Jonke was there, Fräulein Teppert, a Herr vom Sozialamt (a man from the office of social affairs,) and a man with glasses and a grey suit who was not introduced and sat quietly and listened.

They stared at Johann, shocked, then glanced away and began to question him. Johann kept repeating what he had already told me over and over again.

"I want to go home," he said, his voice plaintive. "I want to go back to the farm. I can do some work on the farm. I want to be with my wife, with my children."

He began to talk about his children but they stopped him.

The Herr vom Sozialamt told Johann, as gently as he could, that there was no more East Prussia, there was no farm, his family would not be there. If they had survived, they might be somewhere in Germany.

Johann did not understand. Why should East Prussia no longer exist. Why should his farm no longer exist. It had always existed.

"I want to go home," he repeated. He felt they did not understand him. He turned to me. "Please, Friedel," he pleaded. "Please tell them I want to go home." Soon, I knew, he would begin to cry, tears would run out of those empty, bloody holes.

They asked me to lead Johann back to the barracks and then come back.

They were talking loudly when I returned and knocked at the door.

"*Es ist doch ganz klar* . . . (It's really quite clear . . .)" a sharp, hard voice said, then stopped when I entered. It was the man in the grey suit.

"Is he normal?" he asked me.

"Yes," I said. "I think so. It's just that there are two years missing and he cannot understand the things that happened in that time."

"We cannot send a man like that back to his family," said the Herr vom Sozialamt. "Even if we can find the family."

"*Es ist doch ganz klar,*" the man in the grey suit said decisively, "*der muss ins Heim* (he has to go to a home)."

The "home" was a home for the blind. The man in the grey suit was the director. He asked me to tell Johann he was going to a very good home, a very special home, while they were looking for his family.

I told all that to Johann. It was a lie, of course. The home for the blind was probably real, but they would never look for his family. For them, if they lived, he would always be "missing."

The car came next day, and I helped Johann walk over to it. There the man in the grey suit took charge and gently but firmly manoeuvred Johann into the car. At the last moment Johann realized I was not with him.

"Don't leave me!" he cried. "Friedel, please, don't leave me." He struggled. The door slammed shut. The car began to roll, and for a moment I could still hear his desperate cries: "Don't leave me! Don't leave me!"

I walked back to the barracks feeling a bit sorry, a bit guilty, a bit sour and annoyed but, most of all, relieved. I was on my own again.

Now it was my turn. Fräulein Teppert asked me to write a résumé, including my hopes and plans for the future.

Since much of it was invented, I wrote it very carefully. It was bland, sounded accurate, and today would be called "politically correct." On the subject of hopes and plans I said I wanted to be a teacher.

I was summoned to Herr Jonke's office, and asked a few questions.

"Was your father a member of the Nazi Party?"

"Yes. As a teacher he had to be."

"Were you in the Hitler Jugend?"

"No. I was too young."

"What languages do you speak?"

"German, Polish, Russian."

"How good is your Russian?"

"Fluent. I worked a lot with Russians and spoke it every day."

He made notes. "Our schools desperately need people who speak Russian," he said.

There was one other thing. Herr Jonke handed me a form. By signing it, I declared my willingness to be adopted. I did not want to be adopted, but I signed the form. Like a maltreated dog, I distrusted kindness but was also cautious about rejecting it.

While the wheels of fate and bureaucracy were grinding, I had plans of my own. The only person of my family I might be able to find was Heddy.

However, since I had stated I had "no known relatives," I could not suddenly talk of a "sister in Sumatra"— and furthermore, an aristocratic one. I tried to keep my two personae strictly separated.

I went to Fräulein Teppert and asked permission to go to Berlin. A remote cousin had married a Dutchman before the war. I had remembered the name. Perhaps the Dutch Red Cross could locate the cousin.

Fräulein Teppert understood. A remote cousin in Holland was not nearly as good as that uncle in America who was the dream of every post-war German. Still, she might be an asset. I got the permission and rations for the day.

I had no money, but my prison looks and Russian prison discharge paper allowed me to travel free. I went by train to Berlin and began to search for the Dutch Red Cross.

Berlin in 1939 had had a population of 4.3 million people. In 1945, only 2.4 million remained. Two-thirds of them were women. The men were dead or in prison camps.

Berlin looked strange. From the train I had seen destroyed Russian cities. And I had seen from afar a Warsaw that no longer existed. Now, traversing Berlin by shuddering tram, I saw a sea of ruins (more than two thousand acres of ruins) and here and there islands of buildings that had somehow survived Russian artillery fire and the forty-five thousand tons of bombs the Allies had dropped on Berlin.

There was immense destruction. But there was also life.

Brigades of women cleaned bricks and shovelled debris into carts. These were the *Trümmerfrauen*, or "rubble women," of Berlin. Thousands of them removed the destruction of war. The bricks were saved for new buildings; the debris was piled into *Trümmerberge*, "rubble mountains." The biggest one, the 115-metre high Teufelsberg in the Grunewald, the forest at the edge of Berlin, is made from 25 million cubic metres of war debris. In winters now, when there is snow, Berliners use it as a ski hill.

Amidst the ruins and near them, wherever there was a bit of space and earth, were *Schrebergärten*, Lilliputian gardens kept with infinite care and love. There were tiny gardens on the balconies of houses that had survived the war. Food was life, and very precious.

There were then five categories of ration cards. Category I was for *Schwerarbeiter*, people doing very heavy physical work. Then, in descending order, came categories II, III, IV, and V. I saw a cartoon in a newspaper. It showed an emaciated, naked man with a spider web across his anus. The caption said: "Category V."

There were few cats in Berlin. There were few dogs in Berlin. People could not afford to feed them. But people ate them. Cats were known as *Dachhasen*, "roof rabbits." Their meat was sold as unrationed *Wildbret* ("venison") or as hare or rabbit meat. Some basement restaurants served *Wildbret* soup, made, rumour had it, with dog meat. "*Die Suppe bellt* (There's a bark to that soup)," said the Berliners.

There were few trees left in Berlin. I walked down *Unter den Linden* (Beneath the Linden Trees), once the majestic boulevard of imperial Berlin where, long ago, the Hohenzollern princes of Prussia rode from their castle to hunt in the *Tiergarten* animal park, the royal hunting grounds in mid-Berlin, and later its central park.

The ancient linden trees were gone. The *Tiergarten* had been razed, cut down by freezing people desperately in need of wood and warmth. (Berlin today is a city of young post-war trees.)

There was a shortage of clothing in Berlin. I walked past a busy brigade of *Trümmerfrauen* removing rubble. Many wore working clothes. Some wore kerchiefs and shawls, plus jackets that had once been expensive and chic. Two women wore the remnants of what had been, in happier times, elegant evening gowns.

And yet, they managed. "The worst is over," said the people with whom I spoke in Rüdersdorf. The winter of 1945–1946 had been terrible, with near-starvation and no heat. Now it was better. People worked. They were looking forward. They hoped again.

I spent all day in Berlin. No one seemed to know the location of the Dutch Red Cross. I tried German police stations. They did not know. There were no accurate city directories.

I tried the British military office in Berlin. The problem there was their guardians, their "concierges," as the British called them, Germans employed to screen and help visitors, and now bloated with self-importance. I was obviously a just-released prisoner, and they treated me like shit. They yelled at me to go away.

I waited until a British officer emerged. When he was near, I spoke to him loudly, clearly, in bad English and in my still-high soprano voice. He was a bit startled, both by my appearance and my voice, but listened politely.

"I don't know," he said. "But wait here and I'll try and find out." He went back into the building.

He returned in a few minutes with the correct address of the Dutch Red Cross and detailed directions on how to get there by *U-Bahn* (subway).

The Dutch were a bit aloof at first, but listened to my request about locating Heddy. I said both Reinhold and Heddy were Dutch citizens, and that Reinhold had been a planter in Sumatra.

I wrote down their names: Reinhold and Heddy von Löwis of Menar.

"That's an odd name," said the official. I explained that it was Baltic German, the family of Scottish origin. He called a colleague and, speaking Dutch, explained my case.

The other man was friendly. "Do you know for which company your brother-in-law worked?" he asked. I didn't.

Slowly and distinctly, he said the names of companies important in the Dutch East Indies. When he came to *Senemba Maatschappij*, it clicked.

"I think that's it," I said. "I've heard that name before."

"With that we should be able to find your sister and brother-in-law," he said. "What's your name and where can we reach you?"

I gave him my full name, but no address. "A refugee camp near Berlin," I said vaguely. "I may soon be moved. I'll come again." I thanked him and left.

Ten days later I was summoned to the office of Herr Jonke. My fate had been decided.

"You will take the train tomorrow to Cottbus. Report there to the F.D.J. (Freie Deutsche Jugend — Free German Youth) office. Herr Henkel is in charge of your case."

He gave me train fare. We shook hands. Next day I left Berlin to join the Socialist Youth.

Chapter 18

THE PLUNDERED CASTLE

AT THE F.D.J. OFFICE in Cottbus everyone was busy "building socialism."

It was a simple office, with wooden chairs and rickety tables. On one wall were large pictures of the East German Trinity: Marx, Engels, and Walter Ulbricht, the Moscow-trained, Stalin-anointed general secretary of the S.E.D. (Sozialistische Einheitspartei Deutschlands — Socialist Unity Party of Germany), the only party that mattered in the Russian zone of Germany.

On the other walls of the office were uplifting slogans and pictures of smiling kerchiefed girls harvesting wheat and young men working with gleaming machines. All were happy and all were "building socialism."

All this was quite familiar to me. I had seen similar offices at our factory in the Soviet Union, with similar slogans and similar pictures.

It didn't bother me. Since the Russians were now in charge, it seemed logical that they would create a Soviet Germany. I had learned how to survive in a Soviet state. As I knew, the key word for all survivors in the Soviet Union was *ostoroshnost*, "caution." I was friendly, polite, and very cautious.

The people at the F.D.J. office were a bit shocked by my appearance, but they were nice and helpful.

Herr Henkel, the director, asked me to come into his small private office. He was a man in his early sixties, who, after the Soviet victory in 1945, had presumably unearthed immaculate socialist roots and was now director. He had read my c.v., he said, and he was glad to help me.

"It is very important to us that you speak Russian," he said. "Our schools need Russian teachers. I have spoken to the director of our Teacher Training Institute," he continued, "and he is willing to enrol you next fall. This is really wonderful and most unusual."

He glanced at a paper and then at me. "You will be fourteen years old next year," he said. "Normally you would have to finish high school and then enrol at the institute. But we desperately need Russian teachers. That's why the director is willing to make this exception."

He smiled. "Because it's so urgent, it will be a one-year course. You may be a teacher at age fifteen!

"In the meantime," Herr Henkel said, "we also have a job for you. The F.D.J. has acquired a former *Schloss* (castle) near Cottbus. We plan to convert it into a *Sozialistisches Jugendheim* (a socialist youth home). Unfortunately, the place is war-damaged and will require extensive repairs. The caretaker, Herr Golantz, is a carpenter. You will assist him with his work. He knows you are coming."

He smiled again, benignly. "I believe our staff has a few things for you," he said.

They had indeed. A few girls in their late teens, and early twenties worked in the office along with several much older women, and they now fussed over me and were very kind. They had a box of clothes: a pair of pants, a good jacket that actually fitted me, shirts, a pullover, underwear, socks, gloves. It was pleasant to have underwear again. I had not worn any for more than a year. Soviet slaves do not get underwear.

I received all necessary papers. I was now a Category III worker and received the corresponding ration cards. I was also going to receive a modest salary, plus free room and board at the castle. "Be sure to come and visit us from time to time," they said.

"War-damaged" when applied to castles, I learned, was the currently correct euphemism for "sacked by the Soviet army."

There were quite a few Soviet soldiers stationed in Cottbus, a predominantly industrial city southeast of Berlin, not far from the Neisse River and the new border with Poland. But they were not much in evidence.

After that first glorious orgy of killing, raping, looting, and sacking castles at the very end of the war and during the first months of occupation, the Soviet army had been reined in and was now busy polishing its image.

Most soldiers were confined to barracks. Russian officers in public were usually polite, correct, and tried to be *kulturnie*, "cultured." They went to the opera and attended concerts.

Meanwhile the MGB, the Soviet secret police (successor to the NKGB and renamed the KGB in 1953), quietly created in its image the *Ministerium für Staatssicherheit* (the Ministry of State Security), the nascent but already feared Stasi, the East German secret police.

The castle near Cottbus which now became my home had been occupied by Soviet troops only briefly in the spring of 1945.

The owner, a wealthy count and his family, had fled just in time, taking their most precious and portable possessions, and leaving behind an exquisitely furnished castle that had been owned by the same family for many generations. However in less than two weeks Soviet soldiers turned it into a pathetic ruin. Forever in need of firewood to boil their food, mainly potatoes, they stripped the mahogany panelling off the walls, axed elegant furniture, chopped up chickens on ivory-inlaid tables, smashed every mirror in the house (they were evidently not superstitious), and broke nearly all the windows, because soldiers enjoy breaking windows.

Now only three rooms in the servants' wing were habitable. One was our kitchen–living room with a cast-iron wood-burning range. Herr and Frau Golantz, the caretaker and his wife, lived in one room. I had the other.

Herr and Frau Golantz were kind, sad people, broken by war and fate. They were refugees from Silesia, now part of Poland, and had lost all their belongings. Both their sons had died in the war. Their daughter worked in Leipzig. Now they only had each other and their memories.

A few more Silesian refugee families lived in the nearby village. Every Sunday after lunch, Herr and Frau Golantz went to the village, where most of the Silesian refugees met in one large room, drank ersatz coffee, and talked sadly of "home." All afternoon.

Our lives were quiet, peaceful, and simple. Frau Golantz cooked and kept house. Herr Golantz did some repair work. I fetched firewood from the park.

It was now December 1946, a cold winter. Each day I left after breakfast with a small sled and a saw and axe, collected broken branches, and chopped down and cut up dead trees. Surplus wood I took to the nearby village and exchanged it there for food, mainly potatoes.

It was wonderful. For the first time in two years I felt truly free. There were no guards, no barbed wire, no mess halls, no squatting in communal latrines, no communal *banyas*.

The park was large, once elegant, but now neglected. It was quiet and marvellously peaceful, and I was alone in the park all day and every day, chopping wood and watching birds.

Several flocks of long-tailed tits lived in the park, elfin little birds, round and fluffy, with shiny black eyes. They were terribly busy collecting insect eggs and wintering larvae, for the days were short, the nights long and cold, and they needed a lot of food energy to survive.

The little birds ate and talked incessantly, a sort of excited sibilant whispering, and in the evening they suddenly vanished. After much watching and searching, I found a flock settled for the night. They sat on the branch of a conifer, sheltered by the trunk from the cutting wind, all fluffed out and huddled close together, keeping each other warm.

I tore the unused pages out of a castle ledger that had remained on a shelf, and again kept a nature diary, with detailed notes on bird behaviour.

When the castle had been sacked, one portion of it had been saved and carefully preserved by the dedicated and efficient men and women of the Soviet army's Trophy Division: the castle's famous library.

The Red Army Trophy Division, the *Trophäenkommission*, as it was called in Germany, kept pace with the advancing front-line troops and protected, saved, and confiscated everything and anything of historical, artistic, and financial value from private homes, estates, and state collections: paintings, china, jewellery, tapestries, carpets, furniture, antiques, chandeliers, and entire libraries. The common soldiers were after watches. The trophy people were after Watteaus.

All they gathered was carefully recorded, crated, and sent to the Soviet Union. It was a large division and they worked very hard but they could not be everywhere and they were not always in time.

At a neighbouring, much richer castle, the villagers told me, the owners, leaving everything behind, had fled just before the advancing Soviet troops occupied the castle.

The troops bivouacked in the castle and the castle grounds. It was cold and the soldiers needed firewood to boil potatoes, so they chopped up the antique furniture. They also took the paintings off the walls, burned the heavy gilded frames, and cut up the oily canvases. Among the canvases they burned, the villagers said, was a large painting by Rubens. If true, those Russian soldiers probably ate the most expensive boiled potato supper in history.

Art theft by victorious armies is, of course, an old tradition. Persians plundered Greek art. Greeks looted Egypt. The Romans conquered an empire and brought its art to Rome.

Napoleon was good at it. His armies swept across Europe, winning battles and acquiring art. From the German town of Kassel alone, Napoleon took almost three hundred paintings, including sixteen by Rembrandt, four by Rubens, and one by Titian. The "Mona Lisa" (not looted, but "borrowed" from the Louvre) hung in Napoleon's bedroom in Fontainebleau.

Several of the rulers of the Third Reich were ardent art collectors. Hermann Göring made frequent trips to France and Holland and returned with truckloads of loot. For a short time he owned one of the most valuable art collections in the world.

Adolf Hitler, once a struggling artist who made a meagre living selling his paintings in Vienna and Munich, in his later days, perched upon the peak of power, had a superb private art collection. His favourite painting, Jan Vermeer's "The Astronomer," had been seized for Hitler in 1940 at the Paris home of Baron Edouard de Rothschild.

None of these great looters of art, however, could rival the vacuum-cleaner efficiency of the Red Army Trophy Division. Little escaped them. In our castle near Cottbus the entire library, amassed by generations of bibliophilic owners, had been carefully crated and now awaited shipment to the Soviet Union.

Those crates fascinated me. I hadn't stolen anything since leaving the Soviet Union, being hindered by a strong, child-hood-acquired inhibition about stealing private property.

These crates were different. They now belonged to the Soviet Union, and they were very tempting, though I realized I had to be extremely careful. If caught stealing from the Soviet State, I might be sent again to one of their slave labour camps.

Two things made the theft easy: the Golantz's regular five-to-six-hour Sunday visit to the village, and Herr Golantz's set of carpentry tools.

One Sunday when they were gone, I jimmied open one of the crates, being extremely careful not to leave the slightest mark.

This crate was filled with fat law books, including leather-bound sets of the *Jahrbuch des Deutschen Rechtes* (the *Annual of*

German Law) from the beginning of the century. I removed six books, re-arranged the others to leave no gaps, and cautiously closed the crate.

I hid four volumes in the castle, put two in a sack, and hid the sack in the unused gatehouse at the entrance to the castle grounds.

On Monday I asked Herr Golantz if I could go to Cottbus to visit the F.D.J. office. "Of course," he said. "Take the morning train and come back in the evening."

I left with a small bag, picked up the sack with the books at the gatehouse where no one could see me, and took the train to Cottbus.

After quite a bit of asking and searching, I found an antiquarian bookstore. The owner was a tall man, nearly completely bald, a bit bent, wearing horn-rimmed glasses. He was alone in the store.

"May I help you?" he asked.

"I have some books for sale," I said. "Perhaps they are of interest to you." I showed him the two volumes.

He was interested. He was also cautious. I think he knew the books were stolen. He may even have guessed where they had been stolen. He never asked my name or inquired about the provenance of the books I brought to him.

"Do you have more books?" he asked.

"Yes."

"Can you bring entire sets?"

"No."

"Can you tell me what else you have?"

"No. I'll come about once a week and bring a few books."

We left it at that. He paid me thirty marks per book, more than I had expected. Then I visited the F.D.J. office, had a nice chat, was presented with another pair of socks, and returned to the castle.

This became my routine. All week I cut wood in the park and watched birds. On Sundays I stole books, but never more than six to eight from one crate. On Tuesdays I took the train to Cottbus and sold the books.

To account for my sudden weekly urge to visit Cottbus, I hinted shyly that I had met a nice girl there and Tuesday was her day off.

This was no longer unlikely. Although officially only fourteen, I was in fact going to be eighteen in a few months. Perhaps it was my age, perhaps regular meals, perhaps hard work in the park, or perhaps it was a combination of all these factors that stimulated my body to proceed with the normal process of growing up, and rather suddenly the starvation-delayed puberty kicked in.

My voice dropped fairly abruptly from boy soprano to baritone, and there were quite a lot of other changes as well. With them came a growing-but-so-far-theoretical interest in girls. In practice, however, I was far too shy, solitary, and distrustful to venture out into those pastures.

In the meantime, a putative girlfriend provided an excellent excuse for my weekly visits to Cottbus to sell stolen books.

It was on one of those visits, in April 1947, when, after selling another lot of books, I dropped in at the F.D.J. office, that Herr Henkel, the director, asked me to come into his office.

"We have found a lady who would like to adopt you," he said in his most benign voice. "Please come to our office tomorrow afternoon. I will then introduce you to the lady and we can discuss your future."

I took the train back to the castle and went for a long walk in the park.

I knew that, months ago, at the relocation camp in Rüdersdorf, I had signed, with some misgivings, a form declaring my willingness to be adopted. Time had passed. I had nearly forgotten about it. Now I had to make a decision.

There were at least three good reasons against adoption.

I had had wonderful parents, whom I had loved deeply. They had been murdered, and nothing and nobody could ever replace them.

The years in prison had left me cold and cautious. I wanted neither to receive love, nor give love.

Thirdly, I was not who I said I was, as now stated in my c.v. and on my identity papers. And I was not about to reveal my real identity to anyone. If that leaked out, I might get into serious trouble with the Stasi, the secret police.

Since I was born in Riga, Latvia, and Latvia was now part of the Soviet Union, I was retroactively by Soviet law a Soviet citizen and might be "repatriated." That, I realized, would most probably mean a death camp in Siberia.

But against all these cogent reasons to reject adoption outright, there was that cautious prison shrewdness: "Never refuse anything. If it's no good, then worm out of it somehow."

The next day I travelled to Cottbus to meet the lady who wanted to adopt me.

Chapter 19

THE SOVIET DISCIPLES OF
GENERAL VON CLAUSEWITZ

FOUR PEOPLE ASSEMBLED in the office of the F.D.J. in Cottbus: Herr Henkel, the director, Frau Schreben, who hoped to adopt me, a Fräulein vom Sozialamt (a young woman from the Office of Social Affairs), and I.

The Fräulein, it turned out, was in charge of adoptions, and she did most of the talking. She began with the correct banalities: the evils of Hitler's tyranny, the losses it had inflicted upon Frau Schreben and me, the glorious hope that socialism was bringing to our new workers' Germany . . .

She rattled off the prescribed socialist litany in a let's-get-this-over-with manner, and then became decisively efficient.

"You," she said, looking at me, "have declared your willingness to be adopted. Frau Schreben wishes to adopt you. In situations like this, it is customary to have a *Bekanntschaftsperiode* (get-to-know-each-other period).

"Frau Schreben has a room available at her apartment. I suggest you move into this room as a paying boarder. Please contact me when you are ready to proceed with the adoption." She gave us her office address and phone number and left.

Now it was Herr Henkel's turn. Looking his most benign, he said: "I have found a good job for you in Cottbus. As lab assistant at the Teacher Training Institute, where you will begin studying in the fall. I have spoken with the director. He is expecting you."

I thanked him. He had been most kind and helpful.

Frau Schreben and I left, both feeling shy and awkward. We sat on a park bench for a while and talked.

She was a teacher and looked as one imagines a German teacher should look: straight-backed, neat, prim, with grey hair, nice but simple clothes, and a kind but clear and decisive voice. Her face was lined and I guessed her to be in her late fifties. She was, in fact, only forty-seven years old.

"What were you called at home?" she asked.

"Friedel."

"May I call you 'Friedel' and '*Du*'" [the familiar German 'thou']? she asked.

I agreed, gladly. But I always called her "Frau Schreben" and "*Sie*" (the formal German "you").

I moved to her apartment a few days later. "My" room was nice but sad. It had once been the room of her only son, Gert. He had been nearly exactly as old as I really was.

Her husband had been killed early in the war. Gert, just a boy, her only child, went to school in Cottbus. In February 1945, he was drafted into the *Volkssturm* (the "People's Storm"), that pathetic last-hope army of old men and young boys, thrown together at Hitler's orders and sacrificed to prolong a lost war, and Hitler's life, by a few more days. Gert had been killed near Berlin by Russian machine-gun fire on April 26, 1945. He was sixteen years old. The war ended twelve days later.

I could never replace him, just as she could never replace my parents. The best I could do was to assuage a bit his mother's grief and loneliness.

Shortly after I had moved to her apartment she gave me some of Gert's clothes. "Wear them," she said. "I think they will fit you."

A bit reluctantly I put them on. When I came into the living room, she looked at me and started to cry. I felt badly, somehow guilty. I tried to comfort her. "We'll put these clothes away," I said.

"No," she said. "No. Please, don't. It's just that they remind me so much of Gert."

"I'll pack them and put them away."

"Please don't. They fit you well. I want you to have them. Please keep wearing them."

I did wear them for they did fit me. I was eighteen but very slim, Gert's size when he died at sixteen. After a while, she got used to it, and became more resigned.

There wasn't much I could do for her. But the apartment needed some repairs, the small things normally done by a man.

I returned to the castle one Sunday, told Herr Golantz what needed fixing at the apartment, and asked to borrow some of his tools.

"Sure," he said. "No problem."

I wandered through the castle. The crates with books were gone. "What happened to those crates?" I asked.

"Oh, those. Ivan came and got them. They're gone to Russia." ("Ivan" was the East German generic name for Russians.) Russia never got the nearly one hundred books I had stolen. That pleased me.

I visited the antiquarian. "Any more books?" he asked. "No, I'm afraid that's finished. Now I want to buy a book. Something nice. Not too expensive. For a lady of fifty or so who likes poetry."

He had just the thing. A small book, elegant, linen-and-leather cover, late nineteenth century. "How much do I owe you?" I asked.

He smiled. "Nothing," he said. "It's my last payment for all the books you brought."

I enjoyed my work at the institute from the start. I helped the physics and chemistry teachers prepare experiments and demonstrations, cleaned up, and put things away. I tried to hide my utter ignorance of all things physical and chemical, asked questions, was useful, and learned a lot. A week later, I was offered additional work.

"Could you give German lessons to a Russian officer?" asked the director of the institute.

"Yes," I said. "But I will need the appropriate textbooks."

The institute would provide me with everything I needed, the director assured me.

"His name is Major Belukov and you are to meet him tomorrow at noon at the Russian officers' club."

The major, a good-looking man of about forty, was slightly startled by my age. He had not expected a fourteen-year-old teacher. But he was delighted that I spoke Russian and asked where I had learned it.

"In Russia," I said, without elaborating.

He understood, and asked no further questions. He was polite, nearly formal.

I called him "Comrade major." He called me "Gospodin Bruemmer" (Mr. Bruemmer, the prerevolutionary form of polite address, pronouncing my name the Russian way, "Brjoomer").

He said he was anxious to learn German. It was his dream, he confided, to some day read Clausewitz in the original. He spoke of him with so much respect that I didn't dare ask: "Who's Clausewitz?"

We agreed on three one-hour lessons a week at a room in the officers' club. An encyclopedia at the Cottbus library told me that Karl von Clausewitz, 1780–1831, had been a Prussian general and writer, and that his famous book *Vom Kriege* (*On War*) had enormously influenced military strategy and tactics. War, he wrote, was simply "a continuation of diplomacy by other means." He advocated a war not just between armies, but a "total war," in which the land, the citizens, and the property of the enemy should be attacked and destroyed.

It sounded horribly familiar.

I asked the librarian for Clausewitz's book *Vom Kriege*. I didn't get the book. Instead, I got an angry lecture.

She was evidently a recent convert to Communism, and spoke primarily in slogans. She lit into me for asking for a "Junker book," a book written by a Prussian aristocrat. I should clean myself of the evils of the past. I should read the great, progressive works of socialist writers.

She went on and on, preaching Party doctrine. When she stopped her diatribe, I told her I was teaching German to Russian officers and they were ardent admirers of Clausewitz. Her tone changed abruptly, from arrogant to servile, and I got the book.

It was not an easy time to be a librarian in the Russian Zone of Germany. Information was state-controlled, and doled out on a "need-to-know" basis.

A librarian had to be very cautious and had to decide:

What books were "correct" and could be lent out.

What books were mildly "suspect" and had to be lent out with care.

What books were "evil" and had to be destroyed.

What books had to be locked away.

Who was allowed access to "forbidden" books.

The system was extremely complicated and convoluted — and subject to abrupt shifts in Party thought. Books that had been lent out with a Party-approved *nihil obstat* were suddenly proscribed, and had to be locked away. Being a librarian in the Russian Zone would today be called a high-stress job.

At our first lesson, Major Belukov ushered me into our study room at the officers' club, a small room with a table and four chairs. After he closed the door, he suddenly looked hard at me, put his finger on his lips for silence, and then made a curious circling motion with his hand.

I didn't get it. He made the same motion, then pointed at the ceiling. Suddenly I understood. The room was bugged. We had to be careful what we said.

I knew, of course, that bugging was common and widespread in the Soviet Union — not, however, at the worm's level of my slave existence in Russia. Nonetheless, I had learned all about caution in the Soviet Union. I smiled at the major and nodded that I understood, and we proceeded with our first lesson.

Soon word spread, and I acquired two more Russian officer pupils, both captains, and two German students, both bureaucrats who thought it wise to learn Russian. Since I could no longer steal books, this provided me with a good income, and the Russian officers, as a bonus, occasionally gave me small presents of food and cigarettes.

But I had problems. Having learned Russian orally at a coal mine and in a factory, I could neither read nor write it, my vocabulary was crude and limited (slaves rarely discuss Clausewitz), and my way of speaking was fluent but plebeian.

This amused my Russian officers. They themselves were trying hard to speak the more refined middle-class Russian of prerevolutionary times, a Russian now considered *kulturnie*, "cultured," and they did their best to improve my too-proletarian Russian.

I crammed at home — German grammar for the Russians, Russian grammar for the Germans — and managed to stay several lessons ahead of my pupils.

In June, the institute closed for the summer. I took two weeks off from teaching to visit Dresden, and then made a too-long-delayed visit to the Dutch Red Cross in Berlin.

Chapter 20

THE DEAD CITY

AS A CHILD, IN RIGA and Kleingraben, I had had two dreams: to become a *Naturforscher,* "a naturalist," and to travel.

Now, since thanks to stolen books and private lessons I had quite a bit of money, I decided to make my first trip: to Dresden, or what was left of it, and, beyond it, to the wildly romantic Elb-sandsteingebirge, the fantastically carved cliffs and gorges of the Elbe sandstone massif.

My Red librarian gave me books on the Dresden that once was. "There's nothing left of it," she said with a moue of disgust. *"Das haben die Engländer gemacht!* (That's what the English did!)."

Dresden had once been one of the most beautiful cities in the world, the "Florence on the Elbe."

Due to one of the more complex dynastic deals of the time, some of the electors of Saxony were also kings of Poland. That provided them with great wealth. Two of them, Augustus II (1670–1733), who collected art and mistresses, was known as Augustus the Strong, and could bend horseshoes like spaghetti, and his son, Augustus III (1696–1763), whose taste in women and art were similar to those of his father, hired the best architects of the time (mostly Italians), who built for them, on the banks of the River Elbe, a fairytale city.

It was, said the writer Ian Buruma in his book *The Wages of Guilt*, "one of the architectural wonders of the world," a city of sumptuous baroque palaces, elegant parks, magnificent churches, and the Semper-Oper, perhaps the most beautiful opera house in Europe. In 1939, Dresden had a population of six hundred and twenty thousand.

During most of the war, while other cities were being heavily bombed, Dresden remained untouched. It had an important marshalling yard, but no significant war industries, and was essentially undefended.

In early February 1945, Dresden was a city packed with refugees, fleeing from the advancing Soviet armies, who were then only eighty miles to the east.

At the Yalta Conference in the Crimea, February 4–11, 1945, Stalin urged Roosevelt and Churchill to bomb cities in the eastern part of Germany heavily to help the Soviet advance. As Richard Rhodes mentions in *The Making of the Atom Bomb*, when Stalin mentioned Dresden, Churchill agreed that it would make "an especially interesting target."

During the night of February 13–14, 1945, one thousand four hundred aircraft of the British Bomber Command dropped massive, high-explosive bombs on Dresden, plus nearly six hundred and fifty thousand incendiary bombs. This produced a firestorm so violent it could be seen two hundred miles away.

The next day, February 14, 1945, just after noon, one thousand three hundred and fifty American heavy bombers appeared above the fiercely burning city and blanketed it with their cargoes of high explosives.

The operation was called "a total success" (Rhodes). It wiped out Dresden and killed an estimated one hundred thousand people. About thirty thousand of them, mostly women and children, "were incinerated," said one report.

There were no birds in Dresden.

IT WAS A LOVELY SUMMER morning when I walked out of Dresden's gutted railway station, with its mass of twisted, melted iron girders, into a city that was as still as death. I did not see one bird. Not even a sparrow.

Having admired so many pictures of "beautiful Dresden," photographs, and reproductions of the older, marvellously warm and detailed paintings of Dresden by Bernardo Bellotto, nicknamed Canaletto after his more famous uncle and teacher, the Venetian painter Antonio Canal or Canale, called Canaletto, I was confused to be in a city that no longer existed. It was like seeing the tattered shreds of what had once been the "Mona Lisa" or a pile of marble chips that had once been the Taj Mahal.

"Beautiful Dresden" was now a dream. The reality was rubble, acres and acres of brownish-grey rubble. Here and there were the fire-blackened stumps of church towers and mounds of stone that had once been lavish, baroque castles.

Amongst the rubble lay tear-shaped gobs of glass. The heat in the burning city had been so intense, it had melted the windows.

Dresden, like other "royal" cities of Europe — Versailles, for example — had been a city of palaces and parks.

The palaces were now piles of rubble, the parks ugly wastelands, with fire-blackened stumps of trees. Weeds grew on the former flower beds. The famous fountains had been crushed. Their basins were now covered with a greenish algal slime.

I walked for a while through the city trying to identify where things had been. Most streets had been cleared. Some people worked, removing debris, cleaning stones.

Tired and depressed, I joined an old man who sat on a pile of stones above the Elbe River. He had a friendly round face with red cheeks and snow-white hair. He was probably about seventy-five years old, my age today. Then, he seemed ancient to me.

"Are you from Dresden?" he asked.

"No. I live in Cottbus."

"Did you know Dresden before the war?"

"No, I'm from East Europe. I just arrived in Dresden today. To see."

"I was born in Dresden," he said. "Lived here all my life."

He smiled, a sad, reminiscing smile. "This place," he motioned at the stone and rubble where we sat, "was once the Brühlsche Terrasse (the Brühl Terrace). It was a lovely place, so elegant. And such a beautiful view over the Elbe. My wife and I used to come here. It was our favourite place. We'd sit here. There were trees on the terrace and white tables and chairs. We sat here and drank coffee and ate *Kuchen* (cake).

"Over here," he pointed to the left, "was the Semper-Oper. My wife and I often went to the opera. We both loved music.

"I worked at the clarinet factory. We made other musical instruments, too, but we were famous for our clarinets. They were used by musicians in all the great orchestras of Europe. We even exported clarinets to America," he said proudly.

"Were you in Dresden during the war?" I asked.

He knew what I meant but did not want to ask directly: Had he been here during *die Nacht*, "that night," as it was called.

That smile was again on his face, that melancholy inward smile that looked into the past.

"We had a nice apartment," he said and pointed again. "Over that way, near the Elbe. Our son was at the front, but our daughter-in-law lived with us and the three grandchildren.

"The girls were six and eight. I had given them clarinets, and they took lessons and played quite nicely. The little boy was nearly two. He was just starting to talk. My wife spoiled him awfully. *Oma*, he said, and 'cookie.' Those were his first words. When I came home, the girls would call, '*Opa*, come and play with us,' and we'd sit in the living room and play music. They were such a joy."

His face darkened. "I wasn't in Dresden that night. I had gone to stay with friends in the country. You know, I was hoping to bring back some extra food.

"We were still talking when we heard the planes. A steady, heavy drone. We stood on the lawn and stared at the sky. We couldn't see them. But that drone! It was terrible. 'There's hundreds of them,' said my friend.

"We knew they were going for Dresden. And then came those dull 'thuds' of the explosions, just steady 'thud-thud-thud.' A while later, the fires began. Soon the whole sky was red."

His voice became bitter. "You know how they did that?" he asked. "They first dropped the heavy bombs to collapse the buildings and to scare the people so they would leave the shelters and run out into the street. And then, when the streets were full of people, they dropped the fire bombs to burn them to death.

"We bicycled to Dresden that night. Towards that red sky. Bicycled and prayed.

"The city was still burning. The streets were full of corpses, with their hair and clothing burned away. Black and shrivelled. Often two close together. A mother who had tried to protect a child.

"My family was still in the shelter. There were about sixty people in that shelter. They looked so strange. Untouched. But all of them were dead. That firestorm had sucked all the oxygen out of the air. They'd been asphyxiated. Like being strangled.

"We met others. Searching, trying to find their families. Dazed. Some of them had heard the terrible screaming of burning women and children."

He stopped and looked at me. "You know," he said, "even now, when Dresden children hear a plane, they cry and try to hide."

The dark fears of children.

Many years later, in a house near the Old Jewish Cemetery in Prague, I saw a display of drawings made by children in a concentration camp. That night I wrote in my diary: "Frightening pictures, painted by children in Theresienstadt: all the flowers are black and the trees have no leaves! Pictures that show fear and a feeling of approaching doom and death."

The old man took a heavy round watch from his fob pocket and opened the lid.

"I must go," he said. "I now live with friends in the suburbs. Their house survived. But I come here every day."

An old man and a dead city.

I spent the night in a flophouse. There were no hotels in Dresden.

IN THE MORNING I WALKED down to the river where, I had been told, the flat-bottomed paddle-wheelers ("the oldest wheel-driven riverboats in the world") were again leaving for excursions up the Elbe.

I bought a ticket and walked up the gangplank. At the top stood a man in a dark-grey suit, bluish shirt, and dark tie. I gave him my ticket.

"May I see your Party card, please," he said.

"I have no Party card."

His tone changed. "This is for Party members only," he informed me.

"They didn't say anything about that when I bought the ticket," I protested.

"Well, that's too bad," he sneered. He was now *very important.*

"Get off the ship," he ordered. "Others are coming."

I went to the counter to return my ticket.

"We don't give refunds," said the man.

I began to protest, but he interrupted me.

"Complaints must be sent through the proper channels," he said coldly.

I knew that voice. I knew that type. The bastards! I cursed, in Russian. It's a nice, rich language for cursing.

"What happened?" an amused voice near me asked in Russian.

It was a Russian major, with his wife and two blond children.

"They sold me a ticket," I explained. "And now they won't let me board because I'm not a Party member."

"Why aren't you a Party member?" asked the major.

"I worked two years in the Soviet Union," I said.

He smiled. "I understand. Come with us."

We walked up the gangplank, the wife and children first, and then the major. I followed.

The man in the grey suit bowed and fawned. Then he spotted me and turned on me in vicious anger.

"*Du Scheisskerl! Ich hab Dir doch gesagt* (You shit-bastard! I told you . . .)."

That's as far as he got. The major turned and said clearly and with a touch of menace: "*Er mein Freund!* (He's my friend!)" and to me, in Russian, he added, "Please, come."

The man in the grey suit was terrified.

"I didn't know," he stammered, cringing. "Please forgive me . . ." He was disgusting. A moment more and he'd have kissed my ass.

The best section of the ship was reserved for the Russians. The major and I talked, friendly but cautious. Always cautious.

I told him I was giving German lessons to Russian officers. I mentioned Major Belukov. He knew of him. I said Belukov admired Clausewitz and hoped someday to read him in German.

"Ah, yes. Clausewitz," the major said. "We had to read him at the Military Academy. Did you see Dresden?" he asked.

"Yes."

The major looked straight at me. "Dresden! That's the 'total war' of Clausewitz," he said softly.

I left the boat at the Bastei, the towering sandstone pinnacle high above the Elbe. I said goodbye to the major and his family and thanked him. He smiled and nodded towards the man in the grey suit. "It was a pleasure," he said.

I walked for four days. First through the weirdly sculptured sandstone massif and slowly onward back towards Dresden. It was warm. I slept outside, on meadows near brooks, looked up at the sky and stars, and felt gloriously free, as only those who have once been slaves can treasure and savour freedom.

I'd wake up early in the morning and the birds were busy. This was June, family time in birdland. All the nests were full of hungry, growing chicks, and their parents were busy from dawn to dusk collecting food. I lay still and watched them for hours.

The roads were empty. There were no cars, only an occasional truck or people on bicycles. The air was pure and clear.

I had some food along and the cigarettes given to me by my Russian pupils. Cigarettes were currency, were, in fact, better than money. Like food, cigarettes were rationed. I stopped at a couple of farms and exchanged cigarettes for bread, sausages, and cheese.

The farms and the land were beautiful and peaceful. I dawdled, enjoyed, then walked quickly through Dresden to the railway station. I did not want to see this nightmare city of fire and death again — but I did, many years later.

I have a second family, the family Lackschewitz, Baltic Germans, two girls and three boys who are like sisters and brothers to me. Wolf studied with me in those long-ago days of Kleingraben. They were our neighbours in Poland. I lived with them in West Germany after the war.

Every two years they have a *Familientag*, "a family reunion." The entire Lackschewitz clan, about fifty people scattered across Europe, gathers, and my wife, Maud, and I come from Canada.

The 2003 *Familientag* was in Dresden. We six of the "old generation" are Baltic Germans. Our children and grandchildren are German, Spanish, Swedish, Finnish, and Canadian.

On our last day in Dresden I took Maud to the Brühlsche Terrasse, again as elegant as before the war, and we had coffee and *Kuchen*.

To the right and left of us was the reborn city of Dresden, the Semper-Oper, the glorious Zwinger. The Frauenkirche was being rebuilt. Some of the most generous donors, I noticed, were British.

I told Maud about the dead city, about the white-haired man who sat on the rubble where we were now eating *Kuchen*, and what he had told me about the death of Dresden, the death of his family.

Maud, who has a tender heart, started to cry. We have grandchildren that age.

Our young waiter came over and asked, "Is anything wrong?"

"No," I said. "I was here just after the war and I told my wife about the firestorm."

He shrugged, relieved. "Oh that. Yeah, well, that was long ago."

THE MAN AT THE DUTCH RED CROSS in Berlin was charming but a bit reproachful.

"I have known the address of your sister for a long time," he said. "Why didn't you come?"

I made up excuses. He wrote down addresses: Heddy was in Holland, Reinhold still in Sumatra.

I thanked him and walked away in a daze.

I had been afraid the answer might be "no," afraid of more death, of nothingness. That was probably why I had not come to Berlin.

And now it was "yes." Heddy was alive. Maybe Hella and Arist were alive as well!

I took the train to Rüdersdorf and went to the office of the relocation camp. Fräulein Teppert, the social worker, was there, still overworked, greyer, older. She did not recognize me.

In the ten months since she'd seen me, I had metamorphosed from a kid in rags with a sunken face and shaven head into a neatly dressed young man.

Fräulein Teppert was delighted to see me and sorry that the director was away. I thanked her for all that she and the director had done for me and gave her the little book of poetry.

"May I visit the camp?" I asked.

"Yes, of course," she said. "Another transport just arrived."

I walked into the camp. Men stood in groups, clutching dirty sacks that held all their belongings, men in rags, with hollow, prison faces and shaven heads, and those dull, distant eyes of slaves.

I looked at them, both chilled and a bit triumphant.

That had been me ten months ago!

I took the train back to Cottbus and wrote a letter to Heddy.

Chapter 21

A FAMILY OF PRISONERS

TWO WEEKS AFTER RETURNING from Berlin, I came home for lunch from one of the lessons I gave at the Russian officers' club. Frau Schreben met me as I came into the apartment.

"You have a visitor," she said. Her voice sounded strange.

I walked into the living room.

It was Hella, my "dead sister." All these years I had so terribly feared she was dead. Now here she was, alive and wonderful, and we hugged and cried and were incredibly happy.

It was an immense joy. But I also had an instant problem. To Hella I was one person. To Frau Schreben I was another. Fortunately Hella had just arrived and the two had hardly talked.

When Frau Schreben, kind and tactful, went into the kitchen to make tea, I gave Hella a condensed version of my new identity. She understood, but was slightly confused, because hers now had to match mine — things such as being born in Poland and having parents who were teachers.

We had tea and talked. Hella worked for the Americans in Heidelberg, as a secretary in the Signal Corps. The moment she heard from Heddy that I was alive, darling Hella, impulsive and reckless (the way she used to ride horses in Kleingraben), had invaded the office of some senior American officer and had poured out a tale so tearful and tragic about a dying brother released from Russia, that within less than twenty-four hours he got her a three-day *Interzonenpass*, the hard-to-get permit to travel to the Russian Zone. She had come via Berlin. And, yes, Arist was alive and married. And Heddy had a child, a boy, now already eight years old. We had a lot to catch up on. We talked and talked and talked.

All four of us had survived. But all had been in prisons: Hella in Poland, Arist in an American camp, I in the Soviet Union, and Heddy and her child in a Japanese concentration camp.

Now I found out what had happened nearly two and a half years ago on that terrible day after our parents had been murdered, when I turned to discover that Hella was gone.

"The younger of our two guards hit you," said Hella. "The older guard pushed us women in another direction. He took us to the women's prison in Poznan.

"They had released all the women imprisoned by the Germans. Now they locked up the German women. In some ways, it was the safest place in town!"

"They kept us locked up for a week or so. Just gave us a bit of food and water. Nearly all the women were like us, people who fled too late.

"Then they shoved in another wave of prisoners. Polish women. 'Collaborators' they called them. Some had slept with Germans. But most of them had only worked for Germans. You know how it was. They had no choice. People denounced each other. There was a lot of nasty vengeance."

After the Soviet armies had moved on and some order had been established, the women prisoners cleaned houses that had been occupied by Russian soldiers. I did that with Karl, Manek, and others before we were sent to Russia. "Full of shit!" I said.

"Yes," Hella said and laughed. "It's funny now. But then it was a filthy, miserable job.

"Later we cleaned offices. There were now Polish bureaucrats, and we cleaned their offices.

"After a while, things got better. The food improved. German and Polish prisoners got on fairly well together.

"You know how it is," Hella said again. "Some guards are real bastards, and others are quite nice.

"We had one guard, a guy of forty or so, a leering bastard. And brutal. Pushed the women around. Cut rations. Real mean. We all hated him.

"The Polish women prisoners somehow found out his wife was cheating on him, that she had had an affair with one of his bosses, and they made life hell for him. Poisonous gossip. Made sure he heard it. All the lewd and luscious details!

"They drove him nuts. One day he got so raging mad, he attacked the boss and beat him up. Then he was sent to prison and we had a victory party!"

After ten months, she and other Germans had suddenly been "sent home." Hella, better informed than I, gave the name of a town in West Germany and was sent there.

She found some Baltic Germans, who knew other Baltic Germans, and via that grapevine she found Arist, living in a village in the British Zone.

She lived with him for a while, then heard from Karin von Haken, her childhood friend, who had spent summers with us in Quellenhof. Karin was working in Heidelberg. For the "Amis," as the Americans were called. (The British were "Tommies.") She got Hella a job, first as a waitress while she studied English at the university, and now at the American Signal Corps. She had many friends in Heidelberg. She looked young and happy. It was marvellous to be with her.

Arist, in early April 1945, had been twenty-four years old, a highly decorated *Hauptmann*, "captain," and still in command of half a dozen Panthers, the best tanks of the German army. He was fighting, together with other remnants of a German army, on the southeastern front. The war, he realized, was nearly over.

He called his men together. "If we remain here," he said, "we'll end up dead or as prisoners of the Russians. I suggest we make a run for it and try to reach the West." All the men agreed.

That made them deserters. And, in that end-of-the-war chaos, one part of the German military still functioned to perfection: the SS units dealing with deserters.

Their orders were explicit: "Any soldier found behind the front without orders was to be executed immediately and his body exhibited as a warning." Deserters were shot, or hanged from trees and lampposts, with cardboard signs attached to their legs: "Traitor! I deserted my people."

An order also came from the *Führerbunker* in Berlin (Hitler's subterranean bunker, protected by a 30-metre-thick carapace of concrete): "It is expressly forbidden to fall back to the west. Officers who do not comply unconditionally with this order are to be arrested and shot right away." That order, issued April 21, 1945, was signed by Adolf Hitler. Nine days later, on April 30, 1945, Hitler committed suicide.

Arist and his men raced west. There were roadblocks. There were checkpoints, manned by SS units. There were executed "deserters" hanging from trees. But, as Arist later said, "You don't stop six Panthers!" The forty-five-ton tanks crushed the roadblocks, scattered the SS men, crunched their vehicles.

They reached the Elbe River, the border between American- and Russian-occupied Germany (agreed upon at the Yalta Conference), one day too late. Instead of Germans, Americans occupied the bridge. Honouring their promise to Stalin, they did not allow any Germans (or refugees of other nationalities) to cross to the West.

Arist tried to talk to the officer in charge of the bridge, but it was no good. The officer did not speak German, and Arist had had no English at school in Riga — only Greek and nine years of Latin.

In desperation, he tried Latin. To his amazement, the American officer understood, and, groping for words, tried to answer in Latin.

Suddenly they were not "enemy officers," but young men grappling with nearly forgotten high-school Latin. Both laughed, and that did it.

Speaking in a mixture of sign language and mangled Latin, the American told Arist that this bridge was occupied and no one could pass. But thirty kilometres from there was another bridge, intact, that would not be occupied until tomorrow. Try that. Good luck. They saluted.

Arist and his men reached the other bridge and crossed the Elbe. They were now in the West, but still terrified they might be sent back or turned over to the Russians.

"We had some bedsheets," Arist told me later. "We tore them up, hoisted them as white flags, and kept driving west. It was amazing. No one shot at us. No one stopped us. No one seemed surprised or interested. We just drove on and on, past American military convoys. When the roads were clogged, we'd drive across fields."

Finally, far in the West, they met an American major and surrendered themselves and their tanks to him.

Arist spent five months in an American camp for prisoners-of-war in Germany. He was treated fairly well and spent much of his time learning English.

After his release, also via the Baltic German grapevine, he found Elizabeth von Kursell, whom he had known since high-school times in Riga. Now they were both refugees. They had married and were living in Sehlde, a village in the British Zone.

"You remember how good a carpenter Arist always was," Hella said. "Well, now he's become a turner. He's bought a high-speed lathe and makes beautiful wooden plates and lamps and all sorts of other things."

Heddy had, of course, gone out to the Dutch East Indies with her husband, Reinhold. She had loved Sumatra, loved life on the estate, and quickly learned the common local language: *Passar Malay*, "market Malay."

In 1941, her son, Patric, had been born. On December 7, 1941, Japanese planes attacked Pearl Harbour and destroyed much of the U.S. Pacific Fleet. On December 8, 1941, the Netherlands (and other Allied nations) declared war against Japan.

In February 1942, the Japanese invaded and occupied Sumatra. On March 9, 1942, one hundred thousand Dutch and Allied troops surrendered to the Japanese on Java.

Most Dutch men, including Reinhold, were sent to Burma to work for the Japanese. Dutch women and their children and Indonesian women married to Dutchmen were arrested and herded into concentration camps.

Heddy worked hard, loading and unloading trucks, cutting timber, harvesting rice. Being out of camp, she had a chance to talk with Indonesian women, to make friends. She exchanged whatever of her possessions had value for extra food. She smuggled things out of camp. She was good at it. She had her contacts and fences outside. She began to smuggle for others. (Heddy and I, continents apart, had evidently shared an aptitude for survival and a flair for smuggling.)

Years later, in one of those periodicals published by and for former prisoners of the Japanese, I would read an article a woman had written about the camp she had shared with Heddy.

We all admired [Mrs.] Mevrouw von Löwis. We didn't dare to smuggle, because if you were caught by the Japs you were terribly beaten. Mevrouw von Löwis smuggled for all of us. She was like a cat at night. And she had good contacts with Indonesian women. Thanks to her, many of us had extra food which we terribly needed.

There was a small girl named Maud van den Berg in the same concentration camp. She was five years old when the Japanese took her father away and she and her mother were imprisoned. She lived there for four years.

Her mother and Heddy became close friends. To the little girl, Heddy was always "*Tante*" *Heddy* ("Aunt" Heddy).

Twenty years later, she would become my wife.

Heddy survived camp both physically and mentally in amazingly good shape, but was haunted for many years afterwards by a recurring nightmare: the Japanese were taking her child away. It was always the same. She clung desperately to the child, the soldiers tore it away from her, and she screamed and screamed, then awoke with a start, covered in sweat, with that immense relief: "It was the nightmare."

Prisons scar your soul. I, too, carried within me a deep fear, and about once a month I had a nightmare. With minor variations, it was always the same nightmare and it always had the same ending.

It always began with me attempting to escape from camp. It was a terrible camp, with a high-voltage barbed-wire fence, great moving searchlights, high, black towers, and guards with machine guns.

I tried to escape, got tangled up in the electrified barbed wire like a fly in a spider web, and hung there, struggling and twisting.

Slowly, terribly slowly, the gleaming shafts of the searchlights turned towards me, found me, held me in their brilliant, blinding light, and then the machine guns began to stutter, and I woke up screaming and soaked in sweat.

These nightmares lasted for seventeen years. Before I married, Heddy warned Maud that I might suddenly scream madly at night, but oddly enough, with marriage my nightmares ceased.

Hella had only a three-day pass for the Russian Zone, but she remained five days. It was so wonderful to be together again. I had feared she was dead; she had feared I was dead. And now we were alive and together.

"I'll cross the border in the Harz Mountains," Hella said blithely. "I've heard it's easy."

She promised to write immediately. I would then visit the West.

Chapter 22

SLIPPING THROUGH THE IRON CURTAIN

THREE KILOMETRES WEST OF Yalta is the Livadia Palace, a large, white Italian Renaissance–style building, once the summer palace of the czars. From February 4 to 11, 1945, the fateful Yalta Conference was held at the Livadia Palace.

The huge conference room on the ground floor is now bare, austere: there is only a large table where Roosevelt, Churchill, Stalin, and their translators and advisors sat, a few photographs, the flags of the signatory nations.

In this room, the victors of the Second World War divided post-war Europe. Stalin, farsighted and infinitely cunning, got the best deal.

Roosevelt was a sick man. He died two months later, on April 12, 1945. Churchill had political problems. A few months later he would lose the British election. Both wanted to end the war against Germany and win the war with Japan.

Stalin — considering the war won — looked far ahead. He asked for, and got, all of eastern Europe as his "sphere of influence" by giving a promise of "fair elections."

Of course no "fair elections" were ever held in Soviet-dominated eastern Europe, which now included the Russian Zone of Germany.

The East–West post-war honeymoon first soured, then ended in divorce. Churchill, out of office in 1946 but still immensely influential, saw clearly the danger of Stalin's soaring ambitions. On March 5, 1946, at Westminster College in Fulton, Missouri, Churchill made his famous warning speech:

> From Stettin on the Baltic to Trieste in the Adriatic, an iron curtain has descended across the Continent. Behind that line lie all the capitals of the ancient states of Central and Eastern Europe. I do not believe Soviet Russia desires war. What they desire . . . [is] the infinite expansion of their power and doctrines.

The Cold War had begun, and in Cottbus, I was on the Soviet side of the Iron Curtain.

One problem of living in the Russian Zone was that one saw the world exclusively through Communist-coloured glasses. All news, on radio and in newspapers, was Party-controlled, boring, and repetitive. All we heard were paeans of praise for the Party and its glorious achievements, hymns to Stalin, all-wise, all-wonderful, who would lead us into a glorious tomorrow.

In the Soviet Union the two main newspapers were called *Pravda* (*"Truth"*) and *Izvestia* (*"Information"*). A popular saying was: "There is no truth in *Information*. And there is no information in *Truth*."

In the absence of news, rumours flourished. Everyone knew a rumour. Some were true. Some were not. In this twilight zone, one proceeded with caution. Always caution.

AFTER HELLA WROTE that she had crossed to the West without problems, I told Frau Schreben I wanted to visit Arist, but promised to return in two weeks. To stay longer might arouse suspicion from my pupils, Russian and German, and from neighbours. I still planned to study at the institute and become a teacher in East Germany. Officially I was going to East Berlin to visit relatives. Only Frau Schreben knew I was going to the forbidden West.

Hella had written in detail about her border crossing, and I followed her example. I took the train from Cottbus to the city of Halle, changed to a local train, and arrived at 11 p.m. at the last station in East Germany. There local boys, ten to fifteen years old, awaited the *Grenzgänger*, "the border-crossers," and, for a fee of twenty marks each, offered to lead us safely to the border. "My" boy collected a group of about fifteen people and told us to walk close together and be quiet.

The others stumbled in the dark, cursed, and talked, despite the urgent shushing of the boy. I followed at a distance to have a chance of escape in case the noisy group was arrested.

We crossed fields, meadows, and a small brook and reached a forest. There I caught up with the group. The boy led us through the forest and down a slope. Then he stopped.

"This is the border," he said. We crawled through a few strands of barbed wire and were in the West. "Go straight ahead," said our young guide. "When you come out of the forest, there is a road. Follow it and you'll reach the station." He vanished into the dark.

The twelve days with Arist and Elizabeth were wonderful, and also difficult. Both were shocked and upset that I planned to return to the Russian Zone and become a teacher there. From their western perspective, this seemed like a voluntary return to the "realm of evil." They insisted I must stay in the West, the "free West." And I didn't want that.

I had been on my own for a long time. I had created an alternate persona that, I felt, was quite safe in East Germany. My knowledge of Russian was in great demand. Starting from zero, I had managed quite well.

What was there for me in the West? A factory job or high school. I did not like either idea.

Poor Arist. Now that our parents were dead, he felt strongly that it was his duty to make sure that we were safe and, if possible, successful. Now, here he was stuck with a young brother who was being stubborn, stupid, and, on top of that, smug.

Finally he zeroed in on my weakest point, my biggest fear. "Some day they'll find out that you've been lying," he warned. "That you really are Baltic German. That you were born in Latvia. All the Letts and Ests they caught in East Germany have been 'sent home' to the Soviet Union, and that will happen to you!"

He was right, of course. But I had promised Frau Schreben I would return. She had been very kind to me, and I was determined not to break that promise.

Also, I had a few belongings in the East: some clothes, a second pair of shoes, my diaries, a couple of books on birds, my Russian–German, German–Russian dictionary. These were my first and only possessions. They seemed very precious.

We compromised. I would return to East Germany, stay for a short time, and then come to the West.

Going back to the East, I travelled by train to the last station in the West, a small town in the Harz Mountains. Ten kilometres farther east was the last train station in East Germany. Between these towns, the rail line was dead.

Crossing the border in one direction had been so easy that I was now going to do it in daytime. Hundreds of border crossers who had arrived on the same train, some with suitcases and heavy packsacks, walked east, mostly in small, nervous groups. I waited until all had gone. It rained, and I hoped the Russian border guards, having caught their daily quota, would seek shelter in town. Finally only one other man remained in the station, a doctor who wanted to visit his brother in East Germany.

Like many Germans, the doctor did not accept the fact that Germany had been cut up like a pie by the victor nations and now consisted of four pieces. To him it was one country, somewhat smaller than before the war and temporarily occupied by American, French, British, and Russian troops and administrators, but still one country, whose pieces would soon be reunited into one Germany. It had already started. On January 1, 1947, the United States and Britain had merged their occupation zones.

The doctor considered the East–West border as just a temporary nuisance.

"Have you crossed before?" he asked.

"Yes. At night. Two weeks ago."

"Can I go with you?" he asked.

"Sure," I said. "The train we need to catch will leave at 6 p.m. from the station in East Germany."

We left the western town at noon. In the West there were no border guards, no controls, no interest. We walked through the forest, crossed the few strands of barbed wire that formed the border and kept heading due east. We felt safe in the forest. At the edge of the woods, we stopped. If there were guards, they would be hiding in the shelter of the trees at the edge of the forest.

It rained hard now. No one was in sight. Reluctantly we moved into the open, onto a wide field, feeling terribly exposed, fearing shouts or shots. But all was quiet.

We walked fast; in another hour we would be at the train station. We crossed a meadow, and suddenly there was shouting. A Russian soldier ran up behind us, waving a white handkerchief with one hand, holding a gun in the other.

We turned and walked back. The Russians, three soldiers and a sergeant, were in a railroad underpass, sheltered from the rain.

The sergeant cursed and yelled at us in bits of broken German. We'd be sent to the uranium mines, he threatened. The moment I spoke Russian, he became even angrier.

"You are a spy!" he yelled. "You will be shot!"

He went on like that for a while, then, calmer, asked where I had learned Russian.

"I worked in Russia. For two years. In the south, in the Stalino *oblast* (district)," I said.

"I have a brother in Makeyevka," he said.

"I worked in Makeyevka. In the steel plant," I lied, an easy lie since it is the city's main industry.

"That's where my brother works!" The sergeant was delighted. "Imagine. You worked in the same factory as my brother!"

He gave us cigarettes and hot tea from a sooty kettle above a small fire, and we talked for a while, now warm and friendly.

"Listen," the sergeant said. "There are three more groups of border guards between here and the station. Go back to the forest, then left, skirting the edge of the forest until you come to a road. On that road you can walk safely to the station. There are no guards in that area today."

I thanked him, we shook hands with the sergeant and the soldiers, and said goodbye. We followed his instructions and got safely to the station. I explained it all to the doctor and he was amused and relieved. At one moment, seeing me so chummy with the sergeant, he had feared that I was one of those who, for a reward of food or money, led border crossers straight to Russian guards.

The station was abuzz with more rumours and reports. Many who had crossed the border had been arrested, it was said. A loud man who knew everything claimed most of them would be released, but some men would be sent to the uranium mines.

"People die quickly there," he said. "That's why they need new ones all the time."

Most of us believed him. Atomic bombs, uranium, fission, deadly radiation were vaguely known and greatly feared. In the absence of real knowledge, we accepted rumours.

It seemed logical that uranium mines would be lethal and that the Russians would need a steady supply of men to replace the short-lived miners. That system was familiar to me from the Soviet Union.

MY LAST MONTH in East Germany was sad. I had to tell Frau Schreben that I would leave for the West. She had feared this would happen, and it was hard on her. She had tried to find another son, had been very kind, and now it had to end. She would be alone again with her sorrow, her memories.

I told no one else. To tell people you were going to cross to the West endangered them. They had to report this immediately to the police, and if they failed to do that they were guilty of complicity. They might be questioned at length. They could be punished. A report of the "crime" would go into their file.

Trained and inspired by the Soviet secret police, the East German secret police, the feared Stasi, were busy compiling secret files for virtually every citizen of the Russian Zone of Germany.

A "transgression" (or an anonymous denunciation by a jealous friend, an unpleasant relative, or a nasty neighbour) could result in immediate punishment. It could also be used by the police in many insidious, shadowy ways to ruin a person's life: he might be denied a well-earned promotion; he might be denied a change of jobs or residence; his children might be barred from university.

Being as careful as possible, I sent my few belongings to Arist in *Pfundpäckchen*, the one-pound parcels that were the postal limit of parcels to the West. A pair of shoes was too heavy, so I sent one shoe per parcel.

I said a final, sad goodbye to Frau Schreben. I would not write to her from the West. If she was questioned about my disappearance, she could say I had left to visit relatives in East Berlin, and since then she had not heard from me. If I wrote from the West, she would be in danger. She could lose her job as teacher. She might even lose her apartment.

It was dark in the train to the small border town in the Harz Mountains. Plywood sheets covered broken windows. Light bulbs had been stolen or broken. People talked in worried whispers. Most were planning to cross the border.

German police, some said, had taken over as border guards. They patrolled the border much more efficiently than the Russians. They also arrested people as they got off the train at the border station, assuming they were going to try to cross the border. Several people said they had heard that all the men arrested were sent to work and die in the uranium mines.

The man next to me had served on the Russian front for several years. He said little, but seemed sure of himself. He was one of the tough young-old men of the war, and had been a sergeant when the war ended. Like me, he had only a small rucksack. We agreed to cross the border together and to get out one stop before the border station and walk the extra ten kilometres to avoid arrest.

We walked through the little railway building directly into the arms of the waiting police. Much more efficient than the Russians, they controlled all passengers at several stations before the border. Locals could pass; all others were arrested.

Two policemen checked papers near the door of the station, two armed men kept watch, and four policemen with guns guarded the fast-growing cluster of arrested persons, mostly men, but also women and children. All were standing in the circle of pale yellowish light cast by lamps on a pole near the station. The sergeant and I stood at the very edge of the group.

Four local men approached, walking abreast, heavy, stolid burghers on their way home. As they passed, one said "*Schau doch die armen Esel an*! (Look at the poor asses!)" and in that split second I knew exactly what to do, and so did the sergeant.

We jumped in front of the four men and ran towards the dark. The guards yelled: "Stand! Stand! Or we'll shoot!" But the slow-moving locals were in the way, they did not shoot, and we vanished into the saving darkness.

We ran down the main street of the sleeping village, turned left, away from the border, and hid behind a garden fence. A minute later, two cars raced down the street, stopped, raced on. Maybe they put policemen out to search for us, but no one came near. There were the sounds of the night: the last people going home; gates creaking; doors closing. A dog barked in the distance. Another car raced down the road.

We waited until midnight. All was quiet and, fortunately, it was a very dark night. I walked ahead, since I have good night vision, and we crossed the road and the village, then walked west across fields and meadows. On our right, a dark line in the night, was the railway berm. On our left was a road.

Suddenly a beam of brilliant light shot into the darkness, then swept swiftly yard-high across the fields to spot walking people. We dropped instantly, and the beam swept through the darkness above us.

The policemen in the car on the road, only a hundred yards away, swept their searchlight a few more times across us, then cut the light. "Don't move!" the sergeant whispered. Sure enough, a couple of minutes later, they made another rapid sweep, this time lower. The ground was uneven, so the light did not touch us, but I felt exposed and vulnerable.

They started the car and appeared to drive away, then stopped for more searchlight sweeps. We lay totally still. After half an hour they drove on. We could see the stabbing light in the distance.

We got up and walked, tense in the quiet of the night. A hare, pressed to the ground, jumped up in front of us and raced away. We stopped, rigid with fear, then laughed shakily and walked on.

It was about twenty kilometres to the border. The darkness protected us, but it also made walking difficult, and we were in a hurry for we had to reach the border before dawn. We stumbled, floundered across a creek, got badly scratched in willow thickets, and ran blindly into the barbed-wire fences that enclosed some meadows.

We reached the border forest with the first faint grey light of morning, walked cautiously between the trees, and came to the strands of barbed wire that formed the border between East and West at sunrise.

The rest was easy. We reached the station in the West in broad daylight, tired now, the tension oozing out of us.

There were few border crossers at the station. Of the hundreds who had attempted it that night, less than a dozen had succeeded. All the others had been arrested, the men perhaps headed for the uranium mines and death.

We got on the train and the sergeant instantly fell asleep. He was still sleeping when I got out. I did not say goodbye.

Chapter 23

IN THE REALM OF REFUGEES

WEST GERMANY IN LATE 1947 was a crowded land. An immense wave of displaced humans had surged from east to west, and most of them eventually settled in West Germany.

There were the twelve million Germans expelled from former regions of Germany that now belonged to Poland. There were the millions of ethnic Germans from all of eastern Europe, some from as far away as Russia's Volga River region. In addition, there were groups from the disunited nations of eastern Europe: Serbs, Croats, Ukrainians, Russians, Letts, Ests, Lithuanians. The list was long.

Some had worked in Germany as conscript labourers. Others had fought with Germany against the Soviet Union. Others had fled from their home countries when the Soviet armies occupied their lands.

They often disliked each other. Many also disliked the Germans. One thing all had in common: an icy fear of the creeping, crushing power of Communism, of Soviet rule, now a fait accompli in all of eastern Europe.

Most non-Germans lived in crowded refugee camps, hoping and waiting to emigrate to various promised lands: the United States, Canada, Australia, South America.

The German refugees arrived en masse right after the war in a war-wrecked western Germany occupied and administered by the Americans, British, and French. Initially, they were mostly women and children, since their men, millions of them, were either dead or in POW camps. Nearly all the refugees were penniless, homeless, jobless. The most urgent problems, shelter and food, were solved, as much as possible, by billeting the have-nots with the haves.

And so it came to pass in those days that the rustic village of Sehlde in Lower Saxony, home to a homogenous group of fairly prosperous farmers and their workers, inward-looking and probably content, became abruptly the not-too-happy host to a mass of people from an alien world.

Among them were Arist and Elizabeth. They lived in two tiny attic rooms of a farmer's house, with no water (there was a pump in the yard), no kitchen (Elizabeth cooked on a hot plate), no toilet (there was a privy in the yard), and no heating. To add to this, I now lived with them.

Arist had worked first for a farmer and was paid in food rather than money. Then he changed to the village carpentry shop, and repaired everything from farm wagons to furniture.

Elizabeth sold some of her remaining jewellery. With the money, Arist bought a high-speed lathe and became a master turner, as Hella had reported. He had a marvellous feeling for form, loved to create, and made beautiful wooden plates, lamps, and ornate candelabra. Another refugee, a man from the former *Sudetenland* (now part of Czechoslovakia), an astute salesman, sold all that Arist produced in neighbouring cities.

When I arrived, Arist modified the lathe so that two could work on it. He would design and cut an object from a block of wood. I would sandpaper, polish, and wax it. By now, Arist was a successful and respected village craftsman.

His mother-in-law — known to me as Aunt Vera — painted icons. Vera von Kursell came from a long-vanished world, the St. Petersburg of the czars. Her family, the Amburgers, had been wealthy St. Petersburg merchants. The Russian Revolution in 1917 took all their wealth and nearly took their lives. They just managed to flee to Estonia, and later settled in Riga, Latvia.

She had married Elizabeth's father, a Baltic German, and to earn money, she gave Russian lessons to American and British diplomats in Riga. (After the war, one of her American pupils went to considerable trouble to have her traced. Then, in a gesture of remarkable kindness, he regularly sent his former teacher CARE packages, which, in those lean years, were of great help to Aunt Vera. His name was George F. Kennan, one of America's most influential diplomats and thinkers, U.S. ambassador in Moscow, author, and, later, professor at the Institute for Advanced Study at Princeton.) While she lived in Riga, Aunt Vera had also learned the ancient, sacred art of icon painting from a master, a Russian émigré.

In 1939, when the Hitler–Stalin pact gave Latvia to the Soviet Union, she, like us and like nearly all the Baltic Germans, fled and lived in German-occupied Poland. In 1945, as Soviet armies advanced, she fled again, reached West Germany, and was assigned a room in Sehlde. It had been a harrowing escape, with near-death by hunger and freezing. Her husband died in the war. Her other daughter was "missing." She had probably been murdered by Soviet soldiers.

Despite a life so full of hardship and loss, Aunt Vera was one of the most charming and delightful people I have ever met. She was a devout Russian Orthodox Christian. She lived her faith and loved her faith, and it gave her strength and peace.

When she was young, she must have been like Tolstoy's Natasha in *War and Peace*, strikingly beautiful, vivacious, and brimful of the joy and thrill of being young and alive.

Now she had one room in the house of a Frau Siebenhaar in Sehlde "Siebenhaar, or Sevenhair," was a medieval nickname that had become a surname. There were other names like that in the village: Rollingwagon, Dragfoot, Sourbread.

Frau Siebenhaar was a plump, placid peasant woman. She was born in Sehlde, grew up in Sehlde, married in Sehlde. She had made only one great trip in her life, to the city of Hanover, a hundred miles away. Her world was farm, family, and the village of Sehlde.

Frau Siebenhaar liked to talk. Her husband, Herr Siebenhaar, did not like to talk. He did not like to listen, either. He worked hard, ate supper, then dozed in an easy chair. On Saturdays he went to the pub and had a beer or two. On Sundays he went to church and later read the Bible.

So, nearly every day, Frau Siebenhaar took some of her work to Aunt Vera's room and the two talked, Frau Siebenhaar in a Sehlde-centred Lower Saxony dialect, Aunt Vera in mellifluous, animated, heavily Russian-accented German.

Frau Siebenhaar knew all the village news.

"You know," she would begin, "I was at the baker's this morning and Frau Rollingwagon told me . . ." and on and on she would go, as she told, not unkindly but in great detail, the stories of her village world.

Aunt Vera listened with interest, for she liked people, and painted her icons. The form was sacred and deeply imbued with the mysticism of faith. The technique, ancient and immutable, went back to the time of the Byzantine Empire: to a gesso-coated tablet of well-aged linden wood, Aunt Vera applied layer upon layer of tempera, finely ground mineral paints mixed with egg yolk, which give icons that haunting depth and serenity.

And then, while Frau Siebenhaar peeled potatoes or darned socks (using polished, wooden darning eggs made for her by Arist), Aunt Vera would reminisce about her youth, neither nostalgic nor bitter, but as one who fondly remembers a beautiful play.

She told of glittering balls, young men in gorgeous uniforms, young ladies in exquisite gowns, of elegant soirées, of summer drives *en calèche* along the Neva River in St. Petersburg, of weekend excursions to Peterhof (now Petrodvorets), the glorious park and palace of Peter the Great, a world of barons, counts, and princes, a world of glitter, elegance, and wealth, all laced with dollops of ancient gossip. For Frau Siebenhaar of Sehlde it was like a fairy tale, stories from a wondrous world she could barely imagine but loved to hear about.

Frau Siebenhaar and Aunt Vera were then both about fifty years old. They were very fond of each other.

Chapter 24

FAREWELL TO EUROPE

I HAD FAILED ANOTHER math test. The teacher looked at me, reproachful and resigned.

Someone else, I knew, was also looking at me: a girl, who had tried to prepare me for this test. It was algebra, clear and easy to her, abstruse to me. I didn't get it, failed the test, and the girl was sad, for she had tried so hard to help me.

After four years of deaths, camps, slavery, escapes, and teaching German to Russian officers, I was in class again, a high-school student in the town of Lauterbach in Upper Hesse, in central West Germany.

In January 1948, I visited the Lackschewitz family, our neighbours in Poland, then the Warthegau. They were now in Sickendorf, a village near Lauterbach. Wolf, of course, had lived with us in Kleingraben for a while in 1941, when we shared a tutor and a fascination with nature, collected beetles, and raised moths. His parents were friends of my parents and hence "relatives of choice," and I called them Uncle Theodor and Aunt Hildegard.

Uncle Theodor, tall, kind, and very gentle, managed to cope with the present, but preferred the past. His love was genealogy. He had studied agriculture and now taught agriculture at a nearby town. Aunt Hildegard was practical, decisive, and direct. Within a day, she correctly assessed my situation and proceeded with loving toughness to pound sense into me.

"You must go back to school," she said firmly, "What do you have now? Nothing! You help Arist. Where does that get you?

"You will come and live with us and go to school in Lauterbach."

It was a bit dictatorial but, above all, immensely generous. As a refugee with five children, Aunt Hildegard had been allocated half of a tiny house in the village of Sickendorf, five kilometres from Lauterbach.

Odert, the oldest son, worked and learned agriculture on a neighbouring farm. The youngest son, Klas, went to a boarding school. Wolf and I lived in a tiny A-shaped attic room. It held two bunkbeds with paillasses, two chairs, and a table that we shared.

On the main floor was a small kitchen, where Aunt Hildegard cooked and we all washed. There was a somewhat cramped living–dining room, plus another small room, the bedroom of Aunt Hildegard and her two daughters, Guda and Waldtraut. (Uncle Theodor lived most of the time at the agricultural institute where he taught.)

The privy was at the back of the building.

The pig, our future food, lived in the basement.

An annex to the woodshed was home to a dozen chickens and several geese.

Thanks to Aunt Hildegard's industry and energy we were largely self-sufficient at a time when food was still rationed and very precious.

A large garden near the house yielded all the vegetables we required. A kilometre away, on village land, one-acre plots had been assigned to refugee families. Wolf and I spaded the entire acre. It provided us and the pig with all the potatoes and cabbages we needed.

In fall, we collected pailfuls of wild berries, our jam supply for the year. Wolf and I excelled at gathering beechnuts.

In collaboration with a Lauterbach ornithologist, we banded birds. Some raptors, especially goshawks and buzzards, nested high in the crowns of tall beech trees.

Wolf had obtained the type of climbing irons that telephone repairmen use to climb telephone poles, and after a few heart-stopping slips and near-falls, we became skilled at climbing the smooth-boled, 100- to 130-foot-high beech trees. We banded raptor eyases and shook showers of beechnuts onto blankets spread beneath the trees. They yielded a prized oil. Some of it Aunt Hildegard used; the rest she bartered for the flour needed to bake our bread.

We got up at six in the morning. Wolf fed the pig, the chickens, and the geese. I cleaned the kitchen stove, took out the ash, and brought in the wood for the day. After breakfast we walked the five kilometres to school, watching birds en route, and learning by rote each day twenty new words of Latin, English, or French.

It had been strange to be in school again. I skipped one grade, so I was only a year or two older than most students in my class, but I felt older. I was also behind in all subjects. Some, like French, I had not had before. I crammed, and teachers and other students helped with special lessons.

It was a strange time to go to school, for many of our teachers were not really teachers. During the Nazi era, only teachers who belonged to the Party were allowed to teach. During the post-Nazi era, teachers who had belonged to the Party were not allowed to teach. Therefore, until teachers could be denazified there were hardly any teachers.

And denazification was a slow, cumbersome, and sometimes stupid procedure, rigorous at first and later often only a brief formality.

The charge, essentially, was one of guilt by association. But who was guilty? And how guilty? And guilty of what? Some of Hitler's close associates were not Party members.

Most members of the Wehrmacht, the German army, even its highest officers, were usually not members of the Party. Members of the "Waffen ss," the elite military units of the ss, usually were — but did not have to be — members of the Party, and some, in fact, were not.

Leni Riefenstahl (who died recently at the age of one hundred) was one of the three women Hitler most admired. She filmed the 1934 Nazi rally at Nuremberg for him and created the most brilliant propaganda film of all time, the "*Triumph des Willens*" (the "Triumph of the Will.") Yet she never joined the Party.

On the other hand, she did not have to join the Party. But a teacher in some remote village in Bavaria did have to join the Party. If she didn't, she lost her job. That held true for all other teachers, most government employees, and many other professions.

All this led to a lot of confusion. Denazification became an abstruse ritual, with well-meaning people trying to assess, after the fact, degrees of guilt, the way medieval theologians once tried to define degrees of sin upon which to base punishment or exculpation.

This dragged on and on and left the school in Lauterbach and thousands of other schools in West Germany without the usual teachers. But we had some unusual ones.

Our math teacher, who tried so hard to teach me algebra, had been an artillery officer, a specialist in ballistics, and was a superb mathematician. A few in our class, the truly gifted, benefited greatly from his knowledge. The rest muddled on as best they could. He was kind, and eventually even I got passing grades.

Our music teacher had been a famous choirmaster in Leipzig, the city of Johann Sebastian Bach. He fled to the West and got a job in Lauterbach. He created a choir and poured into us his immense love for music. Within a year we were giving concerts in some of the major cities of West Germany. I sang bass, and the joy of music has remained with me all my life.

Frau Dyrenfurth loved Latin, and her love was so contagious and her teaching so inspired that most of us actually enjoyed learning Latin and read with pleasure Cicero's *Orations against Catiline* and Caesar's *De Bello Gallico*.

She was an excellent teacher, but during the twelve years that Hitler's "Thousand-Year-Reich" lasted, she had not been allowed to teach Latin because her husband was a Jew.

Herr Dyrenfurth survived Hitler's vicious extermination policies by an odd twist of fate. His family, for several generations, had owned a factory in Silesia. The factory made uniforms. It made uniforms for the armies of the Kaiser, for the Reichswehr of the Weimar Republic, for the armies of Adolf Hitler.

The Gestapo arrested him. His workers slowed down, production decreased drastically, the army complained, Herr Dyrenfurth was released and reinstated — not as owner, but as *kriegswichtiger Betriebsleiter* (war-essential manager). It was one of the Gestapo's cynical "we-will-let-you-live-because-we-need-you-but-will-kill-you-later" decisions.

The Soviet armies rushed into Silesia, and the Gestapo fled. The Dyrenfurth family also fled, ending up as refugees in Lauterbach, and we gained a teacher who managed to make us love Latin.

After school, to earn money, Wolf and I did odd jobs in town for an hour or two, chopped wood, repaired fences, painted houses, then walked home to Sickendorf, did our chores, ate supper, did homework until ten or eleven, and passed out.

School and family changed me; I belonged again. The death camp had damaged me. Something within me had atrophied and left me cold, cautious, callous, and old. Now, gradually, I became young again.

I went to parties. I danced the rumba and the samba. I kissed my first girl. I went with her and saw my first colour movie, *Caesar and Cleopatra*, with Claude Rains and Vivien Leigh. I fell in love and suffered. I fell out of love and suffered. I laughed again.

During our holidays we either travelled or we worked. Wolf picked the hardest work, in a brickyard, often working double shifts, sixteen hours in a row, plus walking ten kilometres to work and back.

I worked in the large lumberyard of a sawmill and furniture factory, grading and stacking planks. Having worked in the Soviet Union, my inclination was to do this quickly and easily. Not so my partner. He was a veteran German plank-grader, meticulous and conscientious. Each plank was carefully inspected, turned, and graded, then stacked with great precision, so planks would be well aerated and did not warp.

Quitting time approached. "We'll just finish this," said my partner and we continued for another hour, unpaid, just to do the job well.

I also worked in a hat factory. It was the real-life version of Charlie Chaplin's film *Modern Times*.

The hats were made of felted hairs, mainly rabbit hairs. Initially large and thin, the hats ran through a long series of felting machines. Between each set of machines workers sat on stools opposite each other and changed the shape of the wet and very hot hats as they emerged from one machine and before they entered the next machine.

It was simple. The hat emerged, one put both hands into it, made a sideways motion, and changed its shape.

A jerking motion. Once a second. About fifteen thousand times a day. Every day. Some men had done it for years.

We got an hour off for lunch. And about once every two hours we could take a five-minute break to pee or smoke. I made a rapid signal and a replacement worker came over. As I slid off the stool, he slipped onto it, his hands already jerking.

We worked like marionettes responding to electric jolts, but the pay was fairly good, the money badly needed, and, as of June 20, 1948, money had value again. On that day a new currency, the deutsche mark (DM), was introduced, replacing the reichsmark. Everyone got sixty new marks for sixty old marks. Suddenly stores, until then nearly bare, were full of goods. The barter economy crumbled; the black market economy collapsed.

"*Geld ist wieder Geld*" (Money is money again) was a popular saying. People worked hard to get it, spent it, and the economy inched upwards.

In 1949, Arist and Elizabeth decided to emigrate to Canada. Hella and I were to follow a year later.

This particular twist of fate started with an uncle in America. Herbert Kursell, Elizabeth's uncle, had been, before and during the First World War, engineer for a British-owned gold mine in Siberia. When the Bolsheviks conquered Siberia, he had fled to the United States and rose to chief engineer of a large American mining company.

After the Second World War, he helped his extensive clan of refugee relatives with CARE parcels and with advice. He also urged them all to emigrate. Writing with a pessimistic American world vision, he told Arist: "There is no future for you in Europe. Europe is finished. It may never recover. Canada is the land with the great future."

He also warned: "Leave Europe. Don't ignore *die rote Gefahr* (the red menace)."

To all of us from eastern Europe, that menace was terribly real and frightening. Since 1944, Communism had spread and conquered. All the lands of eastern Europe were obedient satellites.

Now Stalin, immensely shrewd and cunning, set his sights on western Europe and its wealth.

The greatest weakness of western Europe was war-weariness. In the propaganda wars of the late 1940s the Soviet Union used this brilliantly, portraying the United States, flexing its muscles, as the "war monger," the "war monster." The peace movement, directed skilfully by the MGB and promoted by the large Communist parties of France and Italy, demanded the withdrawal of all American forces from Europe. Then there would be peace.

That was the direct attack to get the Americans out of Europe.

The indirect attack was subtle and corrosive. It bolstered and promoted pessimism, an "it can't be avoided" attitude. Communism, it said, was bound to win. That, said the pundits, was "historical imperative." It will happen. So accept it. Don't fight it. Intellectuals quoted Oswald Spengler's *The Decline of the West.* Cynics (male) quoted the old saw: "When rape is inevitable, relax and enjoy it." A common slogan was "Better Red Than Dead!"

That attitude scared people from eastern Europe. Canada to us appeared far away and safe.

Apart from that, Canada was to most of us would-be immigrants "the unknown land." My view of Canada was romantic, coloured by two books I had read as a child: *The Leatherstocking Tales* by James Fenimore Cooper (1789–1851) and *Wild Animals I Have Known* by Ernest Thompson Seton (1860–1946). They spoke of Indians and wilderness, of wolves and coureurs de bois.

Of modern Canada I knew little. It was big, cold, rich in wheat and minerals, had lots of forests. We had geography lessons in school, but Canada, despite its size, got less attention than Belgium.

I was sorry to leave my "family," my friends, the school. I was doing well in high school. Now I would leave before finishing.

Apart from that, I had no roots in Germany, no feeling of loss. My roots had been in Latvia, in the land, in my Baltic German past.

But that had ended in 1939. Since then I had lived in several worlds, but none were really "home." That was even legally true. I was a citizen of no land, except, by retroactive law, the Soviet Union, where I did not want to be. My "passport" said I was "stateless."

Our close-knit Lackschewitz family in Sickendorf began to scatter. I was the first to leave. The others would spread across Europe: Waldtraut married and moved to Spain; Guda married and remained in Germany, but her son is now a chemist in Switzerland; Klas became a high-ranking officer in the German navy; Odert became one of Finland's most famous photographers; and Wolf became director of one of Sweden's largest companies.

Our ship, the *Beaverbrae*, left from Bremerhaven at the end of December 1950. Heddy came from Holland. Emigration was forever. Hella and I said a final goodbye to Heddy and to Europe.

Chapter 25

THE GOLD MINE

CANADA IN 1950 NEEDED farm workers, miners, loggers, and of these, miners did the hardest work and received the best pay. With the help of Uncle Herbert Kursell, Arist got a job in a gold mine in Kirkland Lake, in northern Ontario.

Now the mine had "sponsored" me and advanced my passage money. I was going to mine gold, which sounded vaguely romantic — like my visions of Canada. Arist had advanced Hella's passage money. She was going to be a waitress in a Chinese restaurant in Kirkland Lake.

Since we had been born in Latvia, Canadian immigration officials registered us as Latvians, so my persona changed again. Friedrich von Bruemmer, Baltic German, became Fred Bruemmer, Latvian. I was a twenty-one-year-old high-school dropout.

They asked for English-speaking volunteers on the *Beaverbrae*. Hella and I volunteered. She worked in the purser's office. I washed dishes, was seasick, washed dishes in the kitchen, was seasick . . .

Volunteers were "paid" with cigarettes. Cartons of cigarettes.

The waste of food in that kitchen! I came from a society where food was sacred. It was a gift. To waste it was a sin. Then came years of starvation, and later years of rationed food. Food was life and, like life, precious.

The dinner plates came back from the officers' mess still full of food. They piled their plates, ate some, and sent the rest back as garbage. Buckets of garbage. I lugged it up and threw it overboard. The gulls loved it.

Thus my first image of Canada was of a land of blessed bounty, but a land of profligate waste.

We landed in St. John, New Brunswick, on December 29, 1950, a cold and damp and grey day.

Canadian Customs came aboard and asked for interpreters. Again, Hella and I volunteered, and we were "processed" immediately and rapidly. I had arrived in Canada with two suitcases containing some clothes and a lot of books — dictionaries, books on animals, a paperback edition of Goethe's *Faust*, my diaries.

The 773 immigrants filed off the *Beaverbrae* and, after some chaos and confusion, stood next to their small piles of belongings in the huge customs shed.

Some were farmers from eastern Europe. They had sacks with clothing and blankets, horse harnesses, yokes for oxen, galvanized zinc pails, handmade wooden rakes, spades. Many peasants from Balkan border regions spoke three or four languages fluently: German, Swabian, Hungarian, Romanian, Serb. But none spoke English. They looked bewildered and forlorn.

One man travelled with an oblong wooden crate. It was extremely heavy.

"What's in there?" asked the customs officer.

"A stone," I translated.

"What kind of stone?"

"A gravestone."

"This I got to see," said the customs officer. The box was opened.

In it was a beautifully polished granite gravestone with the man's name, date, and place of birth (a village in Romania).

Place and date of death were blank. At the top was the inscription *Hier schläft in Frieden* (Here sleeps in peace).

"Well, I'll be damned," said the customs officer. He gave orders to have the stone carefully repacked. The man was bound for a remote farming area in western Canada.

Canadian Customs also "paid" interpreters with cigarettes. Cartons of cigarettes.

Hella and I got window seats on the train. Other government officials and people from church groups and sponsoring organizations tried to communicate with their flocks. Hella and I translated.

I walked through the train with an immigration officer. Many people were vague and confused. We stopped with a large family.

"Where are they going?" asked the officer.

"*Nach dem Westen* (Towards the West)," said the man.

"Where in the West?"

"*Ganz weit* (Very far)," said the man.

We checked his papers.

"Tell him to get off the train in Saskatoon, Saskatchewan," said the officer.

The man looked baffled. "What language do they speak there?" he asked me. "When do we get there?" he wanted to know.

"In about four days," said the official.

"*Four days!*" The man stared in disbelief.

Our train moved through Canada: forests, fields, snow. Forests, fields, snow. In Europe, town followed town, city followed city. Cities were full of old stone buildings, soaring church spires. Here the towns were small, the buildings low. All looked neat and new. And all the land and all the towns were covered by snow. We had come to a white and empty land.

Hella and I spent New Year's Eve 1950–1951 at the North Bay, Ontario, railway station. Outside it was minus twenty Celsius. The snow creaked loudly when people walked. The waiting room was very hot, and whenever someone opened the door, a whitish cloud of frost-fog swirled into the room.

On my second day in Kirkland Lake, Arist took me shopping to buy winter clothes for northern Ontario. We got the basic outfit for a hard-rock miner: dirty-grey, scratchy-wool combination underwear, heavy socks, strong working pants, a broad, heavy leather belt to hold the heavy battery for my head lamp, knee-high heavy rubber safety boots with built-in steel toe-caps, and a pair of heavy leather gloves.

I had no money. All was bought on credit, but everyone was friendly. They called me Fred. "Just sign here," they said, "and come again."

"My" mine was called the Toburn, after Tough, Oakes, and Burnside, three Kirkland Lake pioneers. Oakes became Sir Harry Oakes, staked the Lake Shore Mine, by far the most productive mine in Kirkland Lake, grew to be one of the richest men in Canada, and was mysteriously murdered in the Bahamas.

I lived in the Toburn bunkhouse. Built long ago for many men, it now housed only three old-timers, English Canadians who had surface jobs, three newcomers, all Poles, who worked underground, and a French Canadian cook with a wife and eight children. The three groups had little in common. They were on remote-but-friendly terms. I was added to the Poles.

On my fourth day in Canada I began to work underground. Towards 6.30 p.m. the men began to arrive in the "dry," the large change-room, for the night shift.

There was a world of difference between the miners and the surface men. The underground workers of more than a dozen nationalities considered themselves real men, and despised the surface men as softies.

The miners were a tough, rough crowd, skilful and self-reliant. Their work was hard and often dangerous, and they were proud of it. They had both the individualism and the cohesion and comradeship of elite troops.

Among this tough crew I seemed ridiculously out of place, with my soft hands, soft face, and soft body — and, at first, I was pathetically inept. Now that I was one of them, however, they kidded me and made rough jokes, but they also helped and encouraged. That first day, they helped me get dressed in those heavy, awkward mining clothes, picked out a good helmet for me, adjusted it, fixed my battery and lamp, joshed and fussed.

We assembled in the shafthouse. Marino, the Italian-born shift boss, pointed at a man and said to me, "You go with him." The man was Adolfs, a Lett, and from now on my partner.

We took our lunch pails and pressed with many other men into the cage, the cage-tender gave a signal, and the elevator seemed to fall away beneath us, descending at a speed that made my eardrums pop. "Swallow hard!" Adolfs shouted.

Toburn's two shafts reached more than 2,300 feet underground, but it was a shallow mine compared to our immediate neighbour to the west, the Wright Hargreaves Mine, at 8,042 feet (2,452 metres), the deepest mine in North America.

A distinct hierarchy divided underground miners. At the top were the drillers, strong, skilful men who handled their one hundred and sixty pound, high-decibel drills with nonchalant ease. Most were almost deaf, since no one then wore ear protectors. Then came the timbermen (Arist was a timberman), the chute-pullers, the machine men who handled ore cars, and, at the very bottom, the muckers. Adolfs and I were muckers.

In 1951, Toburn had been nearly "mined out." For forty years miners had sunk shafts and had tunnelled outward from them at hundred-foot intervals. They followed gold-bearing quartz veins in kilometre-long, corridor-like "drifts," or horizontal passageways along the veins, then followed the veins upwards from level to level, removing, over the years, millions of tons of rock. They created a hollowed-out, three-dimensional labyrinth of immense complexity that reached far into the earth.

It was said that only one miner, Mickey, our Irish shift boss, knew the entire mine. Yet Toburn was a small mine, near the eastern edge of Kirkland Lake's famous "Mile of Gold" (really three miles), compared to the giants, the Wright Hargreaves and Sir Harry Oakes's Lake Shore Mine, where men mined ore two and half kilometres beneath the surface.

Like all first-day miners, I saw gold everywhere. As we walked along the dark, dank, water-dripping drift, gold glinted enticingly from the walls. But it was all pyrite, "fool's gold." Real gold appeared as minute dull-yellow specks within the quartz veins. Each ton of ore we mined with so much toil contained, on average, about thirteen grams of gold.

A mucker was supposed to shovel a minimum of nine tons of ore each day. For each additional ton, we got a twenty-five-cent bonus.

Mucking, I quickly discovered, was not easy. It took a lot of skill to force the heart-shaped, sharp-edged shovel, using the steel toe of the boot as fulcrum, into a pile of blasted, broken rock.

That first day, while I struggled to muck one ton of rock into an ore car, Adolfs shovelled twenty tons. He was broad, as smoothly muscular as Michelangelo's David, and worked with a fluid, steady rhythm, hour after hour.

I learned much that first day: to always speak to others with an averted head, so as not to blind them with my headlamp; to handle a shovel efficiently; to push a one-ton ore car carefully; to work a lot and cheat a little.

Adolfs taught me how to build with large, flat stones a house-of-cards-like structure into the bottom of the ore car. It filled nearly a quarter of the space and saved us a lot of mucking.

Most miners knew many tricks and cheated, but not too much, because the shift bosses, who had risen through the ranks, knew all the tricks. Mild cheating they accepted and ignored. Blatant cheaters were suddenly assigned to places where the work was extremely hard and cheating impossible. They let you sweat there for a week or two. Then you went to a better place — and henceforth cheated in moderation.

I also learned "Mining English." With Adolfs I spoke Latvian, Polish at the bunkhouse, and German with Hella, Arist, and

Elizabeth. Underground — and only underground — all men spoke "Mining English," a simple-yet-explicit language made up of very basic English, mixed with a lot of mining terms and flavoured with a wealth of swearwords. Most things were "she." "That fucking drill, she no work." "The fucking chute, she hung up."

Through Adolfs I entered the world of "Displaced Persons," the DPs, or "Deepies" as some annoyed Canadians called the newcomers.

They came from war-wrecked Europe, waves of refugees of many nationalities and faiths, arriving with few possessions but a wealth of new and ancient hatreds, feuds, and prejudices, from the "Old Country."

Kirkland Lake got its share of them. Underground they worked hard and behaved, for the mines had a very simple rule: if two men fought, both were fired. The work was dangerous enough without the added risk of ancient DP tribal feuds.

On the surface, however, there were frequent brawls. The immigrant mining population consisted of two main groups that detested each other: the "Old-Timers" who came after the First World War, when Communism was for many the working man's new religion of hope, and the "Newcomers" from eastern Europe, who had experienced Communism and feared and hated it.

Even more bitter was the hatred of those who had suffered under German occupation, had been part of the Underground, and had fought the Germans and their minions (or, at least, said they had fought the Germans and their minions), and those who had collaborated — by choice or by force — with the Germans during the Second World War (or were suspected of having collaborated with the Germans). All this, plus retained and sustained national and religious hatreds that were centuries old, fuelled in bars by booze and bravado, led to nasty fights. After one great brawl, the police rounded up the worst offenders and, still sputtering with rage, they appeared in court.

The magistrate was Siegfried Atkinson, a wise old man who had held this position since 1920. He listened for a while to the furious accusations and counter-accusations, translated from many languages into some sort of English, then stopped the polyglot passions with a very short speech in simple English.

"You come from the Old Country, which is in a terrible mess, to Canada because Canada is a good country. Now you continue to fight here. We don't want that. One more fight and we will send all of you back to the Old Country! Case dismissed!"

It was an empty threat. As magistrate, Atkinson did not have the power to deport anyone. But the immigrants did not know that. No lawyers got involved, and the result was near-instant peace in Kirkland Lake.

Every second weekend, Adolfs and I got drunk. Day shift was from 7 a.m. to 3 p.m. Towards the end of the shift, all blasting was done, and the ventilation system dissipated the potentially lethal post-explosion "gas" (really carbon monoxide) concentrations.

Old-timers, as sensitive to CO as miners' canaries, could "feel" the tasteless, odourless "gas" that sometimes lingered in rock domes. Newcomers occasionally inhaled it, became drowsy, got severe headaches, and collapsed. They usually survived.

Night shift was from 7 p.m. to 3 a.m. With weekly shift changes, this gave us one long and one short weekend. On the short weekend, most miners drank little, because anyone who came to work drunk or badly hung over was sent home and lost the shift. If he did it repeatedly, he was fired.

On long weekends, we worked on Saturdays until 3 p.m., showered, changed, and partied on Saturday night. Sunday we recovered. Monday, cold sober, we reported for evening shift.

Through Adolfs I also became a member of the Latvian community. It was an odd mélange. They were Lett and I was Baltic German, a member of the former ruling class. But what divided us was long in the past. What bound us was now and near: most men were miners, we were all refugees, we had all lost our home, and "home" to them and to me was Latvia. In Kirkland Lake we lived that duality: Canada, the "home" of our choice. Latvia, the "home" of our childhood, our past.

Like most immigrants we were deeply grateful to Canada for having taken us in, for having given us jobs. That strong feeling of gratitude to Canada would stay with most of us for life.

During those Saturday-night parties, we talked a lot, we reminisced, nostalgia for a lost world nicely wrapped in alcohol. Around three or four in the morning I would weave home to my bunkhouse. It was icy cold, and northern lights danced in the sky.

Only one man was a problem. *Lielais Janis*, "Big John." He was tall and powerful. Sober he was a boring braggart; drunk he was a bully. One night he picked on me. I tried to ignore him. Others tried to shush him, distract him. He had just begun to be abusive when suddenly Adolfs stood beside me.

"Let be!" he said quietly but distinctly.

Big John turned on him, his huge hands spread for strangling, with all the fury of a badly drunk bully.

"Come to protect your little —" I think he was going to say "your little baron," but he never got that far. Adolfs's hand shot out, there was a grating crack, a scream, and Big John clutched his hand. Adolfs had broken his index finger.

That ended the party. Some men took the moaning Big John to the hospital. "He fell," they said.

Adolfs and I walked home. I thanked him, but he just laughed. "The big bastard! I've wanted to do that for a long time."

Besides, I was his partner.

Underground we were partners for less than a month. The shift bosses mixed nationalities on the correct assumption that two Italians talk a lot, two Finns talk a lot, but an Italian and a Finn talk much less and may work more.

My new partner was Alex. It was an odd pairing. He was older (about sixty), knotty-lean but very strong with greying hair and a deeply lined face. Alex was a bitter, angry man. He was also a fervent Communist.

Alex came from Galicia, which had been part of the Austrian Empire when he was a boy, and was now part of Poland.

We worked as scrapers in a subdrift, a tunnel into an underground pillar. As upward-leading stopes, gold-bearing ore strata, were excavated, there was a footwall below and a hanging wall above. That hanging wall was supported by wooden pitprops. Thousands of them. There were entire forests underground.

At intervals, to prevent feared cave-ins, extensive rock pillars were left. They contained veins with high-grade ore, and now that Toburn was dying, an attempt was being made to extract some of it from the pillars. We worked in an ancient mine region where no one had been in years.

From the main drift, or tunnel, we clambered down ladders to our subdrift, another tunnel being excavated into the solid rock pillar. The drillers drilled and blasted. The scrapers, Alex and I, moved the broken rock with a machine-operated drag-scraper towards the end of our tunnel. It fell to a chute below, and was taken from there by ore car to the station, and hence to the surface.

We worked, then climbed up to the main drift for lunch. Sitting on empty dynamite boxes, we ate, then talked. Communism was out. We had agreed at the beginning of our partnership to skip that subject. Our views had been forged in different fires.

That left two other of Alex's pet subjects: God and capitalism. He hated both.

Alex had worked in the mines of Kirkland Lake during the Great Depression and he was still bitter. "They hired men, worked them half to death, then fired them and got new ones," he claimed.

"They told us to drill dry or be fired."

That may have been true and, if true, was a vicious form of slow murder.

"Drilling dry," without water, was faster than "drilling wet," and hence more productive, more profitable. But when men drilled dry, they inhaled fine silica dust as sharp as splintered glass, all day. It scarred their lungs and slowly destroyed them.

Several of our older miners, now surface men, had silicosis. They wheezed and suffered. Those with severe silicosis went to hospitals and rest homes and died slowly and in agony.

"Just so the rich could make more money," Alex said.

Now drilling dry was strictly forbidden by mining regulations. Blasted ore was hosed down to bind dust, and after each shift, in the dry, we inhaled vaporized aluminum powder to neutralize any silica dust we might have breathed in underground.

But Alex remembered the times when jobs were scarce and men were ruthlessly exploited. He did not forget and he did not forgive.

Another day, down there, nine hundred feet beneath the surface, closer to hell than to heaven, Alex had had it about God.

"You believe in God?" he asked.

"Yes."

"Then you're stupid!"

"Maybe. But when you die and there is a God, then you'll be the stupid one."

"That's priest talk," Alex snorted. "Them fucking priests! What do they do? Nothing! They say they speak to God. You ever seen them speak with God? You ever seen God? There just ain't no God. It's all a pile of bullshit. To control stupid people. To get money from them."

Between the polemics came angry childhood memories.

"We had to go to confession. Confess our sins. I had stolen some apples. So I confessed to the priest. The bastard told my father and he beat the shit out of me!"

That was probably not true. Priests risk their immortal souls when they betray the confessional. It may have been a coincidence, but it still rankled.

That sentence "my father beat the shit out of me" wandered like a leitmotiv through most of his childhood stories. Alex was full of ancient anger and latent hate.

After lunch and talk, we would turn our headlamps off and have a brief post-prandial nap. It was eerie. The darkness at nine hundred feet within the earth is total and oppressive. One suddenly became aware that between us and the surface, between darkness and light, lay millions of tons of rock. The darkness was so powerful, so massive, so corporeal, few new miners could endure it. After a frightened minute or two, they would turn their headlamps on again.

The mine moved. This was an old, mined-out area, a vast hollow maze within the earth, from which millions of tons of rock had been removed.

We lay in that thick, pressing darkness and listened to the movements of the mine: it creaked and groaned. Old pitprops cracked. Rock ground and crumbled. And throughout, there was the steady drip-drip-drip of water seeping through cracks.

It was warm and humid. Weird fungi grew on the decaying pitprops in these old workings. The logs were festooned with gossamer-fine fungal webs that glowed in weird, unearthly colours in the beams of our headlamps. But if we touched these lovely delicate fungal filaments, they turned into ugly, brownish slime.

OUR SECTION OF THE MINE collapsed just after lunch. We had climbed down the ladders in the forty-five-degree stope to our subdrift. Alex walked to the back of the tunnel to start the scraper, while I remained near the entrance to check the steel cables and pulleys of the drag.

Suddenly the low groaning became a cataclysmic shriek of riven rock. The earth trembled as our area of the mine caved in. Nine hundred feet above, in Kirkland Lake, dishes rattled in cupboards, cups slid off tables, and wives wondered whether their men would come home.

For a moment I could see huge stone blocks hurtling down the slope. Pitprops cracked and crumbled. Then dust obliterated all, and there was only the roar and crash of a collapsing mine, the agony of rock in motion. Our underworld seemed full of chaos, dust, and death.

In our subdrift, the short tunnel into solid rock, we were in fact quite safe, like two rats in a steel pipe buried beneath a collapsing building. We might be trapped, but we would not be crushed.

With that terrible noise and the fear of imminent death, it was difficult to be rational. I walked into the dust-choked tunnel, feeling my way along its walls. And there, at the end of the tunnel on his knees, was Alex, the ardent God-hater, praying. Nearly hysterical with fear, he implored God and the Virgin Mary to save him. He spluttered Hail Marys and bits of half-forgotten prayers.

Maybe it helped him. It did help me. It was so funny, I stopped being scared.

The noise ceased. The odd rock still clattered down the slope. The dust began to settle. An immense slab of rock, thousands and thousands of tons, had slid down from somewhere high in the stope and had become wedged between footwall and hanging wall not far from our subdrift. It now acted as supporting pillar.

We were safe. Our ladders had been damaged but not destroyed. We waited for half an hour, then crawled up and walked out. Our shift was over. We reported to the boss, showered, and got dressed.

"Fred," Alex started with a sheepish grin. "You won't tell what I did, will you?"

"You mean about praying?"

"Yes."

"Sure I'll tell. That was the funniest thing I've seen in years!"

"Jesus, Fred. Don't tell," Alex begged. "Please don't. If they hear about it, they'll make life shit for me." I guessed he was scared of his Communist pals.

"Don't worry, Alex," I assured him. "I was just kidding. I won't tell. To nobody. Ever. Not even Arist."

After all, Alex was my partner.

Apart from hating God (a bit less vehemently after we survived the cave-in), and capitalism, Alex had a quirk. He loved to eat dynamite. All miners were familiar with dynamite and handled the high explosive casually but expertly. Most was used by the drillers to blast their daily rounds. Chute pullers might use a stick of dynamite to free a rock-jammed chute. Muckers used dynamite to shatter big rocks.

The dynamite came in neat wooden boxes. When empty, some of those boxes were our lunchtime seats. Others were used as "shit-boxes," our underground toilets.

Each box contained fifty pounds of dynamite packed in glossy-brown, oily paper, and each stick was individually wrapped in similar paper. Inside, the dynamite looked and felt like a mixture of marzipan and sawdust.

It had a sickly sweet smell, the glycerol odour of nitroglycerine.

Some miners, including Alex, liked to eat bits of dynamite. "It's good for you," they claimed. I tried it. It was so-so. It tasted the way it smelled: sickly sweet.

A few miners, the lonely ones, used dynamite to commit suicide, the way terrorists use it now to blow up both themselves and others.

The miners who committed suicide were usually immigrants who could not cope, sad men who had no families, no home, a destroyed past, an empty future. Some drank themselves into oblivion. Others chose dynamite.

The method was nearly always the same and was based upon the fact that we knew the burning time of a given length of fuse to within seconds. The man who planned to die would sit on an empty dynamite box. He cut a length of fuse that would burn exactly the length of time it took to smoke a cigarette. He inserted fuse and blasting cap into a stick of dynamite and pushed it underneath the front of his broad miner's belt, next to his body. He lit the fuse and, with the same match, lit his last cigarette. He smoked and waited. He had about five more minutes to live.

The blast would cut him in half and scatter the pieces.

AT THE BUNKHOUSE, one of my three Poles had *Liebeskummer*—he was in love and unhappy. Irma, the girl he loved, was still in Germany.

All three Poles had worked as conscript labourers in a factory in western Germany, a small factory in a small town. They had lived in barracks, but there were no guards. They were quite free, went to dances, and, in a Germany where men were scarce, acquired German girlfriends.

With two it had been casual and ended when they emigrated, but Janek was deeply in love with Irma. They were engaged, and she had promised to follow him to Canada.

Janek pined and wrote longing letters. Irma said she pined and asked for money to arrange the trip. I wrote most of Janek's love letters since he had trouble writing German, and I read the ones that Irma wrote.

Over time, I noticed that her letters changed. They were now explicitly sensuous and longing. Woven into this pattern of desire were requests for money. A lot of money.

Janek was a driller. I earned $82.50 a week. Janek earned more than $100 a week—some weeks, with bonuses, he could make $150. The bunkhouse was cheap. We paid $36 a month for ample and excellent food, simple but adequate rooms, and laundry. Janek had, by both Canadian and German standards of the time, a lot of money. And Irma longed for it—and him, she claimed.

Finally, with Janek's somewhat agonized agreement, I wrote a letter to the police chief of the little town, explained the problem, and asked for his help and advice.

Six weeks later I received the answer from the police chief. His advice: send no more money! Irma had married four months before. Poor Janek nearly cried. I wrote one more letter to Irma, a really nasty one, and then the Poles and I went to town and got drunk.

AS I GAINED MORE experience underground, I was assigned to pull chute, alone, at 4-16. Each work place in the mine had a number: 4-16 meant place 16, a chute, on the 400-foot-below-the-surface level.

As upward-sloping stopes were drilled and blasted, the broken ore rushed down and was "pulled" from chutes the way pills are pulled from a pill-dispenser at a drugstore.

The wooden chute, above the tracks, was closed by a strong wooden plank held in place by high steel stanchions. In theory, one lifted the board, the rock rushed out, one filled a one-ton ore car, lowered the plank to stop the flow, pushed the full car the three hundred yards to the station, where it was hoisted to the surface, returned with an empty car, and repeated the procedure.

At 4-16 I was expected to pull twenty tons of ore each day. After that, I got a fifteen-cents-per-ton bonus. On good days I pulled thirty tons.

On bad days, chute pulling was hell. From above, hundreds of tons of ore were funnelled towards the chute. The pressure was immense. Huge chunks of rock rushed down, and it was hard to stop the flow. If it overflowed, it covered the tracks, and I had to shovel for hours.

Much worse was a "hung-up" chute. Somewhere above, the rocks jammed, and the flow stopped. I would have to climb into the car and look cautiously upwards at the hanging rocks. Then I would take a heavy, ten-foot steel rod and begin to poke and pry, trying to free the key rock that held up all the others. If I did it right, one rock came free and an avalanche of ore fell into the chute.

One day I was too slow. The ore hung high. I looked up and touched the rocks, and they fell, driving the steel rod into my face. There was a crashing blow, an explosion of light, then nothing.

When I regained consciousness, I lay on the tracks. It was totally dark.

I'm blind! That was my first thought. I touched my face. It was wet.

Every miner carried a waterproof box with matches. I got the matches out and lit one. I saw the flame! I could see! My headlamp had been smashed.

The matches took me halfway to the station. The rest I groped in the dark. My head throbbed. My left eye socket felt empty.

At the station I gave the emergency signal, and seconds later, the cage tender was on the phone.

"It's me, Fred. At 400. I got hurt."

At the surface, one of the bosses was waiting. He and another man helped me into a car and rushed me to hospital.

A doctor forced my left eye open. He held up one finger.

"How many?" he asked.

"One."

He held up three. I saw three.

"You can see all right," he said, "but you'll have one hell of a shiner."

They X-rayed me. The zygomatic bone near the eye was cracked. A few millimetres further right, and that steel rod would have gone through my eye and skull like a knife through a melon.

Four days later, with a rainbow-coloured face, my left eye swollen shut, I was back at the mine.

"4-16," said Marino, the boss.

That was the rule. When a man was injured he went right back to the place where he got hurt. You had to fight and overcome your fear.

That day, instead of the minimum twenty, I pulled two cars.

"How many?" asked Marino at the end of the shift.

"Two."

He wrote down "two." No comment.

He kept me at 4-16 for another month, until again I pulled twenty to thirty tons each day, until I was free of fear and had both the skill and the caution to handle "hung-up" chutes.

IN SEPTEMBER 1951, I took my two-week holiday. Other miners stayed home during their holidays, rested, puttered in gardens, fished, drank beer. A few ventured south to Toronto, the Big City. I went north.

I took the train to Moosonee, a then largely Indian settlement near the southern tip of James Bay. I lived with a lonely Yugoslav trader in his cabin-cum-store near the great Moose River, and we talked in English, Russian, and Serb about the "Old Country," of the village where he grew up, of other worlds and other times. Indians stopped at the store to buy fuel for their outboard motors, ammunition, tea, sugar, pilot biscuits. I asked to go along on their hunting trips. They hesitated, but agreed when I offered to pay for fuel.

I loved those canoe trips on the great, lonely river. The Indians hunted geese and ducks and zigzagged through the forest checking snare lines.

Late in the evening, far in the forest, we stopped at a lake. The Indians built a fire, skinned two rabbits, and boiled them in a sooty pot. We ate, and smoked, and talked a bit, mainly about rabbits, about good rabbit years and bad rabbit years, the population cycles of the snowshoe hare. The Indians were friendly and relaxed. They knew a lot about rabbits and they told stories and jokes about Canada jays, the ash-grey, cheeky little pilferers that appeared from nowhere to share our meal. This was their life. This was their land.

We slept in the open, on the thin carpet of caribou moss near the lake. Far away, a wolf howled, long-drawn and melancholy, rising on the last note and trailing off into silence. The night wind soughed gently through the spruces, and loons called from the dark lake.

I loved those days and nights, roaming the northern forest with the Indians, camping in the wilderness. Perhaps in its freedom, its simplicity, its nearness to nature, it reminded me of the happiest time of my life, my childhood spent in Quellenhof.

Some evenings, sitting with the Indians by the fire in the forest, I wondered what I should do with my future. There were problems, of course. I had no education, no marketable skills, and only minimal English. Arist, conservative and conscientious, insisted I should finish high school, study, and then march slowly upwards upon the path of duty and respectability, the proper road for rising refugees.

He was, no doubt, right. But that idea did not appeal to me. What I liked was this life in the forest, but I couldn't very well become an Indian. Perhaps I could photograph the lives of Indians, write about life in the forest. The wilderness tales of Ernest Thompson Seton that I had read as a child had left a lasting impression.

Hopes and reality were far apart. As a start, I should learn photography. Perhaps I could become a journalist and combine photography and writing. Perhaps, someday . . . The Indians were asleep. I stared at the dying fire and dreamt of the future and freedom.

WHEN I RETURNED TO TOBURN, I got a new partner. After 4-16 on my own, I was paired with Vainu. I think that match appealed to the boss's sense of humour.

At around one hundred and seventy pounds, a hundred pounds more than I had weighed in Russia, I think I was still the thinnest man in our mine. Vainu was the biggest, heaviest man in our mine, a mountain of a man. He must have weighed close to four hundred pounds.

We were an odd but, on the whole, quite happy couple.

Vainu was mostly muscle, plus a barrel-sized belly, a "pig pelly," as he said. Like most Finns he could not say the "b."

He was by far the strongest man in our mine, the only man who could pick up a derailed one-ton ore car and put it back on the tracks.

His power was immense and so was his appetite. The rest of us came to work with lunchpails. Vainu came with a small suitcase full of food, and ate it all with ease and pleasure.

He was a friendly giant, but he was old and slow. Vainu was past sixty and he stomped slowly through the mine, so I did all the running and fetching, and Vainu did all the heavy hoisting and heaving.

Vainu had grown up on one of the hardscrabble Finnish farms in northern Ontario, farming in summer, logging in winter. When the Second World War broke out Vainu, filled with patriotism, volunteered.

But there was a problem. When his parents had emigrated in the early 1890s, they had travelled via Germany. Vainu was born in Hamburg, Germany, and left Europe as a baby.

Now, when he volunteered, officials looked at his papers and said: "You can't volunteer. You are a German! And you are also too old!"

"I'm not a German!" Vainu protested. "I'm a Finn!" He was very proud to be a Finn.

It didn't help. Technically he was German and for a while they locked him up with other Germans in one of Canada's "enemy alien" camps. When I knew him, he was still angry about that.

Once we were to build a wooden platform in an ancient stope. From it we would be able to drill into a high-grade vein. The two main logs for the platform were huge and heavy, and I couldn't lift them. Vainu, however, could not reach them. His bulging belly was in the way.

I levered up a log, put a rope around it, Vainu pulled it up with ease, swung it onto his shoulder and off we went. He carried the four-hundred-pound log. I carried the lunches.

Once the platform was finished, we drilled, but not as much as we should have. Our lunch breaks were too long. Vainu ate so much, and that took time. Then we talked. Then slept. Then climbed slowly back up to the platform.

This annoyed Mickey, our quick and quick-tempered Irish shift boss, whose nickname was "Quickie-Mickey." All miners worked on their own. A boss would come by once during a shift, one discussed the job, sat, smoked, and then he went again. One shift Mickey climbed up to us, saw how few holes we had drilled, and called Vainu "a big, fat, lazy, fucking Finn!"

It was a bad mistake. He had broken a basic mine taboo. Underground no one ever used an ethnic insult. And Vainu was the wrong man to insult.

Vainu grabbed Mickey by the front of his heavy mining jacket, lifted him up like a puppet, and, his arm outstretched like a crane, swung him off the platform and held him above the deadly void.

"Say dat again!" he challenged.

Mickey said nothing.

Vainu swung him back again and plonked him down upon the platform.

"Don't ever say dat again!" he growled.

It took Mickey a bit to recover. He lit a cigarette. His hands shook.

"You're right," he agreed. "I shouldn't have said that."

Then he grinned. "But you're still a big, fat, lazy, fucking bastard!"

"Yo, dat's right," Vainu agreed amiably.

Mickey went and we drilled out some more of Toburn's remaining high-grade ore.

Toburn closed in the early summer of 1952. I had left some time before.

I had mined gold for fifteen months.

I had bought a motorcycle and a camera.

It was time to start another life.